DATE DUE

P9-EEU-798

HENRY DAVID THOREAU

Modern Critical Views

Continued at back of book

Modern Critical Views

HENRY DAVID THOREAU

Edited and with an introduction by
Harold Bloom
Sterling Professor of the Humanities
Yale University

CHELSEA HOUSE PUBLISHERS ◊ 1987
New York ◊ New Haven ◊ Philadelphia

Library of Congress Cataloging-in-Publication Data

Henry David Thoreau.

  (Modern critical views)
  Bibliography: p.
  Includes index.
  Contents: Words / Stanley Cavell—"The shipwreck" /
James McIntosh—Thoreau's vision of the natural world /
Loren Eiseley—[etc.]
  1. Thoreau, Henry David, 1817–1862—Criticism and
interpretation.   [1. Thoreau, Henry David, 1817–1862—
Criticism and interpretation.   2. American literature—
History and criticism]   I. Bloom, Harold.   II. Series.
PS3054.H38   1987   818'.309   86–31020
ISBN 0–87754–697–5 (alk. paper)

Contents

Editor's Note

This book gathers together a representative selection of the most useful contemporary criticism devoted to the writings of Henry David Thoreau. The critical essays are reprinted here in the chronological order of their original publication. I am grateful to Peter Childers for his aid in editing this volume.

My introduction centers upon Thoreau's relation to his precursor, Emerson. The philosopher Stanley Cavell begins the chronological sequence of criticism with a meditation upon *Walden* that finds in the book an American embodiment of the impulse to philosophical speculation. In a reading of "The Shipwreck," the first chapter of *Cape Cod,* James McIntosh presents one of Thoreau's many visions of the individual mind bereft in its confrontation with an inhuman nature. Loren Eiseley sees in Thoreau's writing a peculiarly unstratified mind working to bring together philosophy, poetry, and science.

Emerson's *Representative Men* is seen as being answered by Thoreau's sketches of American Indians in *The Maine Woods* in the essay of Philip F. Gura. *Walden* is reconsidered in the aura of our contemporary criticism, with its emphasis upon the problematics of reading, in the analysis of Walter Benn Michaels. In a study of Thoreau's first book, *A Week on the Concord and Merrimack Rivers,* Eric J. Sundquist analyzes Thoreau's crucial conceptual metaphors of "cultivation" and "grafting." John Carlos Rowe follows with a study of Thoreau's "language of being" in the same work.

Barry Wood, studying Thoreau's crucial essay, "Civil Disobedience," seeks to read it as an instance of highly personal but structured narrative art. Thoreau's early works receive an overview by Richard Bridgman, who finds in them a distress and confusion that the nature writings sought to overcome. *Cape Cod,* a book that has dwindled into a historical guide for too many, is revived by John Hildebidle as a crucial instance of Thoreau's struggle for literary autonomy.

Michael T. Gilmore explores the ideological relation of *Walden* to the realities of the publishing marketplace in Thoreau's day. In this book's final essay, Robert Weisbuch examines that struggle in relation to Wordsworth and Coleridge, prime English precursors of both Emerson and Thoreau. Weisbuch joyously concludes that *Walden* is a counterannexation, but that returns us full circle to my introduction, where the emphasis is upon what I judge to be Thoreau's failure to counterannex his American precursor, Emerson.

Introduction

All of us, however idiosyncratic, begin by living in a generation that overdetermines more of our stances and judgments than we can hope to know, until we are far along in the revisionary processes that can bring us to a Second Birth. I myself read *Walden* while I was very young, and "Civil Disobedience" and "Life without Principle" soon afterwards. But I read little or no Emerson until I was an undergraduate, and achieved only a limited awareness of him then. I began to read Emerson obsessively just before the middle of the journey, when in crisis, and have not stopped reading him since. More even than Freud, Emerson helped change my mind about most things, in life and in literature, myself included. Going back to Thoreau, when one has been steeped in Emerson for more than twenty years, is a curious experience. A distinguished American philosopher, my contemporary, has written that he underwent the reverse process, coming to Emerson only after a profound knowing of Thoreau, and has confessed that Emerson seemed to him at first a "second-rate Thoreau." I am not tempted to call Thoreau a second-rate Emerson, because Thoreau, at his rare best, was a strong writer, and revised Emerson with passion and with cunning. But Emerson was for Thoreau even more massively what he was for Walt Whitman and all Americans of sensibility ever since: the metaphor of "the father," the pragmatic image of the ego ideal, the inescapable precursor, the literary hero, the mind of the United States of America.

My own literary generation had to recover Emerson, because we came after the critics formed by the example and ideology of T. S. Eliot, who had proclaimed that, "The essays of Emerson are already an encumbrance." I can recall conversations about Emerson with R. P. Blackmur, who informed me that Emerson was of no relevance, except insofar as he represented an extreme example for America of the unsupported and catastrophic Protestant sensibility, which had ruined the Latin culture of Eu-

1

rope. Allen Tate more succinctly told me that Emerson simply was the devil, a judgment amplified in my single conversation with the vigorous Yvor Winters. In many years of friendship with Robert Penn Warren, my only disputes with that great poet have concerned Emerson, upon whom Warren remains superbly obdurate. As these were the critical minds that dominated American letters from 1945 to 1965 (except for Lionel Trilling, who was silent on Emerson), it is no surprise that Emerson vanished in that era. From 1965 through the present, Emerson has returned, as he always must and will, because he is the pragmatic origin of our literary culture. Walt Whitman and Emily Dickinson, Robert Frost and Wallace Stevens, Hart Crane, Elizabeth Bishop and John Ashbery have written the poems of our climate, but Emerson was and is that climate.

How does Thoreau now read in our recovered sense of the Emersonian climate? Is the question itself unfair? Rereading *Walden* and the major essays, I confess to an experience different in degree, but not in kind, from a fresh encounter with Thoreau's verse. As a poet, Thoreau is in the shadow of Wordsworth, towards whom his apotropaic gestures are sadly weak. In prose, conceptually and rhetorically, Thoreau strongly seeks to evade Emerson wherever he cannot revise him directly. But this endless agon, unlike Whitman's, or the subtler subversion of Emerson by Dickinson and by Henry James, is won by the image of the father. Rereading Thoreau, either I hear Emerson overtly or more darkly I detect him in what Stevens called "the hum of thoughts evaded in the mind."

II

During that 1945–1965 heyday of what then was called "the New Criticism," only *Walden,* among all of Thoreau's works, was exempt from censure. I have never understood the New Critical tolerance for *Walden,* except as a grudging bit of cultural patriotism, or perhaps as a kind of ultimate act of revenge against Emerson, the prophet who organized support for John Brown, cast out Daniel Webster because of the Fugitive Slave Act, and burned himself into a premature senility by his fierce contempt for the South and its culture throughout the Civil War. Thoreau, no less an enthusiast for John Brown, and equally apocalyptic against the South, somehow escaped the wrath of Tate, Warren, and their cohorts. This may have something to do with the myth of Thoreau as a kind of American Mahatma Gandhi, a Tolstoyan hermit practicing native arts and crafts out in the woods. Homespun and reputedly naive, such a fellow may have seemed harmless enough, unlike the slyly wicked Sage of Concord, Ralph

Waldo Lucifer, impediment to the United States somehow acquiring a Southern and Latin culture.

The merely actual Thoreau has been so prettified that one does best to begin a consideration of the man with the opening paragraphs of Leon Edel's pungent pamphlet, in which an amiable disenchantment with our American Narcissus is memorably expressed:

> Of the creative spirits that flourished in Concord, Massachusetts, during the middle of the nineteenth century, it might be said that Hawthorne loved men but felt estranged from them, Emerson loved ideas even more than men, and Thoreau loved himself. Less of an artist than Hawthorne, less of a thinker than Emerson, Thoreau made of his life a sylvan legend, that of man alone, in communion with nature. He was a strange presence in American letters—we have so few of them—an eccentric. The English tend to tolerate their eccentrics to the enrichment of their national life. In America, where democracy and conformity are often confused, the nonconforming Thoreau was frowned upon, and for good reason. He had a disagreeable and often bellicose nature. He lacked geniality. And then he had once set fire to the Concord woods—a curious episode, too lightly dismissed in the Thoreau biographies. He was, in the fullest sense of the word, a "curmudgeon," and literary history has never sufficiently studied the difficulties his neighbors had in adjusting themselves to certain of his childish ways. But in other ways he was a man of genius—even if it was a "crooked genius" as he himself acknowledged.
>
> A memorable picture has been left by Hawthorne's daughter of the three famous men of Concord skating one winter's afternoon on the river. Hawthorne, wrapped in his cloak, "moved like a self-impelled Greek statue, stately and grave," as one might expect of the future author of *The Marble Fawn*. Emerson, stoop-shouldered, "evidently too weary to hold himself erect," pitched forward, "half lying on the air." Thoreau, genuinely skillful on his skates, performed "dithyrambic dances and Bacchic leaps," enchanted with himself. Their manner of skating was in accord with their personalities and temperaments.
>
> Behind a mask of self-exaltation Thoreau performed as before a mirror—and first of all for his own edification. He was a fragile Narcissus embodied in a homely New Englander. His

life was brief. He was born in 1817, in Concord; he lived in Concord, and he died in Concord in 1862 shortly after the guns had spoken at Fort Sumter. A child of the romantic era, he tried a number of times to venture forth into the world. He went to Maine, to Staten Island, to Cape Cod, and ultimately to Minnesota, in search of health, but he always circled back to the Thoreau family house in Concord and to the presence of a domineering and loquacious mother. No other man with such wide-ranging thoughts and a soaring mind—it reached to ancient Greece, to the Ganges, to the deepest roots of England and the Continent—bound himself to so small a strip of ground. "He was worse than provincial," the cosmopolitan Henry James remarked, "he was parochial."

Edel's Jamesian slight can be dismissed, since Edel is James's devoted biographer, but the rest of this seems charmingly accurate. The great conservationist who set fire to the Concord woods; the epitome of Emersonian Self-Reliance who sneaked back from Walden in the evening to be fed dinner by Lidian Emerson; the man in whom Walt Whitman (whom he admired greatly, as man and as poet) found "a morbid dislike of humanity"—that, alas, was the empirical Thoreau, as contrasted to the ontological self of Thoreau. Since, to this day, Thoreau's self-mystifications continue to mystify nearly all of Thoreau's scholars, I find myself agreeing with Edel's judgment that the best discussions of Thoreau continue to be those of Emerson, James Russell Lowell, and Robert Louis Stevenson. Magnificent (and subtly balanced) as Emerson's funeral eulogy is, and brilliant as Lowell's much-derided essay continues to be, the best single remark on Thoreau remains Stevenson's: "It was not inappropriate, surely, that he had such close relations with the fish."

Lowell, sympathetic enough to Emerson, had little imagination to countenance the even more extreme disciple, Thoreau:

> This notion of an absolute originality, as if one could have a patent-right in it, is an absurdity. A man cannot escape in thought, any more than he can in language, from the past and the present. As no one ever invents a word, and yet language somehow grows by general contribution and necessity, so it is with thought. Mr. Thoreau seems to me to insist in public on going back to flint and steel, when there is a match-box in his pocket which he knows very well how to use at a pinch. Originality consists in power of digesting and assimilating thoughts,

so that they become part of our life and substance. Montaigne, for example, is one of the most original of authors, though he helped himself to ideas in every direction. But they turn to blood and coloring in his style, and give a freshness of complexion that is forever charming. In Thoreau much seems yet to be foreign and unassimilated, showing itself in symptoms of indigestion. A preacher-up of Nature, we now and then detect under the surly and stoic garb something of the sophist and the sentimentalizer. I am far from implying that this was conscious on his part. But it is much easier for a man to impose on himself when he measures only with himself. A greater familiarity with ordinary men would have done Thoreau good, by showing him how many fine qualities are common to the race. The radical vice of his theory of life was that he confounded physical with spiritual remoteness from men. A man is far enough withdrawn from his fellows if he keep himself clear of their weaknesses. He is not so truly withdrawn as exiled, if he refuse to share in their strength. "Solitude," says Cowley, "can be well fitted and set right but upon a very few persons. They must have enough knowledge of the world to see the vanity of it, and enough virtue to despise all vanity." It is a morbid self-consciousness that pronounces the world of men empty and worthless before trying it, the instinctive evasion of one who is sensible of some innate weakness, and retorts the accusation of it before any has made it but himself. To a healthy mind, the world is a constant challenge of opportunity. Mr. Thoreau had not a healthy mind, or he would not have been so fond of prescribing. His whole life was a search for the doctor. The old mystics had a wiser sense of what the world was worth. They ordained a severe apprenticeship to law, and even ceremonial, in order to the gaining of freedom and mastery over these. Seven years of service for Rachel were to be rewarded at last with Leah. Seven other years of faithfulness with her were to win them at last the true bride of their souls. Active Life was with them the only path to the Contemplative.

It is curious that Lowell should have directed this attack upon Emersonian Self-Reliance at the disciple, not the master, yet Lowell, as he shows abundantly in his fine essay "Emerson the Lecturer," was overcome by the great lecturer's charisma, his mysterious but nearly universally acknowledged personal charm. Even Lowell's argument against Transcendentalist "solitude" would have been better directed against the author of *Society and Solitude* than the recalcitrant author of *Walden*. Lowell's essay survives, despite its unfairness, because of its accuracy, and even because of its ultimate judgment of Thoreau:

> We have said that his range was narrow, but to be a master is to be a master. He had caught his English at its living source, among the poets and prose-writers of its best days; his literature was extensive and recondite; his quotations are always nuggets of the purest ore: there are sentences of his as perfect as anything in the language, and thoughts as clearly crystallized; his metaphors and images are always fresh from the soil; he had watched Nature like a detective who is to go upon the stand; as we read him, it seems as if all-out-of-doors had kept a diary and become its own Montaigne.

To be the Montaigne of all-out-of-doors ought to have been distinction enough for anyone, yet Emerson confessed that he had hoped for more from this rugged and difficult disciple:

> His virtues, of course, sometimes ran into extremes. It was easy to trace to the inexorable demand on all for exact truth that austerity which made this willing hermit more solitary even than he wished. Himself of a perfect probity, he required not less of others. He had a disgust at crime, and no worldly success would cover it. He detected paltering as readily in dignified and prosperous persons as in beggars, and with equal scorn. Such dangerous frankness was in his dealing that his admirers called him "that terrible Thoreau," as if he spoke when silent, and was still present when he had departed. I think the severity of his ideal interfered to deprive him of a healthy sufficiency of human society.
>
> The habit of a realist to find things the reverse of their appearance inclined him to put every statement in a paradox. A certain habit of antagonism defaced his earlier writings,—a trick of rhetoric not quite outgrown in his later, of substituting for the obvious word and thought its diametrical opposite. He praised wild mountains and winter forests for their domestic air, in snow and ice he would find sultriness, and commended

the wilderness for resembling Rome and Paris. "It was so dry, that you might call it wet."

The tendency to magnify the moment, to read all the laws of Nature in the one object or one combination under your eye, is of course comic to those who do not share the philosopher's perception of identity. To him there was no such thing as size. The pond was a small ocean; the Atlantic, a large Walden Pond. He referred every minute fact to cosmical laws. Though he meant to be just, he seemed haunted by a certain chronic assumption that the science of the day pretended completeness, and he had just found out that the *savans* had neglected to discriminate a particular botanical variety, had failed to describe the seeds or count the sepals. "That is to say," we replied, "the blockheads were not born in Concord; but who said they were? It was their unspeakable misfortune to be born in London, or Paris, or Rome; but, poor fellows, they did what they could, considering that they never saw Bateman's Pond, or Nine-Acre Corner, or Becky Stow's Swamp; besides, what were you sent into the world for, but to add this observation?"

Had his genius been only contemplative, he had been fitted to his life, but with his energy and practical ability he seemed born for great enterprise and for command; and I so much regret the loss of his rare powers of action, that I cannot help counting it a fault in him that he had no ambition. Wanting this, instead of engineering for all America, he was the captain of a huckleberry-party. Pounding beans is good to the end of pounding empires one of these days; but if, at the end of years, it is still only beans!

Emerson's ironies are as beautiful here as anywhere, and their dialectical undersong is wholly in Thoreau's favor. Henry Ford, a fervent and overt Emersonian, engineered for all America; clearly Emerson himself, like many among us, would have preferred Thoreau to Ford, and a huckleberry-party to a car factory.

III

Thoreau's crucial swerve away from Emerson was to treat natural objects as books, and books as chunks of nature, thus evading all literary tradition, Emerson's writings not excepted. Unfortunately, Thoreau was not really an oppositional or dialectical thinker, like Emerson, though certainly an oppositional personality, as the sane and sacred Emerson was not. Being also something of a prig and an elitist, again unlike Emerson, Thoreau could not always manage Emerson's insouciant *praxis* of building up a kind of Longinian discourse by quoting amply without citation. Self-consciousness kept breaking in, as it rarely does with Emerson, unless Emerson wills it thus. But if you cannot achieve freedom in quotation, if you cannot convert the riches of others to your own use without a darkening of consciousness, then what can it mean to demand that books and natural objects interchange their attributes? *Walden,* for all its incessant power, is frequently uneasy because of an unspoken presence, or a perpetual absence that might as well be a presence, and that emerges in Thoreau's *Journal:*

> Emerson does not consider things in respect to their essential
> utility, but an important partial and relative one, as works of
> art perhaps. His probes pass one side of their center of gravity.
> His exaggeration is of a part, not of the whole.

This is, of course, to find the fault that is not there, and qualifies only as a weak misreading of Emerson. Indeed, it is to attribute to Emerson what is actually Thoreau's revision of Emerson, since it is Thoreau who considers things as books, not Emerson, for whom a fact was an epiphany of God, God being merely what was oldest in oneself, that which went back before the Creation-Fall. Emerson, like the considerably less genial Carlyle, was a kind of Gnostic, but the rebel Thoreau remained a Wordsworthian, reading nature for evidences of a continuity in the ontological self that nature simply could not provide.

Thoreau on "Reading" in *Walden* is therefore chargeable with a certain bad faith, as here in a meditation where Emerson, the Plato of Concord, is not less than everywhere, present by absence, and perhaps even more absent by repressed presence:

> I aspire to be acquainted with wiser men than this our Concord
> soil has produced, whose names are hardly known here. Or
> shall I hear the name of Plato and never read his book? As if
> Plato were my townsman and I never saw him—my next neigh-
> bor and I never heard him speak or attended to the wisdom of
> his words. But how actually is it? His Dialogues, which contain
> what was immortal in him, lie on the next shelf, and yet I never
> read them. We are under-bred and low-lived and illiterate; and
> in this respect I confess I do not make any very broad distinc-

tion between the illiterateness of my townsman who cannot read at all, and the illiterateness of him who has learned to read only what is for children and feeble intellects. We should be as good as the worthies of antiquity, but partly by first knowing how good they were. We are a race of tit-men, and soar but little higher in our intellectual flights than the columns of the daily paper.

It is not all books that are as dull as their readers. There are probably words addressed to our condition exactly, which, if we could really hear and understand, would be more salutary than the morning or the spring to our lives, and possibly put a new aspect on the face of things for us. How many a man has dated a new era in his life from the reading of a book. The book exists for us perchance which will explain our miracles and reveal new ones. The at present unutterable things we may find somewhere uttered. These same questions that disturb and puzzle and confound us have in their turn occurred to all the wise men; not one has been omitted; and each has answered them, according to his ability, by his words and his life. More-over, with wisdom we shall learn liberality. The solitary hired man on a farm in the outskirts of Concord, who has had his second birth and peculiar religious experience, and is driven as he believes into silent gravity and exclusiveness by his faith, may think it is not true; but Zoroaster, thousands of years ago, travelled the same road and had the same experience; but he, being wise, knew it to be universal, and treated his neighbors accordingly, and is even said to have invented and established worship among men. Let him humbly commune with Zoroaster then, and, through the liberalizing influence of all the worthies, with Jesus Christ himself, and let "our church" go by the board.

The wisest man our Concord soil has produced need not be named, particularly since he vied only with Thoreau as a devoted reader of Plato. The second paragraph I have quoted rewrites the "Divinity School Address," but with the characteristic Thoreauvian swerve towards the authority of books, rather than away from them in the Emersonian manner. The reader or student, according to Emerson, is to consider herself or himself the text, and all received texts only as commentaries upon the scholar of one candle, as the title-essay of *Society and Solitude* prophesies Wallace

Stevens in naming that single one for whom all books are written. It may be the greatest literary sorrow of Thoreau that he could assert his independence from Emerson only by falling back upon the authority of texts, however recondite or far from the normative the text might be.

One can read Thoreau's continued bondage in *Walden*'s greatest triumph, its preternaturally eloquent "Conclusion":

> The life in us is like the water in the river. It may rise this year higher than man has ever known it, and flood the parched uplands; even this may be the eventful year, which will drown out all our muskrats. It was not always dry land where we dwell. I see far inland the banks which the stream anciently washed, before science began to record its freshets. Every one has heard the story which has gone the rounds of New England, of a strong and beautiful bug which came out of the dry leaf of an old table of apple-tree wood, which had stood in a farmer's kitchen for sixty years, first in Connecticut, and afterward in Massachusetts,—from an egg deposited in the living tree many years earlier still, as appeared by counting the annual layers beyond it; which was heard gnawing out for several weeks, hatched perchance by the heat of an urn. Who does not feel his faith in a resurrection and immortality strengthened by hearing of this? Who knows what beautiful and winged life, whose egg has been buried for ages under many concentric layers of woodenness in the dead dry life of society, deposited at first in the alburnum of the green and living tree, which has been gradually converted into the semblance of its well-seasoned tomb,—heard perchance gnawing out now for years by the astonished family of man, as they sat round the festive board,—may unexpectedly come forth from amidst society's most trivial and handselled furniture, to enjoy its perfect summer life at last!
>
> I do not say that John or Jonathan will realize all this; but such is the character of that morrow which mere lapse of time can never make to dawn. The light which puts out our eyes is darkness to us. Only that day dawns to which we are awake. There is more day to dawn. The sun is but a morning star.

The first of these paragraphs echoes, perhaps unknowingly, several crucial metaphors in the opening pages of Emerson's strongest single essay, "Experience," but more emphatically Thoreau subverts Emerson's emphasis upon a Transcendental impulse that cannot be repressed, even if one sets out deliberately to perform the experiment of "Experience," which is to follow empirical principles until they land one in an intolerable, more than skeptical, even nihilistic entrapment. Emerson, already more-than-Nietzschean in "Experience," is repudiated in and by the desperately energetic, indeed apocalyptic Transcendentalism of the end of *Walden,* an end that refuses Emersonian (and Nietzschean) dialectical irony. But the beautiful, brief final paragraph of *Walden* brings back Emerson anyway, with an unmistakable if doubtless involuntary allusion to the rhapsodic conclusion of *Nature,* where, however, the attentive reader always will hear (or overhear) some acute Emersonian ironies. "Try to live as though it were morning" was Nietzsche's great admonition to us, if we were to become Overmen, free of the superego. Nietzsche was never more Emersonian than in this, as he well knew. But when Thoreau eloquently cries out, "The sun is but a morning star," he is not echoing but trying to controvert Emerson's sardonic observation that you don't get a candle in order to see the sun rise. There may indeed be a sun beyond the sun, as Blake, D. H. Lawrence, and other heroic vitalists have insisted, but Thoreau was too canny, perhaps too New England to be a vitalist. *Walden* rings out mightily as it ends, but it peals another man's music, a man whom Thoreau could neither accept nor forget.

STANLEY CAVELL

Words

The very greatest masterpieces, when one is fresh from them, are apt to seem neglected. At such a time one knows, without stint, how unspeakably better they are than anything that can be said about them. An essential portion of the teaching of *Walden* is a full account of its all but inevitable neglect.

I assume that however else one understands Thoreau's topics and projects it is as a writer that he is finally to be known. But the easier that has become to accept, the more difficult it becomes to understand why his words about writing in *Walden* are not (so far as I know) systematically used in making out what kind of book he had undertaken to write, and achieved. It may be that the presence of his mysterious journals has too often attracted his serious critics to canvass there for the interpretation of *Walden*'s mysteries. My opening hypothesis is that this book is perfectly complete, in that it means every word it says, and that it is fully sensible of its mysteries and fully open about them.

Let us begin to read in an obvious place, taking our first bearings, and setting some standards, by looking at his explicit directions in the early chapter entitled "Reading." "The heroic books, even if printed in the character of our mother tongue, will always be in a language dead to degenerate times; and we must laboriously seek the meaning of each word and line, conjecturing a larger sense than common use permits out of what wisdom and valor and generosity we have." This may sound like a pious sentiment, one of those sentences that old-fashioned critics or book clubs like

From *The Senses of Walden.* © 1972 by Stanley Cavell. Viking Penguin, 1972.

to cite to express their high-mindedness. But it is the first step in entertaining Thoreau's intentions and ambitions to understand that he is there describing the pages he has himself readied for our hands. This may not be obvious at first, because the very extremity of his praise for what he calls "classics" and for "reading, in a high sense," together with his devotion to the "ancients," seems to imply that the making of such a book, a heroic book, in the America he depicts and in "this restless, nervous, bustling, trivial nineteenth century," is not a feasible enterprise. But it is axiomatic in *Walden* that its author praises nothing that he has not experienced and calls nothing impossible that he has not tried. More specifically, what is read in a high sense is "what we have to stand on tiptoe to read and devote our most alert and wakeful hours to," and again, "There are probably words addressed to our condition exactly, which, if we could really hear and understand, would be more salutary than the morning or the spring to our lives." Given the appearance of morning and spring in this book, what words could be *more* salutary than these? But then, given such words in the book as, "Morning is when I am awake and there is dawn in me," we recognize that morning may not be caused by sunrise, and may not happen at all. To discover how to earn and spend our most wakeful hours—whatever we are doing—is the task of *Walden* as a whole; it follows that its task, for us who are reading, is epitomized in discovering what reading in a high sense is and, in particular, if *Walden* is a heroic book, what reading *Walden* is. For the writer of *Walden,* its task is epitomized in discovering what writing is and, in particular, what writing *Walden* is.

It is hard to keep in mind that the hero of this book is its writer. I do not mean that it is about Henry David Thoreau, a writer, who lies buried in Concord, Massachusetts—though that is true enough. I mean that the "I" of the book declares himself to be a writer. This is hard to keep in mind because we seem to be shown this hero doing everything under the sun but, except very infrequently, writing. It takes a while to recognize that each of his actions is the act of a writer, that every word in which he identifies himself or describes his work and his world is the identification and description of what he understands his literary enterprise to require. If this seems to reduce the stature of what he calls his experiment, that is perhaps because we have a reduced view of what such an enterprise may be.

The obvious meaning of the phrase "heroic book," supported by the mention of Homer and Virgil, is "a book about a hero," an epic. The writer is aligning himself with the major tradition of English poetry, whose most ambitious progeny, at least since Milton, had been haunted by the call for a modern epic, for a heroic book which was at once a renewed instruction of the nation in its ideals, and a standing proof of its resources of poetry. For the first generation of Romantics, the parent generation to Thoreau's, the immediate epic event whose power their literary epic would have to absorb, was the French Revolution—the whole hope of it in their adolescence, and the scattered hopes in their maturity. The writer of *Walden* alludes to the three revolutions most resonant for his time. Of the Puritan revolution he says that it was "almost the last significant scrap of news" from England. Why almost? We don't really need a key for this, but Thoreau provides one in an essay on Carlyle which he wrote while living at Walden: "What . . . has been English news for so long a season? What . . . of late years, has been England to us—to us who read books, we mean? Unless we remembered it as the scene where the age of Wordsworth was spending itself, and a few younger muses were trying their wings. . . . Carlyle alone, since the death of Coleridge, has kept the promise of England." As against the usual views about Thoreau's hatred of society and his fancied private declaration of independence from it, it is worth hearing him from the outset publicly accept a nation's promise, identify the significant news of a nation with the state of its promise, and place the keeping of that promise in the hands of a few writers.

Of the events which keep burning on the Continent, the writer of *Walden* is apparently dismissive: "If one may judge who rarely looks into the newspapers, nothing new does ever happen in foreign parts, a French revolution not excepted." Marx, at about the same time, puts the point a little differently in his *Eighteenth Brumaire,* suggesting that it is only if you think like a newspaper that you will take the events of 1848 (or 1830) as front-page history; they belong on the theater page, or in the obituaries. But in *Walden*'s way of speaking, its remark also means that *the* French Revolution was not new. For example, the revolution we had here at home happened first, the one that began "two miles south" of where the writer is now sitting, on "our only field known to fame, Concord Battle Ground." For an American poet, placed in that historical locale, the American Revolution is more apt to constitute the absorbing epic event. Only it has two drawbacks: first, it is overshadowed by the epic event of America itself; second, America's revolution never happened. The colonists fought a war against England all right, and they won it. But it was not a war of independence that was won, because we are not free; nor was even secession the outcome, because we have not departed from the conditions England lives under, either in our literature or in our political and economic lives.

I understand the writer of *Walden* to be saying at least these things, in his way, when he announces for the second time the beginning of his

"experiment": "When first I took up my abode in the woods, that is, began to spend my nights as well as days there, which, by accident, was on
Independence Day, or the Fourth of July, 1845, my house was not finished
for winter." Good and learned readers, since at least Parrington, will have
such a passage behind them when they describe Thoreau as having written
a "transcendental declaration of independence." But why does the writer
say "by accident"? Merely to mock America's idea of what independence
comes to, and at the same time ruefully admit that he is, after all, one of
us? But he has been insisting on these things from the beginning. From
what is he supposed to have declared his independence? Clearly not from
society as such; the book is riddled with the doings of society. From society's beliefs and values, then? In a sense—at least independence from the
way society practices those beliefs and values. But that was what America
was for; it is what the original colonists had in mind.

Earlier, as an introduction to the first time we see the hero at his experiment, about to describe the building of his house, he quotes at some
length from two accounts, one contemporary and one nearly contemporary, of the first shelters the colonists made for themselves to get them
through the first winter in the world which for them was new. We know
the specific day in the specific year on which all the ancestors of New England took up their abode in the woods. That moment of origin is the national event re-enacted in the events of *Walden,* in order this time to do it
right, or to prove that it is impossible; to discover and settle this land, or
the question of this land, once for all. This is one reason that taking up
the abode on the Fourth of July is an accident.

Any American writer, any American, is apt to respond to that event
in one way or another; to the knowledge that America exists only in its
discovery and its discovery was always an accident; and to the obsession
with freedom, and with building new structures and forming new human
beings with new minds to inhabit them; and to the presentiment that this
unparalleled opportunity has been lost forever. The distinction of *Walden*'s
writer on this point (shared, I suppose, by the singer of *Leaves of Grass*
and by the survivor in *Moby-Dick*) lies in the constancy of this mood upon
him, his incarnation, one may call it, of this mood at once of absolute hope
and yet of absolute defeat, his own and his nation's. His prose must admit
this pressure and at every moment resolutely withstand it. It must live, if
it can, pressed between history and heaven:

> In any weather, at any hour of the day or night, I have been
> anxious to improve the nick of time, and notch it on my stick

too; to stand on the meeting of two eternities, the past and the future, which is precisely the present moment; to toe that line.

This open acknowledgment of his mysticism, or rather of the path to it, is also a dedication of his prose to that path. This is what "and notch it on my stick too" means—that he is writing it down, that his writing and his living manifest each other. The editor of *The Variorum Walden*, Walter Harding, is surely right to refer here to Robinson Crusoe's method of telling time; but that reference alone does not account for the methods of *Walden*'s writer, for what he would mean by telling time, in particular for what he means in claiming to notch not merely the passing of time but his improvement of it. It is when the writer has just gone over the succession of farms he had bought in imagination, and comes to his abode in the woods, that he says, "The present was my next experiment of this kind, which I purpose to describe more at length." Of course he means that the building of his habitation (which is to say, the writing of his book) is his present experiment. He also means what his words say: that the present is his experiment, the discovery of the present, the meeting of two eternities. ("God himself culminates in the present moment.") The most extended moment of the book which puts together the ideas of art and of the presentness which admits eternity, is the closing parable about the artist from Kouroo, the surface of which relates those ideas to the notching of a stick.

To say that the writer re-enacts the Great Migration and the inhabitation of this continent by its first settlers is not to suggest that we are to read him for literal alignments between the history of the events in his woods and in theirs. That would miss the significance of both, because the literal events of the Puritan colonization were from the beginning overshadowed by their meaning: it was itself a transcendental act, an attempt to live the idea; you could call it a transcendental declaration of freedom. (In his "A Plea for Captain John Brown," Thoreau praised this man once as a Puritan and once as a Transcendentalist.) This means that the writer's claims to privacy, secrecy, and isolation are as problematic, in the achievement and in the depiction of them, as any other of his claims. The more deeply he searches for independence from the Puritans, the more deeply, in every step and every word, he identifies with them—not only in their wild hopes, but in their wild denunciations of their betrayals of those hopes, in what has come to be called their jeremiads. (This is a standing difficulty for America's critics, as for Christianity's; Americans and Christians are prepared to say worse things about their own behavior than an outsider can readily imagine.) His identification extends even to the further meaning of the migration: to perform an experiment, a public demonstration of a truth; to become an example to those from whom they departed; to build, as they said to themselves, "a city on a hill."

This is one way I understand the writer's placing himself "one mile from any neighbor." It was just far enough to be seen clearly. However closely Thoreau's own "literary withdrawal" resembles those of the Romantics, in its need for solitude and for nature, the withdrawal he depicts in *Walden* creates a version of what the Puritan Congregationalists called a member of the church's congregation: a visible saint. On this ground, the audience for the writer's words and acts is the community at large, congregated. His problem, initially and finally, is not to learn what to say to them; that could not be clearer. The problem is to establish his right to declare it.

I have come to trust *Walden* and to trust its accuracy to its intentions when it says, "If you stand right fronting and face to face to a fact, you will see the sun glimmer on both its surfaces, as if it were a cimeter, and feel its sweet edge dividing you through the heart and marrow, and so you will happily conclude your mortal career." I cannot say that this writing always and everywhere brings me to this conclusion. But it often does, often enough so that when it does not I am not quick to determine whether it is failing me, or I it. My subject is nothing apart from sensing the specific weight of these words as they sink; and that means knowing the specific identities of the writer through his metamorphoses, and defining the audiences in me which those identities address, and so create; and hence understanding who I am that I should be called upon in these ways, and who this writer is that he takes his presumption of intimacy and station upon himself. For someone who cannot yield to Thoreau's words, or does not find them to warrant this power to divide him through, my subject will seem empty, even grotesque. Emerson did not quite share this enthusiasm, and yet he knew as well as anyone has known how good a writer Thoreau was, as he proved in his speech at Thoreau's funeral by the sentences he chose to read from the unpublished manuscripts. But in the large of it, the writing made him, as he said to his *Journal,* "nervous and wretched" to read. I find this response also to be accurate and essential to the reading of *Walden*—just not final. (The writer of *Walden* knows how trying his trials can be: "I sometimes try my acquaintances by such tests.")

How far off a final reading is, is something I hope I have already suggested. Every major term I have used or will use in describing *Walden* is a term that is itself in play within the book, part of its subject—e.g., migration, settling, distance, neighborhood improvement, departure, news, obscurity, clearing, writing, reading, etc. And the next terms we will need in order to explain the first ones will in turn be found subjected to examination in Thoreau's experiment. The book's power of dialectic, of self-comment and self-placement, in the portion and in the whole of it, is as instilled as in Marx or Kierkegaard or Nietzsche, with an equally vertiginous spiraling of idea, irony, wrath, and revulsion. Once in it, there seems no end; as soon as you have one word to cling to, it fractions or expands into others. This is one reason that he says, "There are more secrets in my trade than in most men's . . . inseparable from its very nature." But we do not yet know much else about that trade.

We started thinking along one line about what the writer of *Walden* calls "heroic books"; and while I take him there to be claiming an epic ambition, the terms in which he might project such an enterprise could not be those of Milton or Blake or Wordsworth. His talent for making a poem could not withstand such terms, and the nation as a whole to which he must speak had yet to acquire it. (He knows from the beginning, for example, that his book will not come in twelve or twenty-four parts.) In Thoreau's adolescence, the call for the creation of an American literature was still at a height: it was to be the final proof of the nation's maturity, proof that its errand among nations had been accomplished, that its specialness had 'permitted and in turn been proved by an original intelligence. In these circumstances, an epic ambition would be the ambition to compose the nation's *first* epic, so it must represent the bringing of language to the nation, words of its own in which to receive instruction, to assess its faithfulness to its ideal. The call for a new literature came, compounding difficulties, at an inconvenient moment in English literature generally, when it was all a writer like Carlyle could do to keep alive his faith in it. John Stuart Mill, three years younger than Emerson, says in his autobiography that a Romantic poem had helped him recover from the critical depression that preceded his maturity; but once he was recovered, it was Bentham's vision, not Coleridge's, say, that elicited the devotions of a model intellectual. Matthew Arnold, five years younger than Thoreau, spent a life accommodating to his nation's loss of poetry.

According to the assumption that the chapter on reading is meant as a description of the book before us, the one the writer in it went into the woods to write, it is explicitly said to be a scripture, and the language it is written in is what its writer calls the "father tongue."

> Those who have not learned to read the ancient classics in the
> language in which they were written must have a very imperfect

knowledge of the history of the human race; for it is remarkable that no transcript of them has ever been made into any
modern tongue, unless our civilization itself may be regarded as
such a transcript. Homer has never yet been printed in English,
nor Aeschylus, nor Virgil even, works as refined, as solidly
done, and as beautiful almost as the morning itself; for later
writers, say what we will of their genius, have rarely, if ever,
equaled the elaborate beauty and finish and the lifelong and heroic literary labors of the ancients. . . . That age will be rich indeed when those relics which we call Classics, and the still older
and more than classic but even less known Scriptures of the
nations, shall have still further accumulated, when the Vaticans
shall be filled with Vedas and Zendavestas and Bibles, with Ho-
mers and Dantes and Shakespeares, and all the centuries to
come shall have successively deposited their trophies in the fo-
rum of the world. By such a pile we may hope to scale heaven
at last.

The hardest thing to understand or believe about this is that the word
"scripture" is fully meant. This writer is writing a sacred text. This commits him, from a religious point of view, to the claim that its words are
revealed, received, and not merely mused. It commits him, from a literary
point of view, to a form that comprehends creation, fall, judgment, and
redemption; within it, he will have discretion over how much poetry to
include, and the extent of the moral code he prescribes; and there is room
in it for an indefinite amount of history and for a smaller epic or two.
From a critical point of view, he must be readable on various, distinct levels. *Walden* acknowledges this in a characteristic way: " 'They pretend,' as
I hear, 'that the verses of Kabir have four different senses; illusion, spirit,
intellect, and the exoteric doctrine of the Vedas'; but in this part of the
world it is considered a ground for complaint if a man's writings admit of
more than one interpretation." (This is characteristic in its orientalizing of
the mundane. There is just one text in the culture for which he writes that
is known to require interpretation on four distinct levels.)

Ways in which these commitments are to be realized in *Walden* are
made specific in the meaning of "father tongue."

Books must be read as deliberately and reservedly as they were
written. It is not enough even to be able to speak the language
of that nation by which they are written, for there is a memorable interval between the spoken and the written language, the

language heard and the language read. The one is commonly transitory, a sound, a tongue, a dialect merely, almost brutish, and we learn it unconsciously, like the brutes, of our mothers. The other is the maturity and experience of that; if that is our mother tongue, this is our father tongue, a reserved and select expression, too significant to be heard by the ear, which we must be born again in order to speak.

Were it not for certain current fantasies according to which human beings in our time have such things to say to one another that they must invent something beyond the words we know in order to convey them, it would be unnecessary to emphasize that "father tongue" is not a new lexicon or syntax at our disposal, but precisely a rededication to the inescapable and utterly specific syllables upon which we are already disposed. Every word the writer uses will be written so as to acknowledge its own maturity, so as to let it speak for itself; and in a way that holds out its experience to us, allows us to experience it, and allows it to tell us all it knows. "There are probably words addressed to our condition exactly, which, if we could really hear and understand, would be more salutary than the morning." There are words with our names on them—that is to say, every word in our nomenclature—but their existence is only probable to us, because we are not in a position to bring them home. In loyalty both to the rules of interpreting scripture and to the mother tongue, which is part of our condition, the writer's words must on the first level make literal or historical sense, present the brutest of fact. It is that condition from which, if we are to hear significantly, "we must be born again." A son of man is born of woman; but rebirth, according to our Bible, is the business of the father. So *Walden*'s puns and paradoxes, its fracturing of idiom and twisting of quotation, its drones of fact and flights of impersonation—all are to keep faith at once with the mother and the father, to unite them, and to have the word born in us.

Canonical forms of rebirth are circumcision and baptism. True circumcision is of the heart. It has never been very clear how that is to happen; but of course one ought not to expect otherwise: understanding such circumcision requires that you have undergone it; it is a secret inseparable from its very nature. Perhaps it will happen by a line of words so matured and experienced that you will see the sun glimmer on both its surfaces, as if it were a scimitar, and feel its sweet edge dividing you through the heart. Christ is to come with a sword, and in Revelation the sword is in his mouth. Of baptism, two moments are called for. The water of Walden

Pond is unique, but so is every other body of water, or drop, or place; and as universal. John could have used that water in the wilderness as well as any other. The baptism of water is only a promise of another which is to come, of the spirit, by the word of words. This is immersion not in the water but in the book of Walden.

There is a more direct sense in which scripture is written in the father language: it is the language of the father, the word of God; most particularly it is spoken, or expressed, by prophets.

> Then the word of the Lord came unto me, saying, Before I formed thee in the belly I knew thee; and before thou camest forth out of the womb I sanctified thee, and I ordained thee a prophet unto the nations. Then said I, Ah, Lord God! behold, I cannot speak: for I am a child.
>
> But the Lord said unto me, Say not, I am a child: for thou shalt go to all that I shall send thee, and whatsoever I command thee, thou shalt speak. . . . Then the Lord put forth his hand, and touched my mouth. And the Lord said unto me, Behold, I have put my words in thy mouth.
>
> (Jer. 1:4–9)

It is Ezekiel who anticipates most specifically the condition of prophecy in *Walden:*

> And he said unto me, Son of man, go, get thee unto the house of Israel, and speak with my words unto them. For thou art not sent to a people of a strange speech and of an hard language, but to the house of Israel; Not to many people of a strange speech and of an hard language, whose words thou canst not understand. Surely, had I sent thee to them, they would have hearkened unto thee. But the house of Israel will not hearken unto thee; for they will not hearken unto me: for all the house of Israel are impudent and hardhearted.
>
> (Ezek. 3:4–7)

The world of Ezekiel shares other particular features with the world of *Walden:* its writer received his inspiration "by waters"; it is written in captivity (what constitutes our captivity in *Walden* has yet to be outlined); it ends with elaborate specifications for the building of a house.

Milton, in *The Reason of Church Government,* trusted himself to identify with the vocation of Jeremiah and of the author of Revelations in justifying his right and his requirement to write as he did, "to claim . . .

with good men and saints" his "right of lamenting"; and he further attested to his sincerity by announcing that in undertaking this task he was postponing the use of his particular talent, to compose the nation's epic: "to fix all the industry and art I could unite to the adorning of my native tongue; not to make verbal curiosities the end . . . but to be an interpreter and relater of the best and sagest things among mine own citizens throughout this island in the mother dialect. ["For what are the classics but the noblest recorded thoughts of man?"] That what the greatest and choicest wits of Athens, Rome, or modern Italy, and those Hebrews of old did for their country, I in my proportion, with this over and above of being a Christian, might do for mine."

Do we really believe, even when it comes from John Milton, in the seriousness of such an identification and ambition? Or do we believe it, or tolerate it, just because it comes from Milton, who twenty-five years later made good with *Paradise Lost* on some highest promise or other? And if we cannot believe it, is that a skepticism about religion or about literature? And if we may believe it about Milton, would we find it credible that any later writer, and an American to boot, could justly, or sanely, so aspire? Blake's placing of himself on this ground is (though with apparently increasing exceptions) not credited. And by the time Wordsworth finds the seer in the child, the idea of the poet-prophet can conveniently seem to us the sheerest of Romantic conceits.

The writer of *Walden* is not counting on being believed; on the contrary, he converts the problem or condition of belief into a dominant subject of his experiment. As I was suggesting, his very familiarity with the fact that he will not be hearkened to, and his interpretation of it, are immediate identifications with Jeremiah and Ezekiel. His difference from them on this point, religiously speaking, is that the time of prophecy is past; the law has been fulfilled. So for both unbelievers and believers it is a stumbling block that a man should show himself subject to further prophecy. Yet this is New England, whose case rests upon the covenant. It ought to remain accessible to specific identifications with the prophets of the covenant.

The writer of *Walden* establishes his claim upon the prophetic writings of our Scripture by taking upon his work four of their most general features: (1) their wild mood-swings between lamentation and hope (because the position from which they are written is an absolute knowledge of faithlessness and failure, together with the absolute knowledge that this is not necessary, not from God, but self-imposed; and because God's prophets are auditors of the wild mood-swings of God himself); (2) the periodic confusions of their authors' identities with God's—stuck with the words in their mouths and not always able to remember how they got there; (3) their mandate to create wretchedness and nervousness (because they are "to judge the bloody city" and "show her all her abominations" [Ezek. 22:2]); (4) their immense repetitiveness. It cannot, I think, be denied that *Walden* sometimes seems an enormously long and boring book. (Again, its writer knows this; again it is part of his subject. "An old-fashioned man would have lost his senses or died of ennui before this." He is speaking of the lack of domestic sounds to comfort one in the woods, and he is also speaking of his book. In particular, he is acknowledging that it is not a novel, with its domestic sounds.) I understand this response to *Walden* to be a boredom not of emptiness but of prolonged urgency. Whether you take this as high praise of a high literary discovery, or as an excuse of literary lapse, will obviously depend on how high you place the book's value.

Chapter 7, called "The Bean Field," contains the writer's most open versions of his scriptural procedures or, as he puts it later, his revisions of mythology, because he says there explicitly that he is growing his beans not to eat but solely in order to get their message, so to speak: "I was determined to know beans . . . perchance, as some must work in fields if only for the sake of tropes and expression, to serve a parable-maker one day." He acknowledges that he is himself the parable-maker whom his work in the field will serve one day by composing an explicit parable in which his weeding of the field becomes the actions of Achilles before Troy:

> A long war, not with cranes, but with weeds, those Trojans who had sun and rain and dews on their side. Daily the beans saw me come to their rescue armed with a hoe, and thin the ranks of their enemies, filling up the trenches with weedy dead. Many a lusty crest-waving Hector, that towered a whole foot above his crowding comrades, fell before my weapon and rolled in the dust.

It is an uncommonly obvious moment; it gives no further significance either to his or to Achilles' behavior. It has nothing of the force and resonance he can bring to fable or to the mock-heroic when he wants to—e.g., in the comparison of his townsmen with Hercules, in the battle of the ants, or in the new myth of the locomotive. What the writer is mocking in the obviousness of this parable is parable-making itself, those moralizings over nature that had become during the past century a literary pastime, and with which his writing would be confused. With good reason: whatever else *Walden* is, it certainly depends on the tradition of topographical poetry—nothing can outdo its obsession with the seasons of a real place. The writer acknowledges this, too, in allowing the mockery—it is filially gentle—to point at himself and, hence, at Transcendentalism generally. This comes out pointedly in the following paragraph, when, after quoting Sir John Evelyn's "philosophical discourse of earth" and another piece of scientific-pious prose about " 'lay fields which enjoy their sabbath,' " he breaks off abruptly with, "I harvested twelve bushels of beans."

Less obviously, hoeing serves the writer as a trope—in particular, a metaphor—for writing. In the sentences preceding his little parable of the hoer-hero, the writer has linked these two labors of the hand: "—it will bear some iteration in the account, for there was no little iteration in the labor—." So the first value of the metaphorical equation of writing and hoeing is that his writing must bear up under repetitiveness. He takes the metaphor further: "making . . . invidious distinctions with [my] hoe, leveling whole ranks of one species, and sedulously cultivating another." That is, the writer's power of definition, of dividing, will be death to some, to others birth.

As elsewhere in *Walden,* an explicit fable from a foreign classic signals that another parable is under foot. The over-arching parable of the chapter on "The Bean Field" is one that describes the writer-hoer most literally, one which itself takes harrowing to be (a metaphor of) the effect of words:

> See, I have this day set thee over the nations and over the kingdoms, to root out, and to pull down, and to destroy, and to throw down, to build, and to plant.
>
> (Jer. 1:10)

Here is the parable-maker he is serving *this* day, whether hoeing or writing. The tropes and expressions for the sake of which he works in his field had already been employed; to perform "for the sake of them" is to perform because of them, in order that it shall be fulfilled as it is written. So of course he can only be serving "perchance." It is only through chance that he has been singled out for this service; the ordination is not his to confer, though it is his to establish. And only perchance will his service have its effect; there is a good chance that it will not.

If it does not work, he will not know why—whether it is his people's immovability, or God's, or his own. He keeps saying he doesn't much like hoeing, or the way he is hoeing; he is as irritated by it as he is by other men's devotion to nothing else but. And in fact the second half of this

chapter feels thin and irritable; a bad mood is in it. The writer's assertions
of hope or of rebuke do not flex upon themselves and soar, but remain
mere assertions, moralizings; it has been a bad harvest for him. He mani-
fests nothing like the equanimity in his later knowledge of harvesting:
"The true harvest of my daily life is somewhat as intangible and indescrib-
able as the tints of morning or evening. It is a little stardust caught, a seg-
ment of the rainbow which I have clutched." In the first part of "The Bean
Field" the sun is lighting him to hoe his beans, and it comes back at the
end ("We are wont to forget that the sun looks on our cultivated fields and
on the prairies and forests without distinction"). But at the center of the
chapter, the light of nature had gone bad: "I have sometimes had a vague
sense all the day of some sort of itching and disease in the horizon." This
happens "when there was a military turnout of which I was ignorant";
American militarism's conception of patriotism infects even the sky; its
present manifestation is the Mexican War. This is not the only time he as-
sociates despair with a corrupted idea of patriotism: "I sometimes despair
of getting anything quite simple and honest done in this world by the help
of men. They would have to be passed through a powerful press first, to
squeeze their old notions out of them." But "the great winepress of the
wrath of God" (Rev. 14:19) is not perfectly effective. The writer continues: "and there would be someone in the company with a maggot in his
head." In *Walden*'s "Conclusion" the "maggot in their heads" is patriotism.

The writer's next paragraph is uncharacteristically flat in its irony, totally exempting himself from it. "I felt proud to know that the liberties of
Massachusetts and of our fatherland were in such safe keeping; and as I
turned to my hoeing again I was filled with an inexpressible confidence,
and pursued my labor cheerfully with a calm trust in the future." His
mood of mock vainglory persists, and it produces perhaps the most revolted image in the book: "But sometimes it was a really noble and inspiring strain that reached these woods, and the trumpet that sings of fame,
and I felt as if I could spit a Mexican with a good relish." That is, our
bayonets in Mexico are the utensils of cannibals.

He acknowledges this despairing, revolted mood a page or so later
when he again picks up the tilling theme from Jeremiah, this time with a
didactically explicit acceptance of that identity:

> I said to myself, I will not plant beans and corn with so much
> industry another summer, but such seeds, if the seed is not lost,
> as sincerity, truth, simplicity, faith, innocence, and the like, and

see if they will not grow in this soil, even with less toil and ma-
nurance, and sustain me, for surely it has not been exhausted
for these crops. Alas! I said this to myself; but now another
summer is gone, and another, and another, and I am obliged to
say to you, Reader, that the seeds which I planted, if indeed
they *were* seeds of those virtues, were wormeaten or had lost
their vitality, and so did not come up.

It is when Jeremiah is momentarily free of God's voice, and hence of the
ordainment to speak to kingdoms and nations, that he says, and hence says
to himself:

When I would comfort myself against sorrow, my heart is faint
in me. Behold the voice of the cry of the daughter of my people
because of them that dwell in a far country: Is not the Lord in
Zion? is not her king in her? Why have they provoked me to
anger with their graven images, and with strange vanities? The
harvest is past, the summer is ended, and we are not saved.

(Jer. 8:18–20)

"Alas! I said this to myself": What he said to himself was, Alas!—and alas,
that I can say it only to myself. The writer knows that "he that ploweth
should plow in hope" (1 Cor. 9:10). But he has also known, from the beginning, that he is unable to follow that injunction faithfully: "the same
sun which ripens my beans illumines at once a system of earths like ours.
If I had remembered this it would have prevented some mistakes. This was
not the light in which I hoed them."

Hoeing is identified not just with the content and effect of words; it
is also an emblem of the physical act of writing, as though the sheer fact
that a thing is written is as important as what is said. For the writer's hoe,
the earth is a page; with it, the tiller "[makes] the yellow soil express its
summer thought in bean leaves and blossoms rather than in wormwood
and piper and millet grass, making the earth say beans instead of grass."
This is figured when the artist from Kouroo writes a name in the sand with
the point of his stick. The underlying idea of nature as a book is familiar
enough; in Bacon, it justifies the scientific study of nature; in Deism, it
might be used to ornament a teleological argument for the existence of
God. But for an Ezekiel, let us say, these are hardly the issues. In what we
call spring, and what the writer of *Walden* shows to be an Apocalypse,
bringing his life in the woods to an end, the vision of blood and excrement
is transformed into a vision of the earth and its dependents in a crisis of

foliation; these leaves in turn produce a vision of the world as an open book. The idea is literalized when he speaks of "the fine print, the small type, of a meadow mouse"; or speaks of the snow as reprinting old footsteps "in clear white type alto-relievo."

But heroic books are themselves a part of nature: "the noblest written words are as commonly as far behind or above the fleeting spoken language as the firmament with its stars is behind the clouds. *There* are the stars, and they who can may read them." It may seem that the writer is placing his idea of the meaning of nature in a different category altogether from the meaning of words when he turns from the chapter called "Reading" to that called "Sounds" and remarks, "Much is published, but little printed." We know he means that nature is at every instant openly confiding in us, in its largest arrangements and in its smallest sounds, and that it is mostly lost on our writers. But the remark also describes the ontological condition of words: the occurrence of a word is the occurrence of an object whose placement always has a point, and whose point always lies before and beyond it. "The volatile truth of our words should continually betray the inadequacy of the residual statement. Their truth is instantly *translated;* its literal monument alone remains." (As Wittgenstein puts it: "The sign itself is dead.")

This theme is declared as the book opens, in its flat first sentence: "When I wrote the following pages, or rather the bulk of them, I lived alone, in the woods, a mile from any neighbor, in a house which I had built by myself, on the shore of Walden Pond, in Concord, Massachusetts, and earned my living by the labor of my hands only." On a second perusal, this sentence raises more questions than it answers—about where Concord is, and what a pond is, and how far a mile is, and who the neighbor is, and what earning a living is. Now what is "the bulk" of the pages he wrote? We know that Thoreau wrote about half of *Walden* during the years in which his hut was his abode; but *every* page the writer writes, wherever he is and whatever writing is, is merely, or ontologically, the bulk of writing: the mass or matter of it, the body or looming of it, its physical presence. Writing is a labor of the hands. We know from the third paragraph of the book that labor which is not the labor of slaves has a finish; and we know, from what is said about hoeing, that labor at its best "[yields] an instant and immeasurable crop." Writing, at its best, will come to a finish in each mark of meaning, in each portion and sentence and word. That is why in reading it "we must laboriously seek the meaning of every word and line; conjecturing a larger sense."

We are apt to take this to mean that writing, in a high sense, writing which is worth heroic reading, is meant to provide occasions for our conjecturing. That is not wrong, but it is likely to be lukewarm, a suggestion that the puns and paradoxes, etc., are tips or goads to us to read with subtlety and activity, and that we are free to conjecture the writer's meaning. But in *Walden,* reading is not merely the other side of writing, its eventual fate; it is another metaphor of writing itself. The writer cannot invent words as "perpetual suggestions and provocations"; the written word is already "the choicest of relics." His calling depends upon his acceptance of this fact about words, his letting them come to him from their own region, and then taking that occasion for inflecting them one way instead of another then and there, or for refraining from them then and there; as one may inflect the earth toward beans instead of grass, or let it alone, as it is before you are there. The words that the writer raises "out of the trivialness of the street" are the very words or phrases or lines used there, by the people there, in whatever lives they have. This writer's raising of them to us, by writing them down, is only literally, or etymologically, a matter of style, scratching them in. Raising them up, to the light, so to speak, is the whole thing he does, not the adornment of it. The manner is nothing in comparison with the act. And the labor of raising them up is itself one of seeking "the meaning of each word and line," of "conjecturing a larger sense . . . out of what wisdom and valor and generosity" the writer has. Conjecturing is not for the writer, and hence not for the reader, what we think of as guesswork. It is casting words together and deriving the conclusions of each. This is how his labor of the hands earned his living, whatever it was.

Why is the isolation of the written from the spoken word his understanding of the father tongue? Why is it his realization of the faith of the prophets? That is, how does his understanding of his position—in Concord, Massachusetts, "in the Presidency of Polk, five years before the passage of Webster's Fugitive-Slave Bill"—take him beyond the knowledge prophets have always had of the ineffectiveness of God's words in their mouths; or take him to a different resolution of his ordainment?

I understand his strategy as an absolute acceptance of Saint Paul's interpretation of Christ's giving "gifts unto men" (Eph. 4): "I therefore, the prisoner of the Lord, beseech you that ye walk worthy of the vocation wherewith ye are called." According to Paul, the gifts for "the perfecting of the saints, for the work of the ministry, for the edifying of the body of Christ" are divided—among apostles, prophets, evangelists, pastors, and teachers. For the writer of *Walden,* in declaring writing to be such a gift, in such a service, the problem of walking worthy of it is different from, anyway later than, Milton's view of his talent: he must learn not merely what to write, in order that his trust not be buried; he must undertake to write absolutely, to exercise his faith in the very act of marking the word. He puts his hand upon his own mouth.

This fulfillment of his call to prophecy overthrows the mode of the old and the new prophecies of the word—their voicing of it. It directly disobeys the cardinal motivation of Puritan preaching—that the word be spoken and confessed aloud. The time for such prophesying is absolutely over. We have heard it said, "We shall all stand before the judgment seat of Christ . . . every tongue shall confess to God. So then, every one shall give account of himself to God" (Rom. 14:10–12). But *Walden* shows that we *are* there; every tongue has confessed what it can; we have heard everything there is to hear. There were prophets, but there is no Zion; knowing that, Jesus fulfilled them, but the kingdom of heaven is not entered into; knowing that, the founding fathers brought both testaments to this soil, and there is no America; knowing that, Jonathan Edwards helped bring forth a Great Awakening, and we are not awake. The experiment of man ("We are the subjects of an experiment") has failed. Not that any of man's dreams may not come to pass. But there is absolutely no more to be *said* about them. What is left to us is the accounting. Not a recounting, of tales or news; but a document, with each word a warning and a teaching; a deed, with each word an act.

This is what those lists of numbers, calibrated to the half cent, mean in *Walden*. They of course are parodies of America's methods of evaluation; and they are emblems of what the writer wants from writing, as he keeps insisting in calling his book an *account*. As everywhere else, he undertakes to make the word good. A true mathematical reckoning of the sort he shows requires that every line be a mark of honesty, that the lines be complete, omitting no expense or income, and that there be no mistake in the computation. Spoken words are calculated to deceive. How are written words different? The mathematical emblem embodies two ways. First, it is part of a language which exists *primarily* as notation; its point is not the fixing of a spoken language, which had preceded it, but the fixing of steps, which can thereby be remarked. Second, the notation works only when every mark within it means something, in its look and its sequence. Among written works of art, only of poetry had we expected a commitment to total and transparent meaning, every mark bearing its brunt. The literary ambition of *Walden* is to shoulder the commitment in prose.

This ambition, directed toward the establishing of American literature, had to overcome two standing literary achievements with speech:

Wordsworth's attempted redemption of the human voice and of poetry by one another; and America's peculiar exaltation of the oration and the sermon. The task of literature is to rescue the word from both politics and religion. ("God is only the president of the day, and Webster is his orator.") Even Emerson, in his literature of the sermon, has made a false start. However wonderful, it is not a beginning but an end of something. His voice consoles; it is not of warning, and so not of hope.

I will not insist upon it, but I understand the allusion to Emerson in *Walden* to acknowledge this relation to him.

> There was one other with whom I had "solid seasons," long to
> be remembered, at his house in the village, and who looked in
> upon me from time to time; but I had no more for society there.

It may be the most unremarkable paragraph of the book; not just because it is one of the shortest, but because it contributes nothing to the account of the visitors the writer received. What is it there for? "I had no more for society there," beyond saying that no one else visited him, can be taken as saying that he could give no more time or take no more interest in Emerson's social position, which is all he offered. But this writer knows who Emerson is, his necessity as a presence and as a writer. Why would he take a crack at him? Nor can the paragraph be there merely to make the account complete, for the notching must mark not simply the occurrence of time but the improvement of it. So in this case the act of marking must itself be the improvement. There is an earlier notice of a visitor whose name the writer is "sorry I cannot print . . . here." For me, these curiosities come together in Ezekiel's vision which contains the myth of the writer:

> And [God] called to the man clothed with linen, which had the
> writer's inkhorn by his side; And the Lord said unto him, Go
> through the midst of the city, through the midst of Jerusalem,
> and set a mark upon the foreheads of the men that sigh and
> that cry for all the abominations that be done in the midst
> thereof.
>
> And to the others he said in mine hearing, Go ye after him
> through the city, and smite: let not your eye spare, neither have
> ye pity: . . . but come not near any man upon whom is the
> mark.
>
> (Ezek. 9:3–6)

The writer's nameless marking of Emerson is done in order to preserve him and, simultaneously, to declare that his own writing has the power of life and death in it. America's best writers have offered one another the shock of recognition but not the faith of friendship, not daily belief. Perhaps this is why, or it is because, their voices seem to destroy one another. So they destroy one another for us. How is a tradition to come out of that?

Study of *Walden* would perhaps not have become such an obsession with me had it not presented itself as a response to questions with which I was already obsessed: Why has America never expressed itself philosophically? Or has it—in the metaphysical riot of its greatest literature? Has the impulse to philosophical speculation been absorbed, or exhausted, by speculation in territory, as in such thoughts as manifest destiny? Or are such questions not really intelligible? They are, at any rate, disturbingly like the questions that were asked about American literature before it established itself. In rereading *Walden,* twenty years after first reading it, I seemed to find a book of sufficient intellectual scope and consistency to have established or inspired a tradition of thinking. One reason it did not is that American culture has never really believed in its capacity to produce anything of permanent value—except itself. So it forever overpraises and undervalues its achievements.

How is one to write so as to receive the power of life and death? Shelley's "unacknowledged legislators of the world" still had to be poets; Carlyle saw modern heroes in mere men of letters. For Thoreau these are not answers, but more questions. How is writing to declare its faithfulness to itself, in that power? How is it to rescue language?

My discussion suggests the following direction of answer. Writing—heroic writing, the writing of a nation's scripture—must assume the conditions of language as such; re-experience, as it were, the fact that there is such a thing as language at all and assume responsibility for it—find a way to acknowledge it—until the nation is capable of serious speech again. Writing must assume responsibility, in particular, for three of the features of the language it lives upon: (1) that every mark of a language means something in the language, one thing rather than another; that a language is totally, systematically meaningful; (2) that words and their orderings are meant by human beings, that they contain (or conceal) their beliefs, express (or deny) their convictions; and (3) that the saying of something when and as it is said is as significant as the meaning and ordering of the words said.

Until we are capable of serious speech again—i.e., are reborn, are men "[speaking] in a waking moment, to men in their waking moments"—our words do not carry our conviction, we cannot fully back them, because either we are careless of our convictions, or think we haven't any, or imagine they are inexpressible. They are merely unutterable. ("The at present unutterable things we may find somewhere uttered." Perhaps in the words he is now writing.) The written word, on a page, will have to show that a particular man set it there, inscribed it, chose, and made the mark. Set on its page, "carved out of the breath of life itself," the word must stand for silence and permanence; that is to say, for conviction. Until we can speak again, our lives and our language betray one another; we can grant to neither of them their full range and autonomy; they mistake their definitions of one another. A written word, as it recurs page after page, changing its company and modifying its occasions, must show its integrity under these pressures—as though the fact that all of its occurrences in the book of pages are simultaneously there, awaiting one another, demonstrates that our words need not haunt us. If we learn how to entrust our meaning to a word, the weight it carries through all its computations will yet prove to be just the weight we will find we wish to give it.

How is a writer to show, or acknowledge, something true of language as such? I have begun in this chapter to answer that question for the writer of *Walden*—according to my reading of him. So another question has arisen: What will it mean to be the reader of such a writer?

JAMES McINTOSH

"The Shipwreck":
A Shaped Happening

"The Shipwreck," the first chapter of *Cape Cod*, represents ... [a] meeting with inhuman nature, another occasion when the individual mind finds itself bereft and confused in the external world. More specifically, it is an occasion in which Thoreau confronts the fact of human death in the wild landscape of the seashore. As we have seen [elsewhere] in the early journal, when Thoreau meditates on death, he recognizes—albeit reluctantly—a difference between man and other natural beings. The creatures and creations of *phusis* do not experience death in the same way that humans do, in that plants and animals lack the consciousness that they are going to die or that death takes place around them. They thus lack any conception of the morbid; whereas a romantic naturalist so reflective as Thoreau is inevitably aware of the possibilities of decay and nothingness in nature; and this awareness again separates him from nature.

Thoreau handles his uncomfortable awareness of death in several ways when it intrudes in his writing on nature. [Elsewhere] we have already seen him try to rid himself of it as if it were a disease of the mind that could nevertheless be cured or at least made tolerable by proper intercourse with naturally dying and becoming things. When he writes, "I not yet grey on rocks forever gray. I no longer green under the evergreens," he is in a mood to accept his mortality as a mere "phenomenon in the life of nature." But Thoreau will not bask in this tranquil, mollified mood for long; his professions of indolence are but provisional. Like the Puritans he

From *Thoreau as Romantic Naturalist.* © 1974 by Cornell University. Cornell University Press, 1974.

comes back and back to the question of what it is to be truly human, truly regenerate, truly absolved of mortality in a more than natural sense, and when he is in this neo-Puritan state of mind he exhibits reservations about "natural eternity." For example, as he reflects in *A Week on the Concord and Merrimack Rivers* on the pigeons he and John have killed, he generalizes their fate: "They must perish miserably; not one of them is translated." Thoreau shows here obliquely but clearly that he has not renounced the human hope to be "translated," to be removed in death to a realm of happy eternity where souls do not die. The impersonal, unending circulation of an ever-progressing nature is insufficient to satisfy such a hope.

Sometimes, Thoreau sees death in nature not as a mere stage in the endless natural cycle but as a prospect that is a good deal more threatening. Death becomes at moments not a phenomenon in an organic process of recreation but rather a phenomenon of *disorganization,* in which things that die lose their structure and become formless, and the human observer is estranged from the disorder in nature that he now sees in the spectacle of death. This sense of death such writers as Thoreau and Goethe fought with all the strategies at their command, including the strategy of omitting to talk about it. But Thoreau at least on occasion also has the courage to articulate his sense of death-as-disorganization and to try to allow it its place in the totality of his work. One such occasion is "The Shipwreck."

Readers who dismiss Thoreau's imaginative concern with death as abnormal and distasteful, untypical of a healthy-minded naturalist, may miss some of the excitement of his skirmishes with morbidity. He does not allow himself to be comfortably in love with death, as Whitman might, but in his images of death one sometimes feels a surge of controlled, dangerous energy coming into his writing, for example when he wishes for self-dissolution in "The Thaw" or when he invites the reader in *Walden* to look hard at "reality," and feel the bliss of suicide in the perception of the real: "If you stand right fronting and face to face to a fact, you will see the sun glimmer on both its surfaces, as if it were a cimeter, and feel its sweet edge dividing you through the heart and marrow, and so you will happily conclude your mortal career." Here "the nostalgia for the object" is carried to extremes indeed! Such a startling conceit is a fine incidental thought in "Where I Lived and What I Lived For," a fragmentary felicity in the poetry of extra-vagance. Often Thoreau's meditations on death are like this. They are brief excursions into a realm of thought he prefers to visit only briefly, but they are also honest exhibitions of what he perceives there. They are examples of his willingness to cherish a perception or inspiration even if it runs counter to the ordinary grain of his thought.

Thoreau saunters around the problem of death in *Walden,* giving it occasional glancing recognition and engaging it profoundly only by indirection. He reserved most of his more explicit meditations on death for the privacy of his journal. The source of the power of "The Shipwreck," on the other hand, is that he is wrestling with his thoughts and feelings about human and natural death openly and in public, presenting them in their natural incoherence but reflecting on them as a deliberate artist. He tries both to expose his reactions and to shape them artistically, so that they will point the way toward some cumulative meaning, and so that the occasion which prompts them will become a significant episode, will take on the quality of a truthful if obscure recollection of intense experience.

I focus on "The Shipwreck" for three reasons. First, it is another, more effectively shocking encounter between Thoreau and the estranging otherness of nature. Like Keats, Thoreau "saw too far into the sea," and the conclusion to which this seeing leads him in the chapter is less "forgetful," more pessimistic than the final summary of "Ktaadn." Second, it is a rare direct and sustained recognition that the wild nature he desires is the scene and even the cause of death for men and animals. Third, it is a brief but complex example of Thoreau's method in drawing art from the chaos of nature, including the nature of his own mind. I have written of several shaped episodes in his work, among them "Saddleback," "A Walk to Wachusett," and the summit climb in "Ktaadn." All three of these, though they are forceful and engaging narratives, contain conscious or unconscious inconsistencies in Thoreau's attitude toward nature. Yet I do not feel that these inconsistencies necessarily mar the episodes; on the contrary, they may add to the dense liveliness of the narrative, may reflect Thoreau's rash or brave willingness to be double-minded for the sake of a more encompassing truth. "The Shipwreck" is an extreme example of Thoreau's willful but purposeful inconsistency. He seems to throw himself into the encounter and let it guide his reactions. Both the narrative of the events on Cohasset beach and the thoughts that accompany this narrative have the character of a "happening"—a cluster of linked observations, presented seemingly unmodified as they occur to him on the scene. Thoreau does not take one attitude toward the sea, but a succession of different attitudes. Thus he becomes, even more than usually, the speaker or narrator in a dramatic meditation. He responds feelingly to each new thought, and tries by shifts of feeling, not by normal logic, to come to terms with nature and death. He arrives at no final answers—the shipwreck is too compelling and inscrutable an event for that. Instead he throws out solutions, and then finally comes to a definite stance, which he maintains till the end of the chapter but no longer.

"The Shipwreck" is not, however, a chaotic, formless rumination. There is a residue of uncertainty in it; it presents a man caught in the crosscurrents of his own thought. But one may argue that this uncertainty is only "natural." A reaching out for disparate ideas, an attempt to follow paths with uncertain tendencies is characteristic of Thoreau's mind. I would attribute this naturalness of style, this unresolved irregularity of point of view in part to deliberate intention. The naturalness is parallel to the hypaethral quality of the *Week;* and when Thoreau recommends that our lives be part ordered meadow and part unordered forest in "Walking," he gives us a metaphor for his own writing. Moreover, the opposed attitudes in "The Shipwreck" (or some of them) are pitted against each other in dramatic conflict. Part of the nervous force of the chapter comes, as in much of Thoreau, from the attempt to combine and confine polarized opposites in little space. Finally, the last pages of the chapter are "more than natural," are poetic and highly artful. They constitute a beautiful if partial and transient resolution of its earlier uncertainties. The narrator has first recorded the event as it happened, then ruminated over it, and then imposed on it a unifying idea that emerges clearly at the end and functions as a remembering commentary on the issues raised by the wreck.

Like *The Maine Woods, Cape Cod* as a whole is a description of place, drawing on several visits and much reading, not a straightforward narrative of a single experience. The book contains a variety of styles and moods; it is crotchety and entertaining, as well as somber. Parts of it are slow going—Thoreau likes complete descriptions. "The Shipwreck" is, as it were, the first patch in this large quilt: it is bound to the rest but has its own distinctive character. Yet, though it can be treated as a separate unit, it sets the tone for much of the book and presents themes that are recalled and re-emphasized later. Reciprocally, the book as a whole helps us to understand "The Shipwreck." The narrative thread that ties together the various chapters is based on Thoreau's and Ellery Channing's holiday jaunt of October 1849, beginning with their visit to the Cohasset beach. The Cape Cod landscape and weather in this season are especially undomestic and unpredictable. Man and the unstable land are at the mercy of the ocean. "The Shipwreck" and portions of the rest of the book reflect the wildness of the season, and the sense that one walks on the Cape between intervals of storm.

Thoreau seeks in this excursion just such an unfamiliar and unpredictable landscape. He goes to the Cape, he says in the first sentence of the book, "to get a better view than I had yet had of the ocean, which, we are told, covers more than two thirds of the globe, but of which a man who lives a few miles inland may never see any trace, more than of another world." The excursion to the Cape is, in other words, another wandering away from towns and homes into the wild. The ocean, we saw from the early journal, is a symbol of the sublime, of an endless, abundant, terrifying nature. Thoreau's imagination seeks out the "bold," "wild," and "desolate" "grandeur" and "variety" of the sea and shore. He wants, as in his mountain excursions, to get away from narrowly cultured men, to remind himself how small man is and how great nature. "I wished to see that seashore where man's works are wrecks; to put up at the true Atlantic House, where the ocean is land-lord as well as sea-lord, and comes ashore without a wharf for the landing; where the crumbling land is the only invalid, or at best is but dry land, and that is all you can say of it."

But this sea, this wild nature so inspiriting to him still, is nevertheless clearly separate from him, a world entirely different. Perhaps he is influenced by his experience on Ktaadn, or perhaps a landscape similarly vast and inhospitable calls up a similar response; in any case, Thoreau is facing another challenge to his early optimistic holism. Seldom does he find correspondences between man and nature in *Cape Cod*. He does not at all identify himself with particular things in the landscape, as with the white lily, the bittern, or the pond. Similarly, he finds no occasion for a cheerful erotic apostrophe to nature as in his other books—nothing like "Concord River" or the conclusion to "Ktaadn," in which he feels related to nature as to a secret source of nourishing life. If the Greeks were wrong to call the ocean "unfruitful," if, as modern science has shown, it teems with primitive animals and functions as "the laboratory of continents," the walker nevertheless contemplates the laboratory from a safe distance.

There are two stances Thoreau may take toward this separated nature. The first is to affirm it in its full distinctiveness. Though separate from man's mind, nature is yet a great *kosmos* in which all living things not only are related, but also have independent value in themselves. Thoreau's errand in *Cape Cod* is thus to discover, as in the early journal, "how good potato blows are," to observe each thing in and for itself: the sea jellies, mackeral gulls, and mosses, all with delicate organizations and yet able to live in the sea as man cannot, or the phalarope that sports with the waves, "as perfect a success in its way as the breakers in theirs." In such a *kosmos* man plays a real but insignificant role. He is one more "product of the seaslime"; yet this fact of his derivation constitutes his only genuine kinship with the sea.

Human disaster also contributes to the life of the *kosmos*, and from Thoreau's affirming, cosmical perspective it is not important enough to interrupt that life. When Thoreau finds beets growing wild on the Cape, he surmises that their seeds came ashore with the shipwrecked Franklin. He then moralizes, "It is an ill wind that blows nobody any good, and for the time lamentable shipwrecks may thus contribute a new vegetable to a continent's stock, and prove on the whole a lasting blessing to its inhabitants." Though Thoreau first thinks of the "dreary peep of the piping plover" as "a fugacious part in the dirge which is ever played along the shore for those mariners who have been lost in the deep since first it was created," he pulls up short and adds that "the same strain which is a dirge to one household is a morning song of rejoicing to another." The death of men at sea need not be felt as a catastrophe; it is a phenomenon in the life of nature, a necessary occurrence in nature's progress.

Yet even in these attempts to justify nature, shipwrecks are "lamentable." According to a second and equally pervasive point of view in *Cape Cod,* man is all important and alien nature is a grim threat. The book has no references to fancied mariners who gladly lay down their lives in the sublimity of storms. Repeatedly, human death is felt as the great fact revealed on the Cape, to which all other natural facts are subordinate. We keep hearing a muffled dirge for the dead throughout *Cape Cod,* to which the plover's peep contributes. When the thought of death comes to him, Thoreau searches for a way to make a seemly and human response to it. His recourse is often to revert to the anthropocentric, idealist Christianity of his forebears. He finds "Sit Nomen Domini Benedictum (Blessed Be the Name of the Lord)"—the motto on the reverse of a French coin lying on the sand—"a pleasing sentiment to read in the sands of the seashore." His moments of elegy read, in sentiment and cadence, like seventeenth-century prose, though with a Thoreauvian whimsical twist. On finding an ale bottle on the beach, he reflects:

> As I poured it slowly out on to the sand, it seemed to me that man himself was like a half-emptied bottle of pale ale, which Time had drunk so far, yet stoppled tight for a while, and drifting about in the ocean of circumstances, but destined ere-long to mingle with the surrounding waves, or be spilled amid the sands of a distant shore.

The ale bottle is a characteristic example of Thoreau's use of metaphor in *Cape Cod.* Instead of romantic correspondences, he seeks emblematic illustrations of the human fate, which often read like the jottings of a skeptical Father Mapple on holiday. In other words, when his romantic poetics break down, he resorts to the poetics of a Sir Thomas Browne or of one of the more lively Puritan sermon writers. As Sherman Paul points out, Thoreau intends in *Cape Cod* to remind readers of the religious earnestness of the New England past. He honors the Pilgrims as pioneers in spiritual liberty, and appreciates some of their descendents on the Cape for their sober Puritan beliefs and their simple and hardy Puritan habits. Yet Thoreau himself, I would add, is no believer or ignorant provincial. Christian idealism is for him a "fiction" in Frank Kermode's sense, a belief that he experiments with temporarily and poetically in order to deal with the idea of death and the otherness of nature.

From a man-centered viewpoint, the nature Thoreau observes on Cape Cod is inhuman, constantly threatening, the cause of death. In an extended meditation in "The Sea and the Desert," he finds, as in *Contact! Contact!,* a sublime hostility at the heart of things.

> It is a wild, rank place, and there is no flattery in it. Strewn with crabs, horseshoes, and razor clams, and whatever the sea casts up,—a vast *morgue,* where famished dogs may range in packs, and crows come daily to glean the pittance which the tide leaves them. The carcasses of men and beasts together lie stately up upon its shelf, rotting and bleaching in the sun and waves, and each tide turns them in their beds, and tucks fresh sand under them. There is naked Nature,—inhumanly sincere, wasting no thought on man, nibbling at the cliffy shore where gulls wheel amid the spray.

This characterization of nature, however, follows directly on Thoreau's realization that man is a product of the sea-slime. Again, he is not drawing a logical conclusion, but exhibiting a many-sided truth. The ocean has created man; but at the same time nature on the seashore is inhuman. A page later the ocean itself is "a wilderness reaching round the globe, wilder than a Bengal jungle, and fuller of monsters, washing the very wharves of our cities." Yet Thoreau's final reaction to this wildness is not to be appalled by it but to think of it as providing an opportunity for heroic adventure. "To go to sea! Why, it is to have the experience of Noah,—to realize the deluge. Every vessel is an ark." In this conclusion (for the sequence of thought ends here), Thoreau has reverted to his original purpose—joyfully to confront the wild. He has put the thought of the shore as a "vast morgue" and that of the sea as a "Bengal jungle" behind him, has temporarily "forgotten" these disturbing images. Yet the pessimistic view of nature must be remembered as a feature of Thoreau's total vision. It is the predominant view in "The Shipwreck."

Nature is not felt in "The Shipwreck" as an organic whole, but only as power. Whereas the details of Thoreau's descriptions of the river and the woods in *A Week on the Concord and Merrimack Rivers* and "Ktaadn" may be secretly bound together in the body of a *phuendos kosmos,* the texture of details in "The Shipwreck" is more like anarchic patchwork. Objects exist independently alongside each other, like natural objects in the rest of *Cape Cod,* but without the suggestion of functional connection in the *kosmos* we find even there.

> A little further along the shore we saw a man's clothes on a rock; further, a woman's scarf, a gown, a straw bonnet, the brig's caboose, and one of her masts high and dry, broken into several pieces. In another rocky cove ... lay a part of one side of the vessel, still hanging together. It was, perhaps, forty feet long, by fourteen feet wide. I was ever more surprised at the power of the waves, exhibited on this shattered fragment, than I had been at the sight of the smaller fragments before. The largest timbers and iron braces were broken superfluously, and I saw that no material could withstand the power of the waves; that iron must go to pieces in such a case, and an iron vessel would be cracked up like an egg-shell on the rocks.

What connects these fragmentary details is the event of the shipwreck itself, the solemn fact of the power of nature as represented by the rock and as exhibited in the scattering of human things. When that power is exercised, it leads (as the Boston handbill has it) to "Death! one hundred and forty-five lives lost at Cohasset."

In Thoreau's narrative death functions like a magnet, around which diverse objects momentarily cluster. "The Shipwreck" seems entirely "natural"—in the sense that the narrator gives the impression that he is excluding nothing, reporting everything he sees—but it is also focused and unified, around human death. As his narrative proceeds, Thoreau demands, without sentimental overemphasis, our gravest attention for examples of death: for the immigrant woman who lies in a box with her sister's child in her arms, or for the drowned girl who so impressed Robert Lowell that he used Thoreau's account of her in "A Quaker Graveyard in Nantucket."

> I saw many marble feet and matted heads as the cloths were raised, and one livid, swollen, and mangled body of a drowned girl,—who probably had intended to go out to service in some American family,—to which some rags still adhered, with a

string, half-concealed by the flesh, about its swollen neck; the coiled-up wreck of a human hulk, gashed by the rocks or fishes, so that the bone and muscle were exposed, but quite blood-less,—merely red and white,—with wide-open and staring eyes, yet lustreless, dead-lights; or like the cabin windows of a stranded vessel, filled with sand.

This fearful picture appears in Thoreau's context as if in a factual report. We come upon it after details of the geological features of the shore, of the crowds milling about, of the mechanical activities of burial—men hammering and nailing and carting away boxes, "a sober dispatch of business that was affecting." The anarchic-factual quality of the narrative is heightened by Thoreau's feeling for death itself. Death is first a moment of concentration and intensity, then one of disordering, scattering, fragmenting. At death human order dissipates for him into natural disorder, a nature no longer associated with purposeful growth, with the idea of *phusis*. The characteristic quality of his facts and metaphors in the picture of the girl is that they are without relation to each other.

The narrator's immediate response to all that he observes is to feel compassion for the sufferers and moral indignation at those spectators who, unlike those who soberly tend to the dead, are lacking in the humanity called for on such a momentous occasion: the man who stands by "chewing large quids of tobacco, as if that habit were forever confirmed with him"; the man who talks in a loud voice of the particular way the lifeboat painter broke "as if he had a bet depending on it, but had no humane interest in the matter"; the pair of men who come simply for the vulgar thrill of seeing a spectacle and cannot wait for the funeral; and the weed collectors who search about the corpse-strewn remains of the boat for "valuable manure." For one of these last, the bodies of the dead are "but other weeds which the tide cast up, but which were of no use to him." The narrator's critical attitude is humane, moral, man centered. The sea, the rocks, nature—these are by implication the enemy.

But the dialectical, polarizing tendency of Thoreau's mind is at work also in "The Shipwreck." When the narrator ends his account of his visit to Cohasset and adds to it a group of isolated reflections, his direction of mind takes an unexpected turn:

On the whole, it was not so impressive a scene as I might have expected. If I had found one body cast upon the beach in some lonely place, it would have affected me more. I sympathized rather with the winds and waves, as if to toss and mangle these

poor human bodies was the order of the day. If this was the
law of Nature, why waste any time in awe or pity? . . . It is the
individual and private that demands our sympathy. A man can
attend but one funeral in the course of his life, can behold but
one corpse.

The narrator seems to feel that his account has been one-sidedly humane.
Having dwelt on man, he will say a word for nature. (His protest on behalf
of the individual and private is for my purpose secondary to his impulse
to find a way back to nature.) It is as if he wished for the moment to justify
nature in her most drastic manifestations. We feel the constraint of Thoreauvian exaggeration as he sympathizes with destruction, as his "sympathy with persons is swallowed up in a wider sympathy with the universe,"
with the tremendous, amoral natural process that throws up weeds and
wrecks indiscriminately on the sands.

Thus in the midst of human tragedy Thoreau has again set up an exclusive, asocial relation to nature. But his strained sentiments are obviously
not adequate to the whole truth he will convey. His next move is therefore
to qualify his exaggeration. The narrator turns back from nature to consider sober men again. "Yet I saw that the inhabitants of the shore would
be not a little affected by this event. They would watch there many days
and nights for the sea to give up its dead, and their imaginations and sym-
pathies would supply the place of mourners far away." For Thoreau, however, this ground is untenable also. The outlook of the inhabitants of the
shore is too tragic for him to endure. If he cannot affirm nature, he will
effectively take man out of it, denying it any meaningful existence.

Why care for these dead bodies? They really have no friends
but the worms or fishes. Their owners were coming to the New
World, as Columbus and the Pilgrims did; they were within a
mile of its shores; but, before they could reach it, they emi-
grated to a newer world than ever Columbus dreamed of. . . .
I saw their empty hulks that came to land; but they themselves,
meanwhile, were cast upon some shore yet further west, toward
which we are all tending, and which we shall reach at last, it
may be through storm and darkness, as they did. . . . The mariner who makes the safest port in heaven, perchance, seems to
his friends on earth to be shipwrecked, for they deem Boston
Harbor the better place; though perhaps, invisible to them, a
skillful pilot comes to meet him, and the fairest and balmiest
gales blow off that coast, his good ship makes the land in hal-

cyon days, and he kisses the shore in rapture there, while his old hulk tosses in the surf here. It is hard to part with one's body, but, no doubt, it is easy enough to do without it when once it is gone. All their plans and hopes burst like a bubble! Infants by the score dashed on the rocks by the enraged Atlantic Ocean! No, no! If the St. John did not make her port here, she has been telegraphed there. The strongest wind cannot stagger a Spirit; it is a Spirit's breath.

On its face this passage appears to be a piece of quasi-Christian rhetoric, an eloquent but almost conventional funeral sermon. (If the word-play on "old hulk" is Thoreauvian, it would not be out of place in a sermon by Father Edward Taylor of Boston, the original of Father Mapple.) But why does Thoreau preach in this antique style on the immortality of the Spirit? Not, I think, out of a sudden access of piety. Rather, he is trying under the strain of the death scene to improvise a solution to a metaphysical problem. Nature as revealed at Cohasset is incompatible with man— man simply has no generous or loving relation with it. Thoreau cannot here find a way to blend the power of man *and* nature; therefore he must choose man *or* nature. But this he will not do. His stratagem is to affirm one *after* the other, that he may still affirm both. First he sympathizes with a nature devoid of spirit; then he exalts the disembodied and translated souls of the dead. Yet in jumping back and forth between these two poles, he hardly brings them together; they are split as widely apart as in *Contact! Contact!* And both extreme views are unbalanced in terms of Thoreau's usual perspective. When in his reflections the narrator turned to nature, his point of view became practically identical with that of the weed collectors. He too put the bodies of the dead on the same level with objects in nature—wind and waves, fishes and worms. When he now turns to the soul, he denies, as in *Contact! Contact!*, the crucial importance that the body and the senses must have in any wanderer's life in nature. The natives who watch for the drowned are involved, soul and body, with the necessity before them. The narrator, by contrast, emerges from his consideration of death by an idealist escape hatch.

> Quit, now, full of heart and comfort,
> These rude shores, they are of earth;
> Where the rosy clouds are parting,
> There the blessed isles loom forth.

It is in these reflective paragraphs in "The Shipwreck" that the narra-

tor seems particularly uncertain. (His trend of reflection is still less controlled and more varied than my excerpts would indicate.) Adopting a psychological framework, we could agree that Thoreau here is "trying to talk
his way out of death," as Joel Porte puts it; he may be so unnerved by the
spectacle of death as to lose control over the management of his different
points of view. Yet, if these reflections by themselves are confused and obsessive, they nevertheless have an appropriate place in the narrative of
"The Shipwreck." As writer, Thoreau would give us an accurate transcript
of his thoughts. He is bold enough to exhibit his inward indefiniteness, and
then to become definite and coherent again. In an analysis of the composition of "The Shipwreck," then, we may regard the narrator's aberrations
as dramatic outbursts, wayward shifts of mood. For his loss of control is
temporary; the discordant conflicts in his mind are partly resolved, partly
dissolved, in the working out of the chapter.

The last pages of "The Shipwreck," which tell of a second visit to Cohasset, are unique in Thoreau. He has, for once, come to the firm position
that nature is separate from man and indifferent to him. This new attitude
he takes with ease and assurance. He recollects in tranquillity his earlier
experience and manages a beautifully sustained, ironic treatment of alien
nature. The ocean at Cohasset both gives to man and takes from him, but
not in either character does it correspond to man's mind or temperament.
Judiciously, Thoreau balances the advantages and the dangers of the ocean
against each other (he has by now recovered *his* balance, his ability to look
at nature and death with detachment). He makes no attempt, as in the conclusion of "Ktaadn," to regard nature as innocent, and thereby to forget
the terrible aspect of nature to which he has been a witness. Rather, his
knowledge of its underlying terror is an element in his final perspective as
he observes the beach.

True, the beach *seems* innocent to an uneducated observer; it seems
utterly changed from what it was at the time of the wreck. The narrator
visits it on a fiercely hot day, and the intense weather helps to efface the
storm in our minds. The scene is described as pastoral: boatmen call over
the placid water like boys in country barns. The function of the sea at this
moment is to make men and beasts comfortable. It gives relief to the traveler from the heat; horses stand in the water or climb to the top of the fort
at Hull to feel the breeze; the narrator himself goes swimming.

> The sea bathing at Cohasset Rocks was perfect. The water was
> purer and more transparent than any I had ever seen. There
> was not a particle of mud or slime about it. The bottom being

sandy, I could see the sea perch swimming about. The smooth and fantastically worn rocks, and the perfectly clean and tress-like rockweeds falling over you, and attached so firmly to the rocks that you could pull yourself up by them, greatly enhanced the luxury of the bath. . . . There were the tawny rocks, like lions couchant, defying the ocean, whose waves incessantly dashed against and scoured them with vast quantities of gravel. The water held in their little hollows on the receding of the tide was so crystalline that I could not believe it salt, but wished to drink it; and higher up were basins of fresh water left by the rain,—all which, being also of different depths and tempera-ture, were convenient for different kinds of baths. Also, the larger hollows in the smoothed rocks formed the most conve-nient of seats and dressing rooms. In these respects it was the most perfect seashore that I had seen.

This nature is temporarily "convenient"; in other words, "man may use it if he can." The narrator's repeated emphasis on the rocks is clearly ironic—we remember Grampus and the top of Ktaadn, and the weeds too remind us of the Cohasset weed collectors. His bath is only a temporary luxury. Therefore his mind waxes luxurious and fanciful as he describes his pleasure. He indulges in illusions to ornament his hedonistic pose. It is only in fancy that he sees the water in the pools as fresh, the rocks as he-raldic lions. From another, more candid perspective the sea is of the same nature as at the time when the *St. John* split against Grampus.

As I looked over the water, I saw the isles rapidly wasting away, the sea nibbling voraciously at the continent. . . . On the other hand, these wrecks of isles were being fancifully arranged into new shores, as at Hog Island, inside of Hull, where every-thing seemed to be gently lapsing into futurity.

The sea is creative and destructive, gently voracious. It has made this placid scene and will eliminate it. It may be enjoyed on certain days, but a truthful observer will remember its potential wrecking power. Not all the pools it tosses up are convenient for bathing.

I saw in Cohasset, separated from the sea only by a narrow beach, a handsome but shallow lake of some four hundred acres, which, I was told, the sea had tossed over the beach in a great storm in the spring, and, after the alewives had passed into it, it had stopped up its outlet, and now the alewives were

dying by thousands, and the inhabitants were apprehending a
pestilence as the water evaporated. It had five rocky islets in it.

This follows immediately on the narrator's appreciation of his bath. Thoreau's irony is sobering. What is "handsome" on the surface is a natural
graveyard underneath. Where the alewives die is naked nature, presented
factually by the innocent-eyed narrator with the emphasis that only facts
can have. He records the alewives' death and passes on without comment
to the inconsequential, the fact of the "five rocky islets." The salient facts
in nature are apparent only on occasion. The Thoreauvian narrator as reporter of the natural must still give evidence also of the irregularity and
apparent meaninglessness of some of his impressions. The final paragraph
of "The Shipwreck," however, re-emphasizes Thoreau's ironic intent.

> This rocky shore is called Pleasant Cove on some maps; on the
> map of Cohasset, that name appears to be confined to the par-
> ticular cove where I saw the wreck of the St. John. The ocean
> did not look, now, as if any were ever shipwrecked in it; it was
> not grand and sublime, but beautiful as a lake. Not a vestige of
> a wreck was visible, nor could I believe that the bones of many
> a shipwrecked man were buried in that pure sand. But to go on
> with our first excursion.

It is typical of Thoreau that he *goes on* with his excursion; he will not
be caught hamstrung in an attitude. The conclusion he manages so firmly
in the last pages of "The Shipwreck" is meant only for it, not for his attempt to understand nature nor for a stage of his development nor even
for *Cape Cod*. He will allow to each moment its own glory, intensity, and
meaning. Nevertheless, "The Shipwreck" is an integrated and intense artistic moment in itself. It is a learning experience in which Thoreau's first impressions lead inevitably, yet naturally, to his final thoughts on nature's
power and man's vulnerability.

If nature is power, is there a meaningful stance for a man to adopt
toward it? The calm of the last pages of "The Shipwreck" suggests that
Thoreau has temporarily found such a stance. On his second visit to Cohasset he is still attracted to nature and derives enormous sensuous enjoy-
ment from it. But he no longer thinks an I-Thou relation with it possible.
He has accepted the idea that nature is indifferent and dangerous, no
longer a kindly brother. Thus he is detached and circumspect in his attitude, wary of nature and secure in himself. How has he achieved this new
stance? He hints at his method of living with an alien nature, I think, in a
sentence appearing among his troubled reflections on the storm: "I saw

that the beauty of the shore itself was wrecked for many a lonely walker there, until he could perceive, at last, how its beauty was enhanced by wrecks like this, and it acquired thus a rarer and sublimer beauty still." This is one of those momentary attempts to express fragmentary truth that Thoreau sometimes made, because he felt that the finest truths, including those apprehended in nature, were fragmentary and obscure and could be stated best in brief and suggestive sentences of insight. I interpret: The lonely wanderer achieves the detachment of the artist or artistically minded observer. He has indeed been troubled by the evidence of tragedy on the seashore; but he is able to overcome his trouble by the Thoreauvian effort of going again and again to nature (we shall see more of this effort in *Walden*), until he finally attains a new kind of *perception,* which is for Thoreau here a truer and higher perception. He can recognize the fact of death in nature, can perceive that lamentable shipwrecks contribute to its total spectacle, drama, and meaning. From this perspective nature is not kindly or sympathetic; it is simply there for the wanderer to perceive. But when it is viewed with this educated poetic detachment, it may acquire "a rarer and sublimer" beauty than it harbored for him before his initiation into the spectacle of tragedy. Perhaps in Thoreau's own narrative of his second trip to the Cohasset shore he is describing this new beauty, as well as exposing the ironies of his new understanding. He has learned, at least for the moment, to accept nature in all its manifestations as he perceives them. He can thus see and not dismiss events like the wreck of the *St. John.*

This emphasis on educated poetic perception, already present in the passages on seeing in the early journal, appears again in Thoreau's late essays. In "Autumnal Tints" especially he works out at considerable length his idea of the poet as perceiver. Probably it can justly be said that Thoreau moves away in the course of his career from a conception of his relation to nature as one of mutual sympathy toward a soberer conception, according to which he perceives nature without expecting that it will offer him anything but his own perceptions in return. But he never relinquishes the idea of a generous interchange altogether; it is prominent in *Walden,* which is of course a compendium of the thoughts of many years. Moreover, his final view in "The Shipwreck," that nature is an indifferent and voracious power, is not incorporated in any distinctive way in his later work. In *Walden,* in "Chesuncook," and in the late essays he will want back one form or another of the idea that nature is a living and mysteriously beneficent whole. An attitude learned to satisfy the needs of one moment will be unlearned for other needs. Yet, in the total mosaic of Thoreau's imitation of nature, "The Shipwreck" stands out as a brilliant separate piece, the finished expression of a somber experience.

LOREN EISELEY

Thoreau's Vision
of the Natural World

Somewhere in the coverts about Concord, a lynx was killed well over a century ago and examined by Henry David Thoreau; measured, in fact, and meditated upon from nose to tail. Others called it a Canadian lynx, far strayed from the northern wilds. No, insisted Thoreau positively, it is indigenous, indigenous but rare. It is a night haunter; it is a Concord lynx. On this he was adamant. Not long ago, over in Vermont, an intelligent college girl told me that, walking in the woods, her Labrador retriever had startled and been attacked by a Canadian lynx which she had been fully competent to recognize. I was too shy, however, to raise the question of whether the creature might have been, as Thoreau defiantly asserted, a genuine New England lynx, persisting but rare since colonial times.

Thoreau himself was a genuine Concord lynx. Of that there can be no doubt. We know the place of his birth, his rarity, something of his habits, his night travels, that he had, on occasion, a snarl transferred to paper, and that he frequented swamps, abandoned cellar holes, and woodlots. His temperament has been a subject of much uncertainty, as much, in truth, as the actual shape of those human figures which he was wont to examine looming in fogs or midsummer hazes. Thoreau sometimes had difficulty in seeing men or, by contrast, sometimes saw them too well. Others had difficulty in adjusting their vision to the Concord lynx himself, with the result that a varied and contentious literature has come down to us. Even the manner of his death is uncertain, for though the cause is known, some have maintained that he benefited a weak constitution by a rugged outdoor

From *The Star Thrower*, edited by Howard Chapnick. © 1974 by Howard Chapnick. Harcourt Brace Jovanovich, 1978.

life. Others contend that he almost deliberately stoked the fires of consumption by prolonged exposure in inclement weather.

As is the case with most wild animals at the periphery of the human vision, Thoreau's precise temperament is equally a matter of conjecture even though he left several books and a seemingly ingenuous journal which one eminent critic, at least, regards as a cunningly contrived mythology. He has been termed a stoic, a contentious moralizer, a parasite, an arsonist, a misanthrope, a supreme egotist, a father-hater who projected his animus on the state, a banal writer who somehow managed to produce a classic work of literature. He has also been described as a philosophical anarchist and small-town failure, as well as an intellectual aristocrat. Some would classify him simply as a nature writer, others as a failed scientist who did not comprehend scientific method. Others speak of his worldwide influence upon the social movements of the twentieth century, of his exquisite insight and style, of his relentless searching for something never found—a mystic in the best sense of the term. He has also been labeled a prig by a notable man of English letters. There remains from those young people who knew him the utterly distinct view that he was a friendly, congenial, and kindly man. At the time of his funeral, and long before fame attended his memory, the schools of Concord were dismissed in his honor.

In short, the Concord lynx did not go unwept to his grave. Much of the later controversy that has created a Browningesque *Ring and the Book* atmosphere about his intentions and character is the product of a sophisticated literary world he abhorred in life. Something malevolent frequently creeps into this atmosphere even though it is an inevitable accompaniment of the transmission of great books through the ages. Basically the sensitive writer should stay away from his own kind. Jealousies, tensions, feuds, unnecessary discourtesies that are hard to bear in print are frequently augmented by close contact, even if friendships begin well. The writer's life is a lonely one and doubtless should remain so, but a prurient curiosity allows no great artist to rest easy in his grave. Critical essays upon Thoreau now number hundreds of items, very little of which, I suspect, would move the Concord lynx to do more than retire farther into whatever thickets might remain to him. Neither science nor literature was his total concern. He was a fox at the wood's edge, regarding human preoccupations with doubt. Indeed he had rejected an early invitation to join the American Association for the Advancement of Science. The man had never entertained illusions about the course of technological progress and the only message that he, like an Indian, had gotten from the telegraph was the song of the wind through its wires.

As a naturalist he possessed the kind of memory which fixes certain scenes in the mind forever—a feeling for the vastness and mystery contained in nature, a powerful aesthetic response when, in his own words, "a thousand bare twigs gleam like cobwebs in the sun." He had been imprinted, as it were, by his home landscape at an early age. Similarly, whatever I may venture upon the meaning of Thoreau must come basically from memory alone, with perhaps some examination of the tone of his first journal as contrasted with his last. My present thoughts convey only the residue of what, in the course of time, I have come to feel about his intellectual achievement—the solitary memory that Thoreau himself might claim of a journey across austere uplands.

In addition, my observations come mostly from the realm of science, whereas the preponderance of what had been written about Thoreau has come from the region he appeared to inhabit: namely, literature. His scientific interests have frequently been denigrated, and he himself is known more than once to have deplored the "inhumanity of science." Surely then, one cannot, as a representative of this alien discipline, be accused of either undue tolerance or weak sympathy for a transcendental idealism that has largely fallen out of fashion. Yet it is an aspect of this philosophy, more particularly as it is found modified in Thoreau, that I wish to consider. For Thoreau, like Emerson, is an anticipator, a forerunner of the process philosophers who have so largely dominated the twentieth century. He stands at the border between existent and potential nature.

II

Behind all religions lurks the concept of nature. It persists equally in the burial cults of Neanderthal man, in Cro-Magnon hunting art, in the questions of Job, and in the answering voice from the whirlwind. In the end it is the name of man's attempt to define and delimit his world, whether seen or unseen. He knows intuitively that nature is a reality which existed before him and will survive his individual death. He may include in his definition that which is, or that which may be. Nature remains an otherness which incorporates man, but which man instinctively feels contains secrets denied to him.

A professional atheist must still account for the fleeting particles that appear and vanish in the perfected cyclotrons of modern physics. We may see behind nature a divinity which rules it, or we may regard nature itself as a somewhat nebulous and ill-defined deity. Man knows that he springs from nature and not nature from him. This is very old and primitive

knowledge. Man, as the "thinking reed," the memory beast, and the anticipator of things to come, has devised hundreds of cosmogonies and interpretations of nature. More lately, with the dawn of the scientific method,
he has sought to probe nature's secrets by experiment rather than un-
bounded speculation.

Still, of all words coming easily to the tongue, none is more mysterious, none more elusive. Behind nature is hidden the chaos as well as the
regularities of the world. And behind all that is evident to our senses is
veiled the insubstantial deity that only man, of all earth's creatures, has
had the power either to perceive or to project into nature.

As scientific agnostics we may draw an imaginary line beyond which
we deny ourselves the right to pass. We may adhere to the tangible, but
we will still be forced to speak of the "unknowable" or of "final causes"
even if we proclaim such phrases barren and of no concern to science. In
our minds we will acknowledge a line we have drawn, a definition to
which we have arbitrarily restricted ourselves, a human limit that may or
may not coincide with reality. It will still be nature that concerns us as it
concerned the Neanderthal. We cannot exorcise the word, refine it seman-
tically though we may. Nature is the receptacle which contains man and
into which he finally sinks to rest. It implies all, absolutely all, that man
knows or can know. The word ramifies and runs through the centuries,
assuming different connotations.

Sometimes it appears as ghostly as the unnamed shadow behind it;
sometimes it appears harsh, prescriptive, and solid. Again matter becomes
interchangeable with energy; fact becomes shadow, law becomes probabil-
ity. Nature is a word that must have arisen with man. It is part of his
otherness, his humanity. Other beasts live within nature. Only man has
ceaselessly turned the abstraction around and around upon his tongue and
found fault with every definition, found himself looking ceaselessly outside
of nature toward something invisible to any eye but his own and indeed
not surely to be glimpsed by him.

To propound that Henry David Thoreau is a process philosopher, it
is necessary first to understand something of the concepts entertained by
early nineteenth-century science and philosophy, and also to consider
something of the way in which these intellectual currents were changing.
New England's ties to English thought preponderated, although, as is well
known, some of the ideas had their roots on the continent. An exhaustive
analysis is unnecessary to the present purpose. Thoreau was a child of his
time but he also reached beyond it.

In early nineteenth-century British science there was a marked obsession with Baconian induction. The more conservative minded, who dreaded the revelations of the new geology, sought, in their emphatic demand for facts, to drive wide-ranging and useful hypotheses out of currency. The thought of Bacon, actually one of the innovators of scientific method, was being perverted into a convenient barrier against the advance of irreligious science. Robert Chambers, an early evolutionist, had felt the weight of this criticism, and Darwin, later on, experienced it beyond the midcentury. In inexperienced hands it led to much aimless fact gathering under the guise of proper inductive procedures for true scientists. Some, though not all, of Thoreau's compendiums and detailed observations suggest this view of science, just as do his occasional scornful remarks about museum taxonomy.

In a typical Thoreauvian paradox he could neither leave his bundles of accumulated fact alone, nor resist muttering "it is ebb tide with the scientific reports." Only toward the close of his journals does he seem to be inclining toward a more perceptive scientific use of his materials under the influence of later reading. It is necessary to remember that most of Thoreau's intellectual contacts were with literary men, though Emerson was a wide and eclectic reader who saw clearly that the new uniformitarian geology had transformed our conceptions of the world's antiquity.

The one striking exception to Thoreau's lack of direct contact with the scientific world was his meeting with Louis Agassiz after the European glaciologist, taxonomist, and teacher had joined the staff at Harvard in the 1840s. Brilliant and distinguished naturalist though he was, Louis Agassiz was probably not the best influence upon Thoreau. He traced the structural relations of living things, he introduced America to comparative taxonomy, he taught Thoreau to observe such oddities as frozen and revived caterpillars. His eye, if briefly, was added to Thoreau's eye, not always to the latter's detriment. Typically, Agassiz warned against hasty generalizations while pursuing relentlessly his own interpretation of nature.

The European poet of the Ice Age was, in a very crucial sense, at the same time an anachronism. He did not believe in evolution; he did not grasp the significance of natural selection. "Geology," he wrote in 1857, "only shows that at different periods there have existed different species; but no transition from those of a preceding into those of a following epoch has ever been noticed anywhere." He saw a beneficent intelligence behind nature; he was a Platonist at heart, dealing with the classification of the eternal forms, seeing in the vestigial organs noted by the evolutionist only the direct evidence of divine plan carried through for symmetry's sake even when the organ was functionless.

It is this preternatural intelligence which Thoreau is led to see in the protective arrangement of moth cocoons in winter. "What kind of understanding," he writes, "was there between the mind . . . and that of the worm that fastened a few of these leaves to its cocoon in order to disguise it?" Plainly he is following in the footsteps of the great biologist, who, like many other scholars, recognized a spiritual succession of forms in the strata, but not the genuine organic transformations that had produced the living world. It may be noted in passing that this Platonic compromise with reality was one easily acceptable to most Transcendentalists. They were part of a far-removed romantic movement which was to find the mechanistic aspects of nineteenth-century science increasingly intolerable. One need not align oneself totally with every aspect of the Darwinian universe, however, to see that Agassiz's particular teleological interpretation of nature could not be long sustained. Whatever might lie behind the incredible profusion of living forms would not so easily yield its secrets to man.

The mystery in nature Thoreau began to sense early. A granitic realism forced from him the recognition that the natural world is indifferent to human morality, just as the young Darwin had similarly brooded over the biological imperfections and savagery of the organic realm. "How can [man]" protested Thoreau, "perform that long journey who has not conceived whither he is bound, . . . who has no passport to the end?" This is a far cry from the expressions of some of the contemporary Transcendentalists who frequently confused nature with a hypostatized divine reason which man could activate within himself. By contrast, Thoreau remarks wearily, "Is not disease the rule of existence?" He had seen the riddled leaf and the worm-infested bud.

If one meditates upon the picture of nature presented by both the Transcendental thinkers such as Emerson and the evolutionary doctrine drawn from Darwin, one is struck by the contrast between what appears to be a real and an ideal nature. The Transcendentalist lived in two worlds at once, in one of which he was free to transform himself; he could escape the ugly determinism of the real. In Emerson's words, "two states of thought diverge every moment in wild contrast."

The same idea is echoed in the first volume of his journals when the young Thoreau ventures, "On one side of man is the actual and on the other the ideal." These peculiar worlds are simultaneously existent. Life is bifurcated between the observational world and another more ideal but realizable set of "instructions" implanted in our minds, again a kind of Platonic blueprint. We must be taught through the proper understanding of the powers within us. The Transcendentalist possessed the strong optimism of the early Republic, the belief in an earthly Eden to be created.

If we examine the Darwinian world of change we recognize that the nature of the evolutionary process is such as to deny any relationships except those that can be established on purely phyletic grounds of uninterrupted descent. The Platonic abstract blueprint of successive types has been dismissed as a hopeful fiction. Vestigial organs are really what their name implies—remnants lingering from a former state of existence. The tapeworm, the sleeping-sickness trypanosome, are as much a product of natural selection as man himself. All currently existing animals and plants have ancestral roots extending back into Archeozoic time. Every species is in some degree imperfect and scheduled to vanish by reason of the very processes which brought it into being. Even in this world of endless struggle, however, Darwin is forced to introduce a forlorn note of optimism which appears in the final pages of the *Origin of Species*. It is his own version of the ideal. Out of the war of nature, of strife unending, he declares, all things will progress toward perfection.

The remark rings somewhat hollowly upon the ear. Darwin's posited ideal world, such as it is, offers no immediate hope that man can embrace. Indeed, it is proffered on the same page where Darwin indicates that of the species now living very few will survive into the remote future. Teleological direction has been read out of the universe. It would re-emerge in the twentieth century in more sophisticated guises that would have entranced Thoreau, but for the moment the "Great Companion" was dead. The Darwinian circle had introduced process into nature but had never paused to examine nature itself. In the words of Alfred North Whitehead, "Science is concerned not with the causes but the coherence of nature." Something, in other words, held the thing called nature together, gave it duration in the midst of change and a queer kind of inhuman rationality.

It may be true enough that Thoreau in his last years never resolved his philosophical difficulties. (Indeed, what man has?) It may also be assumed that the confident and brilliant perceptions of the young writer began to give way in his middle years to a more patient search for truth. The scientist in him was taking the place of the artist. To some of the literary persuasion this may seem a great loss. Considering, however, the toils from which he freed himself, the hope that he renewed, his solitary achievement is remarkable.

One may observe that there are two reigning models involving human behavior today: a conservative and a progressive version. The first may be stated as regarding man in the mass as closely reflecting his primate origins. He is the "ape and tiger" of Huxley's writing. His origins are sufficiently bestial that they place limits upon his ethical possibilities. Latent aggression makes him an uncertain and dangerous creature.

Unconsciously, perhaps, the first evolutionists sought to link man more closely to the animal world from which he had arisen. Paradoxically this conception would literally freeze man upon his evolutionary pathway as thoroughly as though a similar argument had been projected upon him when he was a Cretaceous tree shrew. Certainly one may grant our imperfect nature. Man is in process, as is the whole of life. He may survive or he may not, but so long as he survives he will be part of the changing, onrushing future. He, too, will be subject to alteration. In fact, he may now be approaching the point of consciously inducing his own modification.

How did Thoreau, who matured under the influence of the Transcendentalists and the design arguments of Louis Agassiz, react to this shifting, oncoming world of contingency and change? It is evident he was familiar with Charles Lyell's writings, that he knew about the development (that is, evolution) theories of Robert Chambers. The final volume of his journals even suggests that he may have meditated upon Darwin's views before his death in 1862.

Now, in the final years, he seems to gather himself for one last effort. "The development theory implies a greater vital force in nature," he writes, "because it is more flexible and accommodating and equivalent to a sort of constant new creation."

He recognizes the enormous waste in nature but tries carefully to understand its significance just as he grasps the struggle for existence. His eyes are open still to his tenderly cherished facts of snow and leaves and seasons. He counts tree rings and tries to understand forest succession. The world is perhaps vaster than he imagined, but, even from the first, nature was seen as lawless on occasion and capable of cherishing unimaginable potentials. That was where he chose to stand, at the very edge of the future, "to anticipate," as he says in *Walden,* "nature herself."

This is not the conservative paradigm of the neo-Darwinian circle. Instead it clearly forecasts the thought of twentieth-century Alfred North Whitehead. Thoreau strove with an unequaled intensity to observe nature in all its forms, whether in the raw shapes of mountains or the travelings of seeds and deer mice. His consciousness expanded like a sunflower. The more objects he beheld, the more immortal he became. "My senses," he wrote, "get no rest." It was as though he had foreseen Whitehead's dictum that "passage is a quality not only of nature, which is the thing known, but also of sense awareness, which is the procedure of knowing." Thoreau had constituted himself the Knower. "All change," he wrote, "is a miracle to contemplate, but it is a miracle that is taking place every instant." He saw man thrust up through the crust of nature "like a wedge and not till the wound heals . . . do we begin to discover where we are." He viewed us all as mere potential; shadowy, formless perhaps, but as though about to be formed. He had listened alone to the "unspeakable rain"; he had sought in his own way to lead others to a supernatural life in nature. He had succeeded. He had provided for others the passport that at first he thought did not exist; a passport, he finally noted, "earned from the elements."

III

To follow the involved saunterings of the journals is to observe a man sorting, selecting, questioning less nature than his own way into nature, to find, as Thoreau expressed it, "a patent for himself." Thoreau is never wholly a man of the Transcendental camp. He is, in a sense, a double agent. He is drawn both to the spiritual life and to that of the savage. "Are we not all wreckers," he asks, "and do we not contract the habits of wreckers?" The term *wreckers,* of course, he uses in the old evil sense of the shore scavengers who with false lights beckoned ships to their doom. And again he queries, "Is our life innocent enough?" It would appear he thinks otherwise, for he writes, "I have a murderer's experience . . ." and he adds, a trifle scornfully, "there is no record of a great success in history."

Thoreau once said disconsolately that he awaited a Visitor who never came, one whom he referred to as the "Great Looker." Some have thought that pique or disappointment shows in these words and affects his subsequent work. I do not choose to follow this line of reasoning, since, on another page of *Walden,* he actually recollects receiving his guest as the "old settler and original proprietor who is reported to have dug Walden pond . . . and fringed it with pine woods." As a somewhat heretical priest once observed, "God asks nothing of the highest soul but attention."

Supplementing that remark Thoreau had asserted, "There has been nothing but the sun and the eye since the beginning." That eye, in the instance of Thoreau, had missed nothing. Even in the depths of winter when nature's inscriptions lay all about him in the snow, he had not faltered to recognize among them the cruel marks of a farmer's whip, steadily, even monotonously, lashing his oxen down the drift-covered road. The sight wounded him. Nature, he knew, was not bound to be kind to man. In fact, there was a kind of doubleness in nature as in the writer. The inner eye was removed; its qualities were more than man, as natural man, could long sustain. The Visitor had come in human guise and looked out upon the world a few brief summers. It is remembered that when at last an acquaintance came to ask of Thoreau on his deathbed if he had made his peace with God, the Visitor in him responded simply, "We have never quarreled."

Thoreau had appropriated the snow as "the great revealer." On it were inscribed all the hieroglyphs that the softer seasons concealed. Last winter, trudging in the woods, I came to a spot where freezing, melting, and refreezing had lifted old footprints into little pinnacles of trapped oak leaves as though a shrub oak had walked upon some errand. Thoreau had recorded the phenomenon over a century ago. There was something uncanny about it, I thought, standing attentively in the snow. A visitor, perhaps the Visitor, had once more passed.

In the very first volume of his journals Thoreau had written, "There is always the possibility, the possibility, I say, of being all, or remaining a particle in the universe." He had, in the end, learned that nature was not an enlarged version of the human ego, that it was not, to use Emerson's phrase, "the immense shadow of man." Toward the close of his life he had turned from literature to the growing, formidable world of the new science—the science that in the twentieth century was destined to reduce everything to infinitesimal particles and finally these to a universal vortex of wild energies.

But the eye persisted, the unexplainable eye that gave even Darwin a cold shudder. All it experienced were the secondary qualities, the illusions that physics had rejected, but the eye remained, just as Thoreau had asserted—the sun and the eye from the beginning. Thoreau was gone, but the eye was multitudinous, ineradicable.

I advanced upon the fallen oak leaves. We were all the eye of the Visitor—the eye whose reason no physics could explain. Generation after generation the eye was among us. We were particles but we were also the recording eye that saw the sunlight—that which physics had reduced to cold waves in a cold void. Thoreau's life had been dedicated to the unexplainable eye.

I had been trained since youth against the illusions, the deceptions of that eye, against sunset as reality, against my own features as anything but a momentary midge swarm of particles. Even this momentary phantasm I saw by the mind's eye alone. I no longer resisted as I walked. I went

slowly, making sure that the eye momentarily residing in me saw and recorded what was intended when Thoreau spoke of the quality of the eye
as belonging more to God than man.

But there was a message Thoreau intended to transmit. "I suspect,"
he had informed his readers, "that if you should go to the end of the
world, you would find somebody there going further." It is plain that he
wanted a message carried that distance, but what was it? We are never entirely certain. He delighted in gnomic utterances such as that in which he
pursued the summer on snowshoes.

"I do not think much of the actual," he had added. Is this then the
only message of the great Walden traveler in the winter days when the
years "came fast as snowflakes"? Perhaps it is so intended, but the words
remain cryptic. Thoreau, as is evidenced by his final journals, had labored
to lay the foundations of a then-unnamed science—ecology. In many ways
he had outlived his century. He was always concerned with the actual, but
it was the unrolling reality of the process philosopher, "the universe," as
he says, "that will not wait to be explained."

For this reason he tended to see men at a distance. For the same reason he saw himself as a first settler in nature, his house the oldest in the
settlement. Thoreau reflected in his mind the dreamers of the westward
crossing; in this he is totally American.

Yet Thoreau preferred to the end his own white winter spaces. He lin-
gers, curvetting gracefully, like the fox he saw on the river or the falcon in
the morning air. He identifies, he enters them, he widens the circumference
of life to its utmost bounds. "One world at a time," he jokes playfully on
his deathbed, but it is not, in actuality, the world that any of us know or
could reasonably endure. It is simply Thoreau's world, "a prairie for out-
laws." Each one of us must seek his own way there. This is his final message, for each man is forever the eye and the eye is the Visitor. Whatever
remedy exists for life is never to be found at Walden. It exists, if at all,
where the real Walden exists, somewhere in the incredible dimensions of
the universal Eye.

PHILIP F. GURA

Thoreau's Maine Woods Indians: More Representative Men

When in 1850 Ralph Waldo Emerson brought out his fourth book of essays, his title accurately conveyed the substance of what had become a major preoccupation in Transcendentalist circles, the identification of individuals who might serve as Representative Men for the age. His published lectures on "representative genius" suggested that in the modern age, and especially in democratic America, while divine truth was discernible in all individuals, biographers should cease to look for "completeness" in any one man. Contrary to the opinions of Emerson's Scottish correspondent Thomas Carlyle, there could no longer be heroes or hero worship. Once someone accepted the premise that the Oversoul manifested itself in all beings, he had to approach a biographical subject in a new way. With true democratic vigor Emerson declared that there were no "common men." All men were at last of a size, and "the true art [of biography] is only possible on the conviction that every talent has its apotheosis somewhere."

But in assembling his list Emerson failed to abide by his own egalitarian proposition. With such subjects as Plato, Swedenborg, Montaigne, Shakespeare, Napoleon, and Goethe, he essentially had composed a hagiography of European intellectual giants, unconsciously committing the sin against America and its democratic principles he had warned against in his 1836 essay "Nature."

While Emerson still groped among the dry bones of the European past, his Concord neighbor and one-time disciple was continuing his own study of a type of man not given attention in Emerson's effort, a man both

From *American Literature* 49, no. 3 (November 1977). © 1977 by Duke University Press.)

very American and representative of traits not even possessed by the multi-faceted Shakespeare, acknowledged by most nineteenth-century Romantics as the genuine embodiment of "genius." If Emerson declared that a representative man "must be related to us" and our lives receive from his "some promise of explanation," it was perfectly consistent with Thoreau's heightened sensitivity to what defined the representative man *in America* that he sought his "explanations" from individuals standing in paradoxically close "relation" to the white Americans of this land. Among Thoreau's few published attempts at extended biography are his sketches of the Penobscot Indian guides whom he met on his exploratory trips to the Maine woods. These sketches, later published in one volume as *The Maine Woods*, offer a revealing insight into this other Concordian's idea of the universal representative genius and understanding of how the new American life could be distinguished from the merely European. If Emerson declared all men richer for appreciating his transcendent pantheon, Thoreau offered his readers yet other models, ones so full of natural and primitive vigor that they seemed to encompass the spirit of their American land.

II

In his journal for February 13, 1859, Thoreau phrased a question which had troubled him for years. Noting how people always had considered America's "indigenous animals so inexhaustibly interesting," he wondered why the American Indian himself had not been treated with similar concern. "If wild men, so much more like ourselves than they are unlike, have inhabited these shores before us," should not an American wish to know "particularly what nature of men they are, how they lived there [and] their relations to nature . . . ?"

Since his youth Thoreau had been interested in what he termed this "indigenous man of America." His first statement about the importance of the American Indian had come as early as 1837 when, as a Harvard College senior enrolled in one of Henry Tyrell Channing's composition courses, he offered a theme on "The Mark or Standard by which a Nation is to be Judged Barbarous or Civilized." In this brief essay he criticized the materialistic tenor of his age and denounced the modern "scientific" view of nature which made men regard natural objects with a constricted and microscopic vision. The Indian, in contrast, did not view nature atomistically but displayed "a liberal and enlarged view of things," what Thoreau felicitously called a "mountain" prospect which took into consideration the entire landscape. With his larger perspective the Indian could live, think, and die "as a man," while the white race deceived itself into thinking that deductive scientific method could explain all.

Part of Thoreau's Romantic defense of the primitive might be attributed to his disgust at the traumatic economic depression into which civilized America (and his family) had just fallen: it was in the depression year of 1837 that Thoreau left Harvard for the world. But even as his attitude toward the native American became more realistic, he retained the sense that the Indian races offered the spectacle of man in a vigorously healthy and cosmically symbiotic relationship with nature and so should stand as "representative" of an attitude critically important to a nation rapidly forgetting its relation to the land which defined its uniqueness. As an early journal entry suggested, "the charm of the Indian" was that he stood "free and unrestrained in Nature" and was "her inhabitant and not her guest." White Americans had only the "habits of the house," and in the economic stampede of the century it was apparent that this domicile had degenerated into a sordid "prison." If nature and the national ego were, as Perry Miller suggests, inextricably linked, instead of worrying about the examples of a Montaigne or a Napoleon, the American man had to be sure that he understood how underdeveloped he remained if he was not able to read the lessons of his own land.

In light of certain biographical facts, Thoreau's interest in the Indian becomes even more suggestive. In 1846, at the same time as he was living so freely at Walden Pond (thinking and writing about himself because by his later admission there was no one he "knew" as well), he took his first extended trip to the Maine woods, not only to satisfy what he called his "singular yearning toward all wildness," but to have an opportunity to study at first hand the Indians' ways. He made another trip in 1853; and in 1857, within three years of bragging as lustily (and, he would have readers believe, as confidently) as Chanticleer to awaken his neighbors to a more wholesome life, again he was in Maine and returned to offer a long study not only of himself but of a Penobscot guide, an alter ego who is as interesting a character as Thoreau presented in his published works. Were these forays into the American forest carried out so that he could decide further what made a life significant? Were his biographical sketches of the Maine guides an indication that Thoreau doubted his own capacity as a "civilized" man, a paleface, to experience fully all that was true and good in nature?

The evidence is persuasive. Long before his death in 1862 he had plans to write a large book on the American Indian, and on his saunterings through New England as well as on his last extended trip (to Minnesota in 1861), he took copious notes on the natural history of the forest tribes. Eleven unpublished notebooks of some 540,000 words remained in manuscript, and biographical folklore has him uttering as his last words "moose" and "Indians." One can claim that part of the unique quality of Thoreau's thought stems from his intuitive sense that to know truly what it is like to be at home with one's self in America he cannot give his hours of study just to the European giants described by Emerson. Thoreau could point to men in New England who by the "wary independence and aloofness" of their "dim forest life" had preserved an intercourse with native gods. They were people admitted "from time to time" to that "rare and peculiar society with nature" after which Thoreau (and such kindred spirits as John James Audubon and Daniel Boone) always longed, and they had to be surveyed for their representative gifts. That few of these men could articulate their thoughts as well as Goethe or Plato was not at issue, especially at that time and in Thoreau's America. Their genius, just like their startling language, ran in different channels.

III

Leaving aside the introspective meditation of *A Week on the Concord and Merrimack Rivers* (1849), in his published works we can best trace Thoreau's search for his own representative man from that significant moment in *Walden* (1854) when he introduces readers to the Canadian woodchopper Alek Therien, "a true Homeric or Paphlogonian man" who sometimes visited Thoreau in his woodland hut. While Joel Porte has convincingly described this relationship as another instance of "the Faustian problem of doubleness" which had been evident in European Romantic literature at least since the time of Goethe, it is not far-fetched to suggest that, rather than just viewing Therien as "the animal soul whom Thoreau must come to terms with before he can hope to be a unified soul," Thoreau's encounters with him also heightened Thoreau's sense that, before he could unequivocally declare his Walden Pond experiment a success, the added perspective offered by people whose lives suggested (as Therien's did) that "there might be genius in the lowest grades of life, however permanently humble or illiterate," had to be acquired. While containing "an exuberance of animal spirits," Therien still seemed as "bottomless even as Walden Pond was thought to be." Thoreau's attempt to define and locate the primitive he encountered in Therien and considered most visible in the American Indian took its mature form in his descriptions of the various Indian guides in the accounts later published as *The Maine Woods*.

One thing to consider is whether or not his association with Therien encouraged Thoreau's first trip to Maine in August 1846. In *Walden* Therien is described as having left Canada in his teens to work in the United States as a lumberman, and proof of his later familiarity with the North Country is evidenced by the fact that on a second trip to Maine in 1853 Thoreau discovered Therien, with twenty or thirty other lumbermen, at "Ansell Smith's clearing" in the middle of the Chesuncook wilderness. We also know that it was during his Walden Pond outing (shortly after he met Therien) that Thoreau left Concord on one of the three trips to the area in which he was most likely to encounter whatever "primitive" men remained in New England. If Thoreau went to the deep woods because he was convinced that, as he had earlier suggested in *A Week on the Concord and Merrimack Rivers,* his genius "dated from an older era than the agricultural," it was equally significant that (as a detailed reading of *The Maine Woods* discloses) he had become interested not only in the wilderness itself but in how a man conceives of himself in relation to it. If America was defined by vast expanses of virgin land, it was important that an American listen for an instant "to the chant of the Indian muse" and understand why an Indian would not "exchange his savageness for civilization." If the biography of such a "wild" man somehow could be assembled, Thoreau might understand better his own race's paradoxical longing for wilderness. His talks with Therien may have crystallized his intent to explore the woodchopper's institutions and to discover whether or not he, Henry Thoreau, was fronting the essential facts of an American life in the civilized wilderness at Walden Pond. He journeyed to the Maine Woods in the hope that he might uncover a man who, in Emerson's words, would become a "lens" through which he could read his own mind more accurately and who could help him adjust the angle of his vision more clearly on an American axis.

But given the sentimentalized popularity the Indian was then enjoying, Thoreau had difficulty in articulating what it was that most attracted him to the Indian genius. Read episodically, *The Maine Woods* reveals Thoreau as a budding, sometimes fumbling, anthropologist whose consecutive journeys to Maine display a gradually increasing sensitivity to the natives he sought to understand. Despite his long-standing interest in the Indians, only on his last trip did he understand precisely what knowledge it was that he had been so long seeking to discover from them. Prior to his actual encounters with the tribes, he labored under the Romantic burden placed on "savages" at least since the time of Rousseau.

This judgment is borne out by the "Ktaadn" essay. As Thoreau later described it, his first trip north of Boston was anything but a success. Beginning to look for his representative man in the Penobscot River settlement of Oldtown, he was disappointed to find the first Indian he encountered not at all the noble savage he expected. His eyes met only a "short, shabby washerwoman-looking Indian" who landed his canoe and took from it "a bundle of skins in one hand and an empty keg or half-barrel in the other." This view of aboriginal man reduced to Yankee trader called forth a lamentation on the white race's influence on these northern tribes, and in a splenetic vein Thoreau reported that by the nineteenth century some Indians had so adopted the white man's ways that their homes had "a very shabby, forlorn, cheerless look" like those further south, and (to Thoreau an even greater disenchantment) it seemed that with them "politics was all the rage," as it presumably was with the Massachusetts citizens he sought to leave behind. After this initial disappointment, Thoreau was understandably eager to locate wilder places populated by wilder men and was pleased that his party quickly secured native Indian guides to lead them toward the Ktaadn wilderness, a place which at that time few white men had explored.

In the youthful spirit of his earlier works, though, the essay "Ktaadn" remains characteristically egotistic: it emerges as the story of Thoreau's encounter with his own spirit in the setting of the primitive forest of which he had always dreamed. The Indians have a place in the narrative; but, as the traveler nears the mountain, Louis Neptune and the other guides retreat to the background as Thoreau steps forward to describe his own emotions when he is exposed to the uninhabited wilderness. Earlier in this essay, as though seeking a parallel to his own life at Walden Pond, he meticulously noted each white man's settlement and had tried to describe the lives of other men influenced by the forest. But soon these pioneers, too, cease to be mentioned as reference points as he continued his inward exploration. These men only struck him as further proof that, with regard to white settlers, "the deeper you penetrate into the woods, the more intelligent, and in one sense, the less countrified do you find the inhabitants." Although adventurous, they were not natives of the vast spaces, but rather shrewd Yankees who remained within the pale of the lumber-camps and riverways from which they hauled their income.

In contrast, what he found when he reached the summit of the mountain was a frightening solitude, a land "vast, Titanic, and such as man never inhabits." There our bachelor of nature felt as though the "inhuman" land held him at a disadvantage and "pilfered him of some of the divine faculty." What surprised him most was not an idyllic solitude but the presence of a force so strange and overwhelming that it was "not bound to be kind" to him; after experiencing his fill of this awesome emotion he descended the mountain with the lonely revelation that "only daring and insolent men" would travel to such places. No one he knew could assimilate such wild tonic into his system. Even the "simple races" do not climb mountains, he admitted. "Their tops are sacred and mysterious tracts never visited by them." The prospective anthropologist would find no material atop Ktaadn, and it became apparent that, if Thoreau wished to discover what was representative about the Indians, he should not wander long in such waste places. On future excursions to Maine he needed to discover some literal or figurative middle ground on which to study the aboriginal hunter race, an environment at least conducive to the fellowship of man. The inhabitants of that space perhaps could mediate between the values of civilization and solitude, just as the Transcendentalist poet spun his verse from the relationship between words and things, object and spirit.

The urge Thoreau felt to unearth such truly representative Americans did not weaken; in September 1853 he made another trip, this time to the Chesuncook Lake region of Maine. At this date, with his youthful expectations of the Indians and their forest environment tempered after his first troubled exploration, Thoreau seemed better able to appreciate the seeming inconsistencies in the natives he met along the way, the combination of civilized and savage gifts which had been so disconcerting in Oldtown. But even though the descriptions of the Indians' habits were more sympathetic in "Chesuncook" than in "Ktaadn," what is most significant in the later relation is Thoreau's outrage at the unfeeling savagery in which the Indian partially lived. Just as the earlier essay described Thoreau's initiation into the frightening loneliness of this continent, here one sees a further deflation of his vision of the Red Man, as Thoreau learned that there were civilized amenities sorely missing along the Allagash and its tributaries.

The chief character of this essay, Joe Aitteon, son of the "Governor," had been engaged by Thoreau's party with an understanding that he would be allowed to hunt meat for the market. The usually noncarnivorous Thoreau was unconcerned by this agreement. He had seen animals killed, and it was more to his delight that at last he had found someone resembling the primitive man he was seeking, a "goodlooking Indian, twenty-four years old, apparently of unmixed blood, short and stout, with a broad face and reddish complexion . . . answering to the description of his race." So eager was Thoreau to believe in this man's natural vigor that, although he heard Aitteon display his corruption by whistling "O Susanna and other such airs" while paddling their canoe, Thoreau still narrowly watched his motions and "listened attentively to his observations," as though ascertaining precisely what gifts this Red Man offered our race when his tunes more truthfully reflected his native background.

He reported closely on Aitteon's activities, but as the trip progressed Thoreau became most interested in the man in his role as hunter, stalking the game by which he and his fellow tribesmen lived. Thoreau carried no firearms, preferring to go as "reporter or Chaplain to the hunters," but he began to admit to a deep curiosity to see a moose "near at hand" and was not sorry "to learn how the Indian managed to kill one." But when the moment finally came, the man from Concord who felt "a strange thrill of savage delight" when he saw even a woodchuck crossing his path (also recall that he was tempted to seize the animal and devour it raw) was shocked by Aitteon's slaughter of the moose. Thoreau's response reveals how much his savage hyperbole always was for rhetorical effect. Even Mr. Sylvester Graham's unbolted flour must have been preferable to meat thus slaughtered on the hoof!

His description of the event records an interesting transformation. Initially Thoreau was fascinated by Aitteon's behavior when the moose's blood was shed. No matter what civilized tunes the Indian had whistled, he now offered a thrilling sight as he chased the wounded creature "lightly and gracefully, stealing through the bushes with the least possible noise, in a way which no white man does." But once the huge animal was tracked and found floating dead in the stream, Thoreau's attitude turned to outright revulsion. Watching Aitteon attack the carcass with his pocket knife, Thoreau regarded the scene (with true New England fastidiousness and a bit of humanitarian outrage) as nothing but a "tragical business" which "affected the innocence" and simply "destroyed the pleasure" of his adventure in Maine. Rather than taking savage delight in the kill, he was repulsed to see "the warm and palpitating body pierced with a knife" and "the warm milk stream from the rent udder." His description of this denouement did not reflect admiration for the native's skilled woodcraft: the scene only reminded Thoreau of "what a coarse and imperfect use Indians and hunters" often made of the nature which to him most often offered purely spiritual food.

The pastoral innocence of his own bean fields in mind, he admitted that for weeks afterward whenever he considered the episode he could not at all cherish the memory, but felt "the coarser for this part of his woodland experience." Having felt cosmically estranged on top of Ktaadn when he knew for the first time the terror of the infinite spaces, now he realized that, while this novel (to him) experience of savagery was still commonplace in the land he was crossing, the best life for him, and his race, had to be lived not in such violence and gore but "as tenderly as one would pluck a flower." Was he still naive about the Indian's lifestyle? What raw experience was he seeking on those trips to the heart of the country?

IV

My contention thus far has been that Thoreau, as much as Emerson, was interested in discovering and defining representative men for his age and that the nature and intensity of this search is explicitly visible in his discussion of the American Indians he offered in the essays comprising *The Maine Woods*. It is, of course, important to note that Thoreau wrote other brief "lives." One immediately thinks of the astute essays on Raleigh and Carlyle, and more importantly of his impressively outraged eulogy for Captain John Brown, whom he canonized with the names "Christian" and "Transcendentalist." Anyone studying the concept of the representative man in Transcendentalist circles cannot ignore these productions. But my point is what was earlier epitomized when Emerson told the audience assembled in 1862 in the Concord meetinghouse to hear him deliver his funeral oration for Thoreau, that by Thoreau's own admission three men of late had greatly influenced his life: John Brown, Walt Whitman, and "his Indian guide in Maine, Joe Polis." The question of Thoreau's fascination with Indian life, raised by Emerson as he bid a final goodbye to his neighbor, forces the critic to reconsider what it was that, even after the fright and disgust of the first trips in search of his hypothetical nobleman, made him continue his study of this race until he discovered someone commensurate to the capacity for wonder toward the Red Man he had so long carried with him.

With the critic's gift of hindsight we question at what point Thoreau realized that the genius the Indians possessed *already* had been vouchsafed him as he had recorded his own Concord experiences. For earlier he had acknowledged that it was man's awareness of and willingness to confront reality that made the lives of some men more meaningful than others. "The frontiers," he had noted, "are not east or west, north or south, but wherever a man *fronts* a fact." With intriguing wordplay he added that a man should "build for himself a log house with the bark on where he is, *fronting* IT, and wage there an old French war for seventy years, with the Indians and Rangers, or whatever else may come between him and reality, and save his scalp if he can." The essence of Thoreau's long-awaited discovery would be that many of the Indians he encountered, despite their obvious failings and corruptions attributable to their exposure to white society, met this test more squarely than his Concord acquaintances, and that in his profoundly simple life the Indian's own consciousness and all outside it (Emerson's Me and Not-Me) were somehow imaginatively linked. This closeness, this blood-knowledge of the final significance of *things,* was what so impressed him about the Red race. Years had passed since his first youthful mention of it, but by the time he met the Penobscot Indian Joe Polis he was able to recognize and appreciate what in his college years he had called the "mountain" prospect the Indians enjoyed. The reticent yet affectionate admiration he felt for his Maine guide who everyday saw facts flower into truths is convincing proof that Joe Polis stands as a central figure in any pantheon of representative men Thoreau implicitly established.

Joe Polis makes his appearance on the first page of the essay on "The Allagash and East Branch," and from the outset it is apparent that Thoreau's relationship to him was more intimate than that with any other Indian. Anthropologically speaking, he again first sought assurance of his subject's authenticity: he carefully noted how typical a native it was he had found as a companion. Stoutly built, with a broad face, and, "as others said, with perfect Indian features and complexion," Joe deserved the appellation as one of the "best" Indians in Oldtown, part of the "aristocracy" of his tribe.

But before he could attempt to plummet this man's depths, Thoreau had to learn patience: the Indian's favors were not bestowed indiscriminately. Emerson's task in describing his subjects had been a much easier one, for the men he considered were all dead and their normal "lives" openly published to the world; with a living specimen, Thoreau had to labor to penetrate what he described as that "strange remoteness in which the Indian ever dwells to the White man." But the lessons of his last trip to Maine had been well learned, and as he accustomed himself to the Indian's natural reticence he began to take this "remoteness" in stride. Within a day Thoreau's own reserved manner had so won Joe's confidence that Thoreau was able to suggest to the Indian that he should "like to go to school to learn his language." Joe thought well of the idea, and these two unlikely pupils soon decided that during the course of their voyage each would teach the other *all* that he knew!

It is important, and perfectly consistent with the pervasive concern with language in the Transcendentalist movement, that Thoreau's attempts to "know" the Indian took most productive form through an inquiry into his vocabulary. In "Chesuncook" Thoreau had already admitted the awe he felt while lying awake listening to the Indians converse in their primitive tongue. Taking strange delight in that experience, he concluded that these "purely wild and aboriginal sounds" which had first issued from the wigwams "before Columbus was born" were supreme proof that the Indian was not "the invention of historians and poets" but a being still existing with such primitive vitality that any man listening acutely to the Indian language was brought back to the origin of his own race's experience in the New World. Newly schooled to the meaning of such words as Musketicook (the Indian name for Concord River) and hearing Joe's quaint singing in his own vital language, Thoreau's imagination returned him "to the period of the discovery of America" when Europeans "first encountered the simple faith of the Indian." The words of that moving song, expressing Joe's faith in the one spirit who created the world, were so full of "sentiments of humility and reverence" that Thoreau knew he was with someone who had felt a spiritual presence as he himself had. Here was no rancorous Christian but a truly religious man: Joe's natural piety, his heightened sense that the world was animated and that his words were so expressive that they became one with the things they named, marked him a man to be treated with utmost respect. Through him Thoreau received further confirmation that what makes a life significant, the marrow of its representativeness, often was defined by how one came to know, and to touch, those simple things which were magically alive with spirit.

I could cite numerous instances of the effect Joe had on Thoreau's perceptions, but this new awareness is best illustrated by an anecdote related shortly after Thoreau's noctural reflections on the haunting piety of the Indian's song. Awakening about midnight to rake over the coals of the campfire, Thoreau witnessed a strange sight:

> partly in the fire, which had ceased to blaze, I saw a perfectly regular elliptical ring of light . . . fully as bright as the fire, but not reddish or scarlet like a coal, but a white and slumbering light, like the glow-worm's.

Mustering the courage to approach this shimmering light, he discovered it to be a piece of decaying moose-wood shining with phosphorescent glow, the mysterious "foxfire" celebrated in countless myths of the forest. Thoreau was so excited by this discovery that he woke his companion, Edward Hoar, to display this legendary will-o'-the-wisp and soon triumphantly noted how after this fortunate moment he "felt paid" for the hardships of his journey. He wrote that (in a telling phrase which reveals his profound interest in the various communications of nature) the light could hardly have thrilled him more if it had "taken the form of letters, or of the human face" as it revealed itself against the darkness. With the disturbing memories of the preceding trips still with him, he acknowledged that this spectacle had come at a time in his journey when he was "just in the frame of mind to see something wonderful." Then, shifting to a religious metaphor, he acknowledged that prior to this excursion he little had thought that there would be such "a light shining in the darkness of the wilderness" for him.

The episode does not close here, for the following morning, still unable to contain his amazement, Thoreau related his nighttime adventure to Joe Polis. The Indian then revealed more about the native mythology of this bewitching phenomenon, and our traveler, with the native's vital and picturesque language still ringing in his ears, finally understood what made the Indian different from his own race. If Joe were so familiar with the natural history of this mysterious event, "nature must have made a thousand [such] revelations to him," most of which remained inaccessible secrets to white men. Thoreau felt privileged to walk for a moment in this charmed circle and noted how he became perfectly content not to dissect the experience further but to "let science slide" while he rejoiced in the light "as if it had been a fellow creature." Scientific explanations of phenomena seemed inappropriate to such graceful moments; and Thoreau, in a vein reminiscent of Emerson when he traced the uses of nature from "commodity" upward, understood that with the Indians' superior vision there was always something magical to be seen within the fabric of nature.

Joe Polis's sophistication aside—he had represented his tribe in the state legislature at Augusta and once even had traveled to Washington, D.C.—he still had insight infrequently granted to people of Thoreau's acquaintance. "One revelation has been made to the Indian, another to the white man," Thoreau humbly admitted. After all his years as a naturalist he knew he had "much to learn of the Indian," a type of knowledge qualitatively different from anything white missionaries, religious or scientific, could present to him. With the Penobscot Joe Polis as a companion, traveling did not become what Emerson had called "a fool's paradise." Polis had taught Thoreau to get the axis of his eyes coincident with the axes of things, and he came to feel for a moment what for the white man would always be the evanescent unity of the Me and Not-Me. In so simple a fact as a piece of wood by a campfire had appeared a divine and supernatural light.

Thoreau's relationship to Joe immediately took on new dimensions.

After the Indian had explained the simple event in his mythological way, Thoreau could better verbalize the affinity he felt toward the Indian and further discover how expanded his own Concord horizon had become because of their rapport: the woods were no longer "tenantless, but chokefull of honest spirits as good as myself anyday." His friendship with the primitive man on this more solid footing, Thoreau now detected "a little fun" in the Indian's eyes, something which yielded to Thoreau's "sympathetic smile." He added, with the pun probably intended, that he even found Joe to be "thoroughly good-humored."

Revelation followed revelation as the Indian taught Thoreau to distinguish the values their differing cultures held. "The Anglo-American can indeed cut down and grub up all this waving forest, and make a stump speech, and vote for Buchanan on its ruins," but for all his pretension to superiority the white man could not "converse with the spirit of the trees he fells" nor read the poetry and mythology which "retire as he advances." Moreover, Joe Polis represented the man who, although he was enough interested in the civilized world to call on Daniel Webster after hearing him deliver his renowned Bunker Hill Oration, derived more pleasure and wisdom from less sophisticated recreations like an affectionate conversation with native wildlife. The day Thoreau heard Joe call to the muskrats in "a curious, squeaking, wiry sound" he knew that at last he had gotten "into the wilderness," a place not so much defined by land and space as by a receptivity to the promptings of the natural spirit. With the spread of white settlements, civilization and its discontents were becoming known to the Indian, but his ability to read the poetry and mythology of his environment gave him the stability to lead a life as meaningful as it had been among his ancestors. The Indian's representativeness finally was defined by his being a man who knew in the deepest sense the anima of the land he inhabited.

With precious understatement, Thoreau reminded the reader that Joe Polis was "a wild man, indeed, to be talking to a musquash!" and to the prosaic mind Joe might seem far removed from the giants with whom Emerson had concerned himself in his book on great men. This man had founded no religions, written no great books, conquered no continents but was merely a Penobscot Indian, one so domesticated that by his own admission he was a practicing Christian who agonized, as any good Protestant would, over excessive work on the Sabbath. What marked him apart was that in his youth he had been fortunate enough to acquire a natural wisdom "from a wise old Indian with whom he associated" and thus could still see and speak the native wonder his race had always perceived. Now he had transferred some of this wisdom to a traveler from Concord, Massachusetts, who was profoundly moved by the new simple ideas presented to him.

With all this in mind it is significant that in Thoreau's narrative Joe Polis, like Aitteon, kills a moose, but that Thoreau displays no adverse reaction to the incident. He was learning that, contrary to the veiled innocence preached by his friend Emerson, violence and evil were present in the world. But they were to be discerned and then transcended through one's understanding that the uses of nature are, indeed, various, and that in this particular case the animal had been slaughtered by a man who knew in the most poetic, as well as the most practical, sense what it meant to perpetrate the deed. Because of his new tolerance our traveler can be forgiven for indulging in a bit of wry humor when Polis became ill with the colic and "lay groaning under his canoe on the bank, looking woebegone." "It was only a common case of colic," Thoreau remarked, but it seemed that the Indian, "like the Irish," made "a greater ado about his sickness than a Yankee does." Such inconsequential failings could be overlooked in one of those representative men who in their characters and actions answered questions which ordinary men did not even have the skill to ask.

V

Thoreau was a man who, as his personal philosophy matured, became increasingly concerned with role models, men who could be termed representative of the gifts necessary to comprehend the complexity that had come to define America. The chaos of the Age of Jackson required that new roles be established—and Thoreau came to view the American Indian as providing an important example of what virtues Americans needed to retain significance in their lives. Unlike others who saw in the Red Man an uncivilized threat to organized society, Thoreau sympathetically probed the aboriginal mind of his continent and ascertained what it was in the Indian spirit that white men sorely lacked in the decadence of their nineteenth-century prosperity, a theme he had addressed differently in *Walden*.

Earlier in life Thoreau had noted in his journal that what he admired most about seventeenth-century exploration writers, the first men who had walked on the virgin continent and encountered the Indian mind, was that their generation, unencumbered by the weight of civilized baggage, "stood nearer to the facts, than this, and hence their books had more life to them." In later years he came to believe that his own inspiring contact with the Indians had returned him, at least imaginatively, to those same days, "to the period of the discovery of America, to San Salvador, and the Incas," when the secrets of the world were unraveled naturally as travelers stood open eyed at the New World's wonder. By understanding the Red Man Thoreau jarred his memory into the association between the shimmering present and an ever-vital past; and, at least momentarily, the constricted consciousness of a white American had been dissolved as Thoreau glimpsed what T. S. Eliot later called a timeless world still in time. Well before D. H. Lawrence and William Carlos Williams (and certainly in a more profound way than his older contemporary James Fenimore Cooper) Thoreau sensed that these Red Men possessed a gift so distinct from his whiteness that without an adequate understanding of it the fair-skinned race had to be driven to lives of quiet desperation.

On his trips to Maine Thoreau sadly realized that even by the 1850s the corruption of the Christian world had penetrated to the heart of the American wilderness. But he also discovered, and revealed it impressionistically in his essay on the adventures of Henry Thoreau and Joe Polis in the Allagash wilderness, that it did not matter *where* a man was as long as he drenched himself in reality with the same intensity as the native Americans. "There is really the same difference between our positions wherever we may be camped," he wrote. We must realize that "some are nearer the frontiers on featherbeds in the towns than others on fir twigs in the backwoods." *The Maine Woods* offers the important lesson that, as with any story of (and by) a representative man, an author is most to be respected because he knows what representative "genius" is. For Thoreau it resided in the breadth of one's imagination.

If the experience of Walden Pond was to remain important in his eyes (and if it is to remain meaningful to us) Thoreau had to learn the lesson that, as his village neighbor often reminded him, the integrity of one's personal vision is all important. Not one of Emerson's representative men had displayed the same genius as the American Indian, Joe Polis. Swedenborg talking to a muskrat, Plato paddling a canoe, Napoleon explaining the eerie foxfire: all are unimaginable. We need a Joe Polis, and a Henry Thoreau, to remind us that truth is spherical and best approached from any tangent drawn from integrity, be it on State Street or in the Maine woods.

WALTER   BENN   MICHAELS

Walden's *False Bottoms*

Walden has traditionally been regarded as both a simple and a difficult text, simple in that readers have achieved a remarkable unanimity in identifying the values Thoreau is understood to urge upon them, difficult in that they have been persistently perplexed and occasionally even annoyed by the form his exhortations take. Thoreau's Aunt Maria (the one who bailed him out of jail in the poll-tax controversy) understood this as a problem in intellectual history and blamed it all on the Transcendental Zeitgeist: "I do love to hear things called by their right names," she said, "and these *Transcendentalists* do so transmogrophy . . . their words and pervert common sense that I have no patience with them." Thoreau's Transcendentalist mentor, Emerson, found, naturally enough, another explanation, blaming instead what he called Henry's "old fault of unlimited contradiction. The trick of his rhetoric is soon learned: it consists in substituting for the obvious word and thought its diametrical antagonist. . . . It makes me," he concluded, "nervous and wretched to read it." That old fault of contradiction is in one sense the subject of this essay, so is wretchedness and especially nervousness, so, in some degree, are the strategies readers have devised for feeling neither wretched nor nervous.

The primary strategy, it seems to me, has been to follow a policy of benign neglect in regard to the question of what *Walden* means; thus, as Charles Anderson noted some ten years ago, critics have concerned themselves largely with "style," agreeing from the start that the book's distinction lies "more in its manner than its matter." Anderson was referring

From *Glyph* 4 (1977). © 1977 by the Johns Hopkins University Press.

mainly to the tradition of essentially formalist studies ushered in by F. O. Matthiessen's monumental *American Renaissance* in 1941, in which Thoreau is assimilated to the American tradition of the "native craftsman," and *Walden* itself is compared to the "artifacts of the cabinet maker, the potter and the founder." Anderson himself has no real quarrel with this procedure; his chief complaint is that Matthiessen's successors have not taken their enterprise seriously enough. The concern with *Walden*'s style, he says, "has not usually been pursued beyond a general eulogy. Perhaps it is through language that all the seemingly disparate subjects of this book are integrated into wholeness." "Why not try an entirely new approach," he suggests, "and read *Walden* as a poem?"

From our present perspective, of course, it is hard to see how reading *Walden* "as a poem" constitutes an entirely new approach; it seems, if anything, a refinement of the old approaches, a way of continuing to bracket the question of *Walden*'s meaning in at least two different ways. The first is by introducing a distinction between form and content which simultaneously focuses attention on the question of form and reduces content to little more than a banality, typically, in the case of *Walden,* a statement to the effect that the book is fundamentally "a fable of the renewal of life." But from this first move follows a second, more interesting and more pervasive: the preoccupation with *Walden*'s formal qualities turns out to involve a more than tacit collaboration with the assumption that *Walden*'s meaning (what Anderson might call its content and what Stanley Cavell will explicitly call its "doctrine") is in a certain sense simple and univocal. The assertion implicit in this approach is that to examine the form of any literary "artifact" (in fact, even to define the artifact) is precisely to identify its essential unity, thus the continuity between Matthiessen's concern with *Walden*'s "structural wholeness" and Anderson's project of showing how well "integrated" the book is. Where nineteenth-century critics tended to regard *Walden* as an anthology of spectacular fragments and to explain it in terms of the brilliant but disordered personality of its author (his "critical power," wrote James Russell Lowell, was "from want of continuity of mind, very limited and inadequate"), more recent criticism, by focusing directly on the art of *Walden,* has tended to emphasize the rhetorical power of its "paradoxes," finding elegant formal patterns in what were once thought to be mere haphazard blunders. Thus, in accepting unity and coherence not simply as desiderata but as the characteristic identifying marks of the work of art, these critics have begun by answering the question I should like to begin by asking, the question of *Walden*'s contradictions.

Thoreau himself might well have been skeptical of some of the claims made on behalf of *Walden*'s aesthetic integrity. He imagined himself addressing "poor students," leading "mean and sneaking lives," "lying, flattering, voting." "The best works of art," he said, "are the expression of man's struggle to free himself from this condition, but the effect of our art is merely to make this low state comfortable and that higher state to be forgotten." In this context, what we might begin to see emerging as the central problem of reading *Walden* is the persistence of our own attempts to identify and understand its unity, to dispel our nervousness by resolving or at least containing the contradictions which create it. It is just this temptation, Thoreau seems to suggest, which must be refused. And in this respect, the naive perspective of someone like Lowell, who saw in Thoreau the absolute lack of any "artistic mastery" and in his works the total absence of any "mutual relation" between one part and another, may still be of some provisional use, not as a point of view to be reclaimed but as a reminder that resolution need not be inevitable, that we need not read to make ourselves more comfortable.

One way to begin nurturing discomfort is to focus on some of the tasks Thoreau set himself as part of his program for living a life of what he called "epic integrity." There were, of course, a good many of them, mostly along the lines of his own advice to the unhappily symbolic farmer John Field—"Grow wild according to thy nature," Thoreau urged him, "Rise free from care before the dawn. Let the noon find thee by other lakes and the night overtake thee everywhere at home." Some other projects, however, were conceived in less hortatory terms and the possibility of their completion was more explicitly imaginable. One, "To find the bottom of Walden Pond and what inlet and outlet it might have," worked its way eventually out of Thoreau's *Journal* and into a central position in the experiment of *Walden* itself. What gave this quest a certain piquancy were the rumours that the pond had no bottom, that, as some said, "it reached quite through to the other side of the globe." "These many stories about the bottom, or rather no bottom, of this Pond," had, Thoreau said, "no foundation for themselves." In fact, the pond was "exactly one hundred and two feet deep," his own "soundings" proved it. This is, he admits, "a remarkable depth for so small an area; yet not an inch of it can be spared by the imagination. What if all ponds were shallow? Would it not react on the minds of men? While men believe in the infinite some ponds will be thought to be bottomless."

If Thoreau's final position on bottoms seems to come out a little blurred here, this has an interest of its own which may be worth pursuing.

On the one hand, the passage seems to be asserting that a belief in the potential bottomlessness of ponds is a Bad Thing. The villagers predisposed
in this direction who set out to measure Walden with a fifty-six-pound
weight and a wagon load of rope were already entrapped by their own
delusions, for "while the fifty-six was resting by the way," Thoreau says,
"they were paying out the rope in the vain attempt to fathom their truly
immeasurable capacity for marvellousness." On the other hand, it isn't
enough that the pond is revealed to have a "tight bottom," or even that it
turns out symbolically "deep and pure"; it must be imagined bottomless
to encourage men's belief in the "infinite." Thus, the passage introduces
two not entirely complementary sets of dichotomies. In the first, the virtues
of a pond with a "tight bottom" are contrasted with the folly of believing
in bottomless ponds. But then the terms shift: the tight bottom metamorphoses into the merely "shallow" and the bottomless becomes the "infinite." The hierarchies are inverted here: on the one hand, a "tight bottom"
is clearly preferable to delusory bottomlessness, on the other hand, the
merely "shadow" is clearly not so good as the symbolically suggestive "infinite." Finally, the narrator is thankful that the pond was made deep, but
"deep" is a little ambiguous: is he glad that the pond is *only* deep so that
tough-minded men like himself can sound it and discover its hard bottom,
or is he glad that the pond is so deep that it deceives men into thinking of
it as bottomless and so leads them into meditations on the infinite? This
second explanation seems more convincing, but then the account of the
experiment seems to end with a gesture which undermines the logic according to which it was undertaken in the first place.

Sounding the depths of the pond, however, is by no means the only
experimental excavation in *Walden.* There is perhaps a better-known passage near the end of the chapter called "Where I Lived and What I Lived
For" which helps to clarify what is at stake in the whole bottom-hunting
enterprise. "Let us settle ourselves," Thoreau says, "and work and wedge
our feet downward through the mud and slush of opinion, and prejudice,
and tradition, and delusion, and appearance . . . through church and state,
through poetry and philosophy and religion, till we come to a hard bottom
and rocks in place which we can call *reality,* and say This is, and no mistake; and then begin, having a *point d'appui* . . . a place where you might
found a wall or a state." Measurement here is irrelevant—the issue is solid-
ity, not depth, and the metaphysical status of hard bottoms seems a good
deal less problematic. They are real, and "Be it life or death," Thoreau
says, "we crave only reality." It is only when we have put ourselves in
touch with such a *point d'appui* that we really begin to lead our lives and

not be led by them, and the analogy with the *Walden* experiment itself is obvious—it becomes a kind of ontological scavenger hunt—the prize is reality.

But there is at least one more hard bottom story which unhappily complicates things again. It comes several hundred pages later in the "Conclusion," and tucked in as it is between the flashier and more portentous parables of the artist from Kouroo and of the "strong and beautiful bug," it has been more or less ignored by critics. "It affords me no satisfaction to commence to spring an arch before I have got a solid foundation," Thoreau begins in the now familiar rhetoric of the moral imperative to get to the bottom of things. "Let us not play at kittlybenders," he says, "There is a solid bottom everywhere." But now the story proper gets underway and things begin to go a little haywire. "We read that the traveller asked the boy if the swamp before him had a hard bottom. The boy replied that it had. But presently the traveller's horse sank in up to the girths, and he observed to the boy, 'I thought you said that this bog had a hard bottom.' 'So it has,' answered the latter, 'but you have not go half way to it yet.' " And "so it is with the bogs and quicksands of society," Thoreau piously concludes, "but he is an old boy that knows it."

This puts the earlier story in a somewhat different light, I think, and for several reasons. For one thing, the tone is so different; the exalted rhetoric of the evangelist has been replaced by the fireside manner of the teller of tall tales. But more fundamentally, although the theme of the two stories has remained the same—the explorer in search of the solid foundation—the point has been rather dramatically changed. The exhortation has become a warning. The exemplary figure of the heroic traveller, "tied to his mast like Ulysses," Thoreau says, who accepts no substitutes in his quest for the real, has been replaced by the equally exemplary but much less heroic figure of the suppositious traveller drowned in his own pretension. In the first version, Thoreau recognized death as a possibility, but it was a suitably heroic one: "If you stand right fronting and face to face to a fact," he wrote in a justly famous passage, "you will see the sun glimmer on both its surfaces, as if it were a cimeter, and feel its sweet edge dividing you through the heart and marrow, and so you will happily conclude your mortal career." The vanishing traveller of the "conclusion" knows no such happy ending, when he hits the hard bottom he will just be dead, his only claim to immortality his skill in the art of sinking, dispiritedly, in prose.

The juxtaposition of these three passages does not in itself prove anything very startling but it does suggest what may be a useful line of inquiry. What, after all, is at stake in the search for a solid bottom? Why is the concept or the project of foundation so central to *Walden* and at the same time so problematic? At least a preliminary answer would seem justified in focusing on the almost Cartesian process of peeling away until we reach that point of ontological certainty where we can say "This is, and no mistake." The peeling away is itself a kind of questioning: what justification do we have for our opinions, for our traditions? What authorizes church and state, poetry, philosophy, religion? The *point d'appui* has been reached only when we have asked all the questions we know how to ask and so at last have the sense of an answer we are unable ourselves to give. "After a still winter night," Thoreau says, "I awoke with the impression that some question had been put to me, which I had been endeavouring in vain to answer in my sleep, as what—how—when—where? But there was dawning Nature in whom all creatures live . . . and no question on *her* lips. I awoke to an answered question, to Nature." The *point d'appui* then, is a place we locate by asking questions. We know that we've found it when one of our questions is answered. The name we give to this place is Nature. The search for the solid bottom is a search for justification in Nature, wedging our way through "appearance," that is to say human institutions, like church and state and philosophy, until we hit what is real, that is, natural, and not human.

That nature in its purest form should exclude humanity is perhaps a somewhat peculiar doctrine, and one which runs counter to much of what Thoreau often says, and to much of what we think about him and his enterprise. But the logic and the desires which generate this conception are made clear in "Civil Disobedience" when Thoreau attacks the "statesmen and legislators" who, "standing so completely within the institution, never distinctly and nakedly behold it." In an essay called "What Is Authority?" Hannah Arendt has described what she calls "the dichotomy between seeing truth in solitude and remoteness and being caught in the relationships and relativities of human affairs" as "authoritative for the (Western) tradition of political thought," and it is precisely this privilege of distance and detachment to which Thoreau seems to be appealing in "Civil Disobedience." He goes on, however, to diagnose more specifically what is wrong with the legislators: "They speak of moving society, but have no resting-place without it." Webster, for instance, "never goes behind government and so cannot speak with authority about it." The appeal here is to the example of Archimedes—"Give me a place to stand and I will move the earth"—and the suggestion in *Walden* is that nature must be much more than a place of retreat. She is a "resting-place" only in the sense of the *"point d'appui,"* the place to stand, and she is an authoritative *point d'ap-*

pui only insofar as she is truly "behind," first, separate, and other. Thus, through most of *Walden,* when Thoreau is addressing himself to the problem of his search for a cogito, a political and philosophical hard bottom, the human and the natural are conceived as standing in implicit opposition to each other. Nature has a kind of literal authority precisely because she is not one of men's institutions. She serves as the location of values which are real insofar as they are not human creations. She is exemplary. "If we would restore mankind," Thoreau says, "let us first be as simple and as well as Nature ourselves." The force of this conception is expressed most directly, perhaps, in the short essay "Slavery in Massachusetts," written to protest the state's cooperation with the Fugitive Slave Law of 1850. The image of Nature here is a white water lily, an emblem, like Walden Pond itself, of "purity." "It suggests what kind of laws have prevailed longest," Thoreau writes, "and that there is virtue even in man, too, who is fitted to perceive and love it." And, he goes on to say, "It reminds me that Nature has been partner to no Missouri Compromise. I scent no compromise in the fragrance of the water-lily." The point again is that it is Nature's independence which makes her exemplary, which, from this standpoint, justifies the retreat to Walden and authorizes the hope that something of real value may be found and hence founded there.

But this conception of nature, as attractive and useful as it is, turns out to be in some ways a misleading one. In "Slavery in Massachusetts," the encomium on the lily is preceded by a brief excursion in search of solace to "one of our ponds" (it might as well be Walden). But there is no solace to be found there. "We walk to lakes to see our serenity reflected in them," Thoreau says, "when we are not serene we go not to them." For "what signifies the beauty of nature when men are base?" If the water lily is a symbol of nature free and clear, sufficient unto itself, the pond in its role as reflector symbolizes a nature implicated in human affairs. It fails as a source of consolation because, unlike the water lily, it participates in the world of Missouri Compromises and Fugitive Slave Laws. And this vision of nature compromised finds a significant position in *Walden* as well. In the chapter called "Sounds," Thoreau devotes the beginning of one paragraph to a sound he claims he never heard, the sound of the cock crowing. This is no doubt a kind of back-handed reference to his own declaration at the beginning of the book: "I do not propose to write an ode to dejection, but to brag as lustily as chanticleer in the morning . . . if only to wake my neighbors up." The writing of *Walden* makes up for the absent cock-crow. But he goes on to speak of the cock as a "once wild Indian pheasant" and to wonder if it could ever be "naturalized without being domesticated." Here *Walden*'s customary opposition between nature and civilization turns into an opposition between wilderness and civilization, and nature ("naturalized") appears as a third term, at one remove from "wild" and in constant danger of being domesticated and so rendered useless. Furthermore, this danger appears most pronounced at a moment which has been defined as that of writing, the cockcrow. The dismay at seeing only one's face reflected in the pond repeats itself here for a moment as the text imagines itself as a once wild voice now tamed and defused.

These two accounts suggest, then, the kind of problem that is being defined. The attraction of Nature as a bottom line is precisely its otherness—"Nature puts no question and answers none which we mortals ask"—and touching bottom is thus (paradoxically) a moment of recognition; we see what "really is" and our relation to it is basically one of appreciation (and perhaps emulation). The paradox, of course, is our ability to recognize something which is defined precisely by its strangeness to us, a difficulty Thoreau urges upon us when he insists that "Nature has no human inhabitant who appreciates her," and that "she flourishes most alone." But, as I have said, this aloneness is the chief guarantee of authenticity—when we have reached the bottom, we know at least that what we are seeing is not just ourselves. And yet this is also what is most problematic in the symbolic character of Walden Pond itself; looking into it, we find ourselves sounding the depths of our own "nature," and so the reflection makes a mockery of our enterprise. "For his genius to be effective," one critic has written, Thoreau recognized that he "had to slough off his civilized self and regain his natural self," and this seems innocuous enough. But the cosmological continuity which would authorize a notion like the "natural self" is exactly what is being questioned here. For us to recognize ourselves in Nature, Nature must be no longer herself, no longer the *point d'appui* we were looking for when we started.

But even if Nature proves inadequate as a final category, an absolute, *Walden*'s response is not to repudiate the notion of intrinsic value. The pond remains a precious stone, "too pure," he says, to have "a market value," and so it provides at least a symbolic alternative to the commercial values of the first chapter, "Economy." "Economy" has usually been read as a witty and bitter attack on materialism, perhaps undertaken, as Charles Anderson has suggested, in response to Mill's *Political Economy* and/or Marx's *Communist Manifesto* (both published in 1848), motivated, in any event, by a New Testament perception: "Men labor under a mistake. . . . They are employed . . . laying up treasures which moth and rust will corrupt and thieves break through and steal." But it isn't simply a mistake in

emphasis—too much on the material and not enough on the spiritual—
that Thoreau is concerned with here, for the focal point of "Economy"'s
attack is not wealth per se but "exchange," the principle of the marketplace. Thus, he questions not merely the value of material goods but the
process through which the values are determined; "trade curses everything
it handles," he says, "and though you trade in messages from heaven, the
whole curse of trade attaches to the business." In some degree this can be
explained as a nineteenth-century expression of a long-standing ideological
debate between the political conceptions of virtue and commerce, which
depended in turn upon an opposition between what J. G. A. Pocock has
called "real, inheritable, and, so to speak, natural property in land," and
property understood to have only what Pocock calls a "symbolic value,
expressed in coin or in credit." One of the phenomena Pocock describes
is the persistence with which various social groups attempted to convince
themselves that their credit economies were "based on the exchange of real
goods and the perception of real values." Failing this, he says, "the individual could exist, even in his own sight, only at the fluctuating value imposed
upon him by his fellows."

Thoreau was obviously one of those unconvinced and unhappy about
it. Not only did he repudiate what he perceived as false methods of determining value, not only did he rail against the maintenance of a standing
army and even reject at times the validity of the entire concept of representative government (all these, as Pocock depicts them, classical political positions); he also attacked real, so-called natural property as well, and precisely at the point which was intended to provide its justification, its
inheritability. "I see young men," he says at the very beginning of *Walden,*
"my townsmen, whose misfortune it is to have inherited farms, houses . . .
for these are more easily acquired than got rid of." Here he blurs the customary distinction between real or natural and symbolic or artificial property, insisting that all property is artificial and so exposing laws of inheri-
tance as mere fictions of continuity, designed to naturalize values which in
themselves are purely arbitrary.

This points toward a rather peculiar dilemma—Thoreau's doggedly
ascetic insistence on distinguishing natural values from artificial ones leads
him to reject the tokens of natural value which his society provides, and
so the category of the natural becomes an empty one. But this doesn't
mean that the natural/arbitrary distinction breaks down. Quite the contrary: the more difficult that it becomes to identify natural principles, the
more privilege attaches to a position which can be defined only in theoretical opposition to the conventional or institutional. The "resting-place

without" society that Thoreau speaks of in "Civil Disobedience" now turns out to be located neither in nature nor in culture but in that empty space he sometimes calls "wilderness." This is perhaps what he means when he describes himself once as a "sojourner in civilized life" and another time as a "sojourner in nature." To be a sojourner everywhere is by one account (Thoreau's own in "Walking") to be "at home everywhere." In *Walden,* however, this vision of man at home in the world is undermined by the Prophetic voice which proclaims it. He denounces his contemporaries who "no longer camp as for a night but have settled down on earth and forgotten heaven" by comparing them unfavorably to the primitive nomads who "dwelt . . . in a tent in this world," thus invoking one of the oldest of western topoi, the moral authority of the already atavistic Hebrew nomads, the Rechabites, relating the commandments of their father to the prophet Jeremiah: "Neither shall ye build house, nor sow seed, nor plant vineyard, nor have any: but all your days ye shall dwell in tents; that ye may live many days in the land where ye be strangers" (Jer. 35:7). The Rechabites were at home nowhere, not everywhere. Jeremiah cites them as exemplars not of a healthy rusticity but of a deep-seated and devout alienation which understands every experience except that of Yahweh as empty and meaningless. Thus, to be, like Thoreau, a self-appointed stranger in the land is to repudiate the values of a domesticated pastoral by recognizing the need for a resting place beyond culture and nature both, and to accept the figurative necessity of living always in one's tent is to recognize the impossibility of ever actually locating that resting place.

Another way to deal with this search for authority is to imagine it emanating not only from a place but from a time. In *Walden,* the notion of foundation brings these two categories uneasily together. The solid bottom is a place where you might "found a wall or a state," but the foundation of a state is perhaps more appropriately conceived as a time—July 4, for example, the day Thoreau says he moved to the woods. This constitutes an appeal to the authority of precedent which would justify also the exemplary claims *Walden* makes on behalf of itself. The precedent has force as the record of a previous "experiment," and since "No way of thinking or doing, however ancient, can be trusted without proof," the "experiment" of *Walden* can apparently be understood as an attempt to repeat the results originally achieved by the Founding Fathers. But the scientific term *experiment,* precisely because it relies on the notion of repeatability, that is, on an unchanging natural order, turns out to work much less well in the historical context of human events. "Here is life," Thoreau says, "an experiment to a great extent untried by me; but it does not avail me that they have tried it." This now is a peculiar kind of empiricism which stresses not only the primacy of experience but its unrepeatability, its uniqueness. (What good is *Walden* if not as a precedent?) The revolutionary appeal to foundation as a new beginning seems to be incompatible with the empiricist notion of foundation as the experience of an immediate but principled (i.e., repeatable) reality. The historical and the scientific ideas of foundation are clearly at odds here, and Thoreau seems to recognize this when he speaks of his desire "to anticipate not the sunrise and the dawn merely, but if possible Nature herself," that is, to achieve a priority which belongs to the historical but not the natural world. Coleridge had written some twenty years before that "No natural thing or act can be called an originate" since "the moment we assume an origin in nature, a true beginning, that moment we rise above nature." Thoreau speaks of coming before rather than rising above, but the sense of incompatibility is the same. Once again the desire for the solid bottom is made clear, but the attempt to locate it or specify its characteristics involves the writer in a tangle of contradictions.

What I have tried to describe thus far is a series of relationships in the text of *Walden*—between nature and culture, the finite and the infinite, and (still to come) literal and figurative language—each of which is imagined at all times hierarchically, that is, the terms don't simply coexist, one is always thought of as more basic or more important than the other. The catch is that the hierarchies are always breaking down. Sometimes nature is the ground which authorizes culture, sometimes it is merely another of culture's creations. Sometimes the search for a hard bottom is presented as the central activity of a moral life, sometimes that same search will only make a Keystone Cop martyr out of the searcher. These unresolved contradictions are, I think, what makes us nervous reading *Walden*, and the urge to resolve them seems to me a major motivating factor in most *Walden* criticism. Early, more or less explicitly biographical criticism tended to understand the inconsistencies as personal ones, stemming, in Lowell's words, from Thoreau's "want of continuity of mind." But as the history of literary criticism began to deflect its attention from authors to texts, this type of explanation naturally began to seem unsatisfactory. Allusions to Thoreau's psychological instability were now replaced by references to *Walden*'s "literary design," and paradox, hitherto understood as a more or less technical device, was now seen to lie near the very center of *Walden*'s "literariness." In one essay, by Joseph Moldenhauer, Thoreau's techniques are seen in easy analogy to those of Sir Thomas Browne, Donne, and the other English Metaphysicals, and generally the "presentation of truth through paradox" is identified as Thoreau's characteristic goal, although sometimes the truth is mythical, sometimes psychological, sometimes a little of both. In any event, the formalist demand that the text be understood as a unified whole (mechanical or organic) is normative; what Moldenhauer calls the "heightened language of paradox" is seen as shocking the reader into new perceptions of ancient truths.

More recently, the question of *Walden*'s hierarchies has been raised again by Stanley Cavell in a new and interesting way. Cavell recounts what he calls the "low myth of the reader" in *Walden*. "It may be thought of," he says, as a one-sentence fabliau:

> The writer has been describing the early spring days in which he went down to the woods to cut down timber for his intended house; he depicts himself carrying along his dinner of bread and butter wrapped in a newspaper which while he was resting he read. A little later, he says: "In those days when my hands were much employed, I read but little, but the least scraps of paper which lay on the ground . . . afforded me as much entertainment, in fact answered the same purpose as the *Iliad*."
>
> If you do not know what reading can be, you might as well use the pages of the *Iliad* for the purpose for which newspaper is used after a meal in the woods. If, however, you are prepared to read, then a fragment of newspaper, discovered words, are sufficient promptings . . . The events in a newspaper, our current lives are epic, and point morals, if we know how to interpret them.

The moral of this interpretation, as I understand it, is that just as the hierarchical relation between nature and culture is uncertain and problematic, so there is no necessary hierarchy among texts—a Baltimore *Morning Sun* is as good as an *Iliad* if you know how to read it. But it is interesting that one of the passages Cavell elsewhere refers to (from *Walden*'s chapter on "Reading") is concerned precisely to specify a hierarchy of texts. "I kept Homer's *Iliad* on my table through the summer," Thoreau writes, "though I looked at his page only now and then. . . . Yet I sustained myself by the prospect of such reading in the future. I read one or two shallow books of travel in the intervals of my work, till that employment made me ashamed of myself, and I asked where it was then that *I* lived." The contrast here is between the epic and the travelogue, and for Thoreau the latter was a particularly vexing genre. "I would fain say something, not so much concerning the Chinese and Sandwich Islanders as you who read these pages, who are said to live in New England," he proclaims in *Walden*'s first chapter, and in its last chapter he renounces any "exploration" beyond one's "private sea, the Atlantic and Pacific Ocean of one's being alone." In his personal life, too, he shied away from voyages; until his last years, he never got any farther from Concord than Staten Island, and it took only several youthful weeks on that barbaric shore to send him scurrying for home. But he was at the same time inordinately fond of travel books; one scholar's account has him reading a certifiable minimum of 172 of them, and as any reader of *Walden* knows, these accounts make frequent appearances there. In fact, in "Economy," no sooner has Thoreau announced his intention to ignore the lure of Oriental exoticisms than he plunges into a series of stories about the miraculous exploits of certain heroic "Bramins." *Walden* is, in fact, chock full of the wisdom of the mysterious East. The epics which Thoreau opposes to "shallow books of travel" are, in almost the same breath, described as "books which circulate around the world," that is, they are themselves travelling books.

All this serves mainly to reinforce Cavell's point; judging by subject matter at least, epics and travelogues turn out to look pretty much the same—the significant distinctions must then be not so much in the books themselves as in the way we read them. And along these lines, Thoreau suggests in "Reading" another, perhaps more pertinent way of distinguishing between the two genres: travel books are "shallow," epics presumably are not, which is to say that in reading epics, we must be prepared to conjecture "a larger sense than common use permits." The mark of the epic is thus that it can be, indeed must be, read figuratively, whereas the travel book lends itself only to a shallow or literal reading. Thoreau goes on to imagine the contrast between classical literature and what he calls a "cheap, contemporary literature" as a contrast between the eloquence of the writer who "speaks to the intellect and heart of mankind, to all in any age who can *understand* him" and the lesser eloquence of the orator who "yields to the inspiration of a transient occasion, and speaks to the mob before him, to those who can *hear* him." Thus the opposition between the epic and travelogue has modulated into an opposition between the figurative and the literal and then between the written and the oral. In each case, the first term of the opposition is privileged, and if we turn again to the attempt to sound the depths of Walden Pond, we can see that these are all values of what I have called *bottomlessness*. A shallow pond would be like a shallow book, that is, a travel book, one meant to be read literally. *Walden* is written "deep and pure for a symbol."

But this pattern of valorization, although convincing, is by no means

ubiquitous or final. The chapter on "Reading" is followed by one called
"Sounds," which systematically reconsiders the categories already introduced and which reasserts the values of the hard bottom. Here the written
word is contrasted unfavorably with the magical "noise" of nature. The
"intimacy" and "universality" for which Thoreau had praised it in the first
chapter are now metamorphosed into "confinement" and a new kind of
"provincialism." But not only is the hierarchical relation between the written and the oral inverted, so is what we have seen to be the corresponding
relation between the figurative and the literal. What in the chapter on
"Reading" was seen to be the greatest virtue of the classic texts, their susceptibility to interpretation, to the conjecturing of a larger sense "too significant," Thoreau says, "to be heard by the ear," a sense which "we must
be born again to speak," all this is set aside in favor of the "one articulation of Nature," the "language which all things and events speak without
metaphor." In "Sounds," Nature's voice is known precisely because it resists interpretation. The polysemous becomes perverse; the models of communication are the Puri Indians who, having only one word for yesterday,
today, and tomorrow, "express the variety of meaning by pointing backward for yesterday, forward for tomorrow, and overhead for the passing
day." Where the classic texts were distinguished by their underdetermined
quality—since the language they were written in was "dead," their "sense"
was generated only by the reader's own interpretive "wisdom," "valor,"
and "generosity"—nature's language in "Sounds," the song of the birds,
the stirring of the trees, is eminently alive and, as the example of the Indians shows, correspondingly overdetermined. Theirs is a system of words
modified only by gestures and so devised that they will allow only a single
meaning. No room is left for the reader's conjectures; the goal is rather a
kind of indigenous and monosyllabic literalism, so many words for so
many things by the shores of Gitcheegoomee. This means, of course, that
the values of bottomlessness are all drained away. The deep is replaced by
the shallow, the symbolic by the actual—what we need now, Thoreau says,
are "tales of real life, high and low, and founded on fact."

This particular set of inversions helps us to relocate, I think, the problem of reading *Walden,* which we have already defined as the problem of
resolving, or at least containing, its contradictions, of establishing a certain
unity. Critics like Lowell domesticated the contradictions by understanding
them as personal ones; to point out Thoreau's (no doubt lamentable) inconsistencies was not, after all, to accuse him of schizophrenia—the parts
where he seemed to forget himself or ignore what he had said before were
evidence only of certain lapses of attention. The formalists, turning their

attention from the author to the text, transformed Thoreau's faults into *Walden*'s virtues; theirs was already the language of paradox, apparent inconsistencies pointing toward final literary (i.e., not necessarily logical) truths. Now Cavell takes this process of resolution, of replacement, as far, in one direction, as it can go; the unity which was claimed first for the personality of the author, then for the formal structure of the text itself, now devolves upon the reader. *Walden*'s contradictions are resolved, he says, "if you know how to interpret them." The reader who knows how, it turns out, can discern in *Walden* "a revelation in which the paradoxes and ambiguities of its doctrine achieve a visionary union." And more recent writers like Lawrence Buell have extended this principle to others among the Transcendentalists. "Emerson's contribution," Buell writes, "is to show through his paradoxical style the inoperability of doctrine, to force the auditor to read him figuratively, as he believes that scriptures should be read."

But Cavell's position has its own peculiarity, for while it recognizes and even insists upon the difficulty of maintaining hierarchies in the text of *Walden,* it goes on simply to reinscribe those hierarchies in *Walden*'s readers. Knowing how to read for Cavell and for Buell is knowing how to read figuratively, and this is one of the things, Cavell says, that *Walden* teaches us. Thus the coherence that the formalists understood as the defining characteristic of the text becomes instead the defining characteristic of the reader, and the unity which was once claimed for the object itself is now claimed for the reader's experience of it. But, as we have just seen, the power of figurative reading is not the only thing *Walden* teaches us; it also urges upon us the necessity of reading literally, not so much in addition to reading figuratively as *instead of* reading figuratively. In the movement from "Reading" to "Sounds," the figurative and the literal do not coexist, they are not seen as complementary; rather the arguments Thoreau gives in support of the one take the form of attacks on the other. If, following Thoreau's guide, we conceive the literal as a meaning available to us without interpretation (i.e., the unmediated language of nature) and the figurative as a meaning generated by our own interpretive "wisdom," we find that the very act of reading commits us to a choice, not simply between different meanings, but between different stances toward reality, different versions of the self. Thus books must inevitably be "read as deliberately and reservedly as they were written" because to read *is* to deliberate, to consider and decide. "Our whole life is startlingly moral," Thoreau says, "There is never an instant's truce between virtue and vice." This is a call to action in the most direct sense, and the action it imagines is reading,

conceived as an explicitly moral activity. Elsewhere he writes, "it appears
as if men had deliberately chosen the common mode of living because they
preferred it to others. Yet they honestly think there is no choice left." Thoreau's concern in *Walden* is, of course, to show us that we do have choices
left and, by breaking down hierarchies into contradictory alternatives, to
insist upon our making them. But this breakdown, which creates the opportunity, or rather the necessity for choosing, serves at the same time to
undermine the rationale we might give for any particular choice. If there
is no hierarchy of values, what authority can we appeal to in accounting
for our decisions? What makes one choice better than another?

     This is what the search for a solid bottom is all about, a location for
authority, a ground upon which we can make a decision. *Walden* insists
upon the necessity for such a search at the same time that it dramatizes the
theoretical impossibility of succeeding in it. In this sense, the category of
the bottomless is like the category of the natural, final but empty, and
when Cavell urges upon us the desirability of a figurative reading, he is just
removing the hard bottom from the text and relocating it in the reader.
The concept remains equally problematic, our choices equally unmoti-
vated. The result is what has been described in a different context, precisely and pejoratively, as "literary anarchy," a complaint which serves,
like Emerson's attack of nerves, as a record of the response *Walden* seems
to me to demand. In a political context, of course, the question of authority is an old one. Thoreau raises it himself in "Civil Disobedience." "One
would think," he writes, "that a deliberate and practical denial of its authority was the only offence never contemplated by a government." The
form this denial takes in "Civil Disobedience" is "action from principle—
the perception and the performance of right," but the perception of right
is exactly what *Walden* makes most equivocal, and the possibility of action
from principle is exactly what *Walden* denies, since the principles it identifies are always competing ones and hence inevitably inadequate as guide-
lines.

     To be a citizen or to be a reader of *Walden* is to participate always in
an act of foundation or interpretation which is inevitably arbitrary—there
is as much to be said against it as there is for it. The role of the citizen/
reader then, as Thoreau said in "Civil Disobedience," is "essentially revolutionary," it "changes things and relations ... and does not consist
wholly with anything that was." But not only is it revolutionary, it is divisive: it "divides states and churches, it divides families," it even "divides
the *individual*," that is, it divides the reader himself—he is repeatedly con-
fronted with interpretive decisions which call into question both his notion

of the coherence of the text and of himself. In "Civil Disobedience," however, as in most of the explicitly political texts, Thoreau professes no difficulty in locating and identifying legitimate principles of action. It is only in *Walden* itself that the principle of uncertainty is built in. "Let us not play at kittlybenders," he wrote in *Walden*'s "Conclusion," "There is a solid bottom everywhere." Kittlybenders is a children's game; it involves running or skating on thin ice as quickly as you can so that you don't fall through. If the ice breaks, of course, you're liable to find the solid bottom and so, like the traveller in the story, "conclude your mortal career." The traveller is an image of the writer and, as we can now see, of the reader too. *Walden,* as it has been all along, is a book. To read it, as Thoreau suggested some hundred pages earlier, you "lie at your length on ice only an inch thick, like a skater insect on the surface of the water, and study the bottom at your leisure." But, he goes on to say, "the ice itself is the object of most interest." To read *Walden,* then, is precisely to play at kittlybenders, to run the simultaneous risks of touching and not touching bottom. If our reading claims to find a solid bottom, it can only do so according to principles which the text has both authorized and repudiated; thus we run the risk of drowning in our own certainties. If it doesn't, if we embrace the idea of bottomlessness and the interest of the ice itself, we've failed *Walden*'s first test, the acceptance of our moral responsibility as deliberate readers. It's heads I win, tails you lose. No wonder the game makes us nervous.

ERIC J. SUNDQUIST

"Plowing Homeward": Cultivation and Grafting in Thoreau and the Week

A person to spend all his life and splendid talents in trying to achieve something naturally impossible,—as to make a conquest over Nature.
—HAWTHORNE, *The American Notebooks*

As we drew near to Oldtown I asked Polis if he was not glad to get home again; but there was no relenting to his wildness, and he said, "It makes no difference to me where I am." Such is the Indian's pretence always.
—THOREAU, *The Maine Woods*

When the roof of Marmaduke Temple's new house is found to protrude unnaturally into the landscape in *The Pioneers*, Richard Jones tests three colors of paint—"sky blue," "cloud," and "invisible green"—in his attempt to cover up civilization's incursion into the wilderness; all fail, of course, and renouncing concealment, Richard decides instead to "ornament the offensive shingles" with a gaudy "sunshine" paint, as though to blaze the way for further waste under the guise of enlightenment. The boat in which Thoreau and his brother John sail up and down the Concord and Merrimack Rivers is painted half blue, half green, at best a rather half-hearted attempt to hide, if only symbolically, the fact that the trip they are on is a suspicious enterprise—suspicious not because they have a criminally ulterior motive, but because, as Thoreau recognizes, they are un-

From *Home as Found: Authority and Genealogy in Nineteenth-Century American Literature.* © 1979 by the Johns Hopkins University Press.

avoidably civilization's agents. The two-week voyage is ostensibly a return to "Nature," a tooting out of the primitive and an engagement with the uncertain origins of American history. What *A Week on the Concord and Merrimack Rivers* records, though, is the unrelenting difficulty Thoreau has in finding Nature, that is, in uncovering something which is sufficiently far removed from his own defilement to qualify as that American garden at once primitive and Edenic. When Thoreau's tools themselves—his faculties of observation, his speech, and his writing—are brought to test and found lacking, he is forced to reevaluate the categories of Nature and the primitive with dramatic urgency. Unlike the river itself, which "steals into the scenery it traverses without intrusions," Thoreau cannot quite sneak into Nature without leaving behind the scars of his entrance. Although the *Week*'s trip for a good part of the time is veiled as a leisure charade "on the placid current of our dreams, floating from past to future," it is frequently rifled by Thoreau's disturbing recognition that his every encampment, if not the river journey itself, marks "the first encroachment of commerce on this land."

A brief remark from Thoreau's journals may be one of the more incisive critiques of, if not all of his writings, at least of the *Week:* "It is vain to dream of a wilderness distant from ourselves. There is none such. It is the bog in our brain and bowels, the primitive vigor of Nature in us, that inspires that dream. I shall never find in the wilds of Labrador any greater wilderness than in some recess in Concord, *i.e.* than I import into it." What this fierce circularity—that an interior wilderness inspires the dream of its own exterior distance—underlines, is an intricate awareness on Thoreau's part that his hunt for unravished and "original" American frontiers, so much his pervasive concern, especially in the *Week,* is necessarily one in which the pioneer is constantly frustrated by the elusiveness of that which he would possess. Thoreau is again and again overly conscious of the fact that his *essays* out of Concord do not quite allow him to escape its civilized encumbrances, but only leave him torn between two worlds— one which he seemingly wants to repudiate, but which trails naggingly behind as soon as he shoves off in search of that other one he can never have. Like Natty Bumppo, Thoreau might well be called the archetypal "man without a home." But in the long run it may be no different to say, as he does in "Walking," that Thoreau has "no particular home, but [is] equally at home everywhere." Yet it is only a short step then to Thoreau's admission in *The Maine Woods* that whatever place you select "for your camp . . . begins at once to have its attractions, and becomes a very centre of civilization, to you: 'Home is home, be it never so homely.' "

Cooper's home in *Home as Found* is literally *found;* it is that which he returned to, though as we have discovered, Cooper goes to an extravagant length to *found* that home in another sense. Thoreau's case is equally ambiguous when scrutinized under the vocabulary of *finding* and *founding*. *Walden* has often been taken to be the primary text on the American way of taking up residence, of founding a home in the most basic sense, though it is again and again unsettled by civilized doubts and savage eruptions that threaten to tear its elegantly labored edifice apart at the seams. What is most unnerving about the book, however, is that despite Thoreau's constant parading of simplicity and economy, a more rhetorically ornate volume is hard to imagine. *Walden* recounts an experiment in settlement, one that strips itself down to essentials of a sort, but the record finally contains far more showmanship than primitivism. In this respect, Thoreau's *Week* may be a more forceful account of his head-on encounter with the frontier that America itself is; and the book's very power lies in the fact that it is less refined than *Walden,* as though the very wildness Thoreau is after has entered into the written record of the journey. The *Week,* as Thoreau wrote of it in his journal of 1851, is a much more "hypaethral or unroofed book, lying open under the ether and permeated by it, open to all weathers, not easy to be kept on a shelf."

But if Thoreau did not "cultivate" or "domesticate" the *Week* as carefully as he did *Walden,* it is not because these actions do not inform and qualify the motives of his exploration. Rather, the domestication of the wilderness is what the *Week* is so anxiously about: it is to be avoided if the wilderness is to be preserved, but is inevitable in the labor Thoreau himself undertakes, not least the labor which forms the book. The same writing which produces his account is inextricably bound up with the incursion into an unprofaned terrain that eludes his grasp and leaves him stranded on the frontier, then returns him "home" to elegize the fall recapitulated by his own adventure. "Men plow and sail for [the Wild]," writes Thoreau in "Walking"; he does both in the *Week,* but as the term plowing suggests, it may be that the very act of searching for the wild undermines all hope of its attainment, renders its existence suspect, or even destroys it. Before elaborating the melodrama of circularity that his notions about traveling and writing produce, however, it is worth determining what, in fact, Thoreau goes in search of.

I

When he notes early on in the *Week* that "it is worth the while to make a voyage up this stream . . . only to see how much country there is in the rear of us" and much later that "facts are being so rapidly added to the sum of human experience, that it appears as if the theorizer would always be in arrears, and were doomed forever to arrive at imperfect conclusions," Thoreau is being crucially, if paradoxically, exact about both the journey and his written record of it. The ambiguity of the "rear" in the first remark—is the rear upstream or is it downstream?—is one we will find Thoreau playing with continually in his contemplation of the ratio between the natural and the historical; and as the second remark suggests, the completion of the journey issues not in a settled account of that which is "in the rear" but rather in its circular displacement. The recovery of that which is "in the rear" can but add to the journey, driving a final conclusion always into a deeper recess. But since what is "in the rear"—the origins of American history, the primitive Indian language, the pure wilderness—is almost by definition unavailable to recovery, Thoreau's search becomes an exercise in evasion which perhaps succeeds theoretically, but, because it is only theoretical, fails. Thoreau is doomed always to be "in arrears," and his debt is an exact measure of his nervousness not just about civilization's destruction of "Nature," but also about America's relative lack of a documentary history.

Thoreau's vocabulary of debt is hardly peculiar to him, no more than his ambivalence about the contending benefits and deficiencies which accrue from an act of revolution and the foundation of a new society. Cooper had already lamented in *Home as Found* that "the American nation," despite in brief tenure, was already "lamentably in arrears to its own avowed principles." The advance of Cooper's career found him less and less optimistic about the possibility of recouping the debt to a Jeffersonian dream, a debt which only became magnified as the dream played itself out in the westward expansion it had sanctioned. And some seventy years later, one of James's bizarre ventriloquistic voices in *The American Scene,* presumably that of "one of the painted savages" America has "dispossessed," complains that the "pretended message of civilization is but a colossal recipe for the *creation* of arrears, and of such as can but remain forever out of hand." James is no Thoreauvian lover of the wilds, but his sentiment is not far from that of the beleaguered Concord explorer; the American act of settlement, ruthlessly imperialistic and wantonly regardless of tradition, remains in debt to an ideal which is as yet unfulfilled but which began itself with an erasure of debt, a revolutionary denial of America's dependence on the models of history in its "rear." The American position has been marked by this paradox: while its disavowal of the past portended a clean slate, a new social and political Eden, the pressure to enact the fantasy of a new beginning at once disfigured the dream and fell short, in the eyes of both foreign and native observers, of those conventions and institutions which had initially been repudiated. While James makes America's blank past his constant whipping boy, Thoreau desires on the one hand to search out a justification for the blankness, and on the other to fill it in with authentic native lore. But as he keeps realizing, once the blank is filled, it no longer functions as the lost innocence avidly pined after; paying up the debt merely displaces, or in fact augments, its demand. What is striking, though, is Thoreau's subtle alertness to the fact that the very figures with which he fills the blank of America, the figures of his own writing, perpetuate both the dream and the debt, and turn him into an entrepreneur who corrupts his Edenic property at the same time he advertises its value.

Thoreau's position is precarious, and combined with his allegiance to the American Indian, its playful and tricky logic chopping often quickly turns remorseful. Since the *Week* is not so formidably braced with paradox and pun as *Walden,* its melancholy undercurrent is much plainer, its regret more forthright. Thoreau seeks to recover the lost state of Nature, the simple life of the Indian; that much is a common enough way of putting it. Like Rousseau, however, Thoreau recognizes that "it is no light undertaking to separate what is original from what is artificial in the present nature of man, and to know correctly a state which no longer exists, which perhaps never existed, which probably never will exist, [but] about which it is nevertheless necessary to have precise notions in order to judge our present state correctly." The confusing use of the terms *nature* and *state* in Rousseau's statement is indicative of the thinness of the line separating "original" and "artificial," and the state of Nature finally remains as much a hypothesis for him as it does for Thoreau. What distinguishes the American position, though, and makes Thoreau's a more exacting and acrobatic undertaking, is that going *back* and going *forth* are the same: the primitive is past, but it is also West, and West is future. As a result, Thoreau's pioneer must walk a line which goes both ways at once, and to this extent, the Rousseauvian state which "probably never will exist" is a much more emphatic vector on Thoreau's map and a more forceful index of the debt which cannot be paid up. The *Week* is marked throughout by the torque of this paradox, for not only is it a haunting elegy for the passing of the American Indian and an unspoiled state of Nature, but it also must account for its own implication in the act of violation, one that goes nearly under its auspices.

Two passages in particular from the *Week* point up a telling ambivalence in Thoreau's attitude toward the Indian's uprooting and displacement, and moreover toward his own uprooting of a narrative about this part of America's story:

> The honey-bee hummed through the Massachusetts woods, and sipped the wild-flowers round the Indian's wigwam, perchance unnoticed, when, with prophetic warning, it stung the Red child's hand, forerunner of that industrious tribe that was to come and pluck the wildflower of his race up by the root.
>
> The white man comes, pale as dawn, with a load of thought, with a slumbering intelligence as a fire raked up, knowing well what he knows, not guessing but calculating ... a laboring man, despising game and sport; building a house that endures, a framed house. He buys the Indian's moccasins and baskets, then buys his hunting-grounds, and at length forgets where he is buried and plows up his bones. And here town records, old, tattered, time-worn, weather-stained chronicles, contain the Indian sachem's mark perchance, an arrow or a beaver, and the few fatal words by which he deeded his hunting-grounds away.
>
> Such is Commerce, which shakes the cocoa-nut and bread-fruit tree in the remotest isle, and sooner or later dawns on the duskiest and most simple-minded savage. If we may be pardoned the digression, who can help being affected by the thought of the very fine and slight, but positive relation, in which the savage inhabitants of some remote isle stand to the mysterious white mariner, the child of the sun?—as if *we* were to have dealings with an animal higher in the scale of being than ourselves. It is a barely recognized fact to the native that he exists, and has his home far away somewhere, and is glad to buy their fresh fruits with his superfluous commodities.

We will return to these passages in several other contexts, since as well as any in the book they disturbingly yoke Thoreau's archeology with his imperialism. For now it is enough to note the way in which the white man's "load of thought," which strikingly plays off his "superfluous commodities" and underscores the position of the theorizer always in arrears, is subtly transfigured into the capital for a laborious and ruinous purchase of the primitive hunting grounds. The second passage, however, is less decisive in its bargaining. With characteristic syntactical ambiguity, Thoreau leaves the reference of "animal" unsettled. It can refer to the "white mariner," leaving *"we"* to be fused with the savages, a possibility certainly germane to Thoreau's playful enterprise; or in an equally paradoxical trap it can refer to those savages "higher in the scale of being" with whom the "white mariner"—for example, Thoreau himself in the *Week*—has dealings, getting in trade for his commodities the savage's "fresh fruits."

But of course once the white mariner lays hold of the fresh fruits, they will wither in his grasp. Thoreau's various relics of wildness unendingly coax and wheedle his attention only to slip out of reach at the last instant, and in so doing leave him still further in arrears, as though the price of the primitive rises as a correlative function of Thoreau's willingness to involve himself in the negotiations of its surrender. That Thoreau found the very act of writing to be concurrent with the frustrated attempt to recover the fresh fruits of an innocent, primitive state raises the stakes of his game precipitously. He intimates the violence of his seemingly routine act when he remarks that the writer must "grasp the pen firmly so, and wield it gracefully and effectively, as an axe or a sword"; but the more devious and accurate figure for Thoreau's craft is exposed in his further claim that "a sentence should read as if its author, had he held a plow instead of a pen, could have drawn a furrow deep and straight to the end." Writing, like the commerce of agriculture, is figured as a violent scarring of the land, and the two are made to form a mutually despoiling force that perpetuates itself by adding continually to the profane load of both thought and commodities with which a presumably once virgin land is encumbered: "what have [settlers] not written on the face of the earth already, clearing, and burning, and scratching, and harrowing, and plowing, and subsoiling, in and in, and out and out, and over and over, again and again, erasing what they had already written for want of parchment." In Thoreau's case, the term *cultivation* could not be more appropriate. His traveling and his writing, both endorsed figuratively by the literal plowing he also did, are acts inflicted on a pristine landscape that at once violate its soil and instigate production.

Thoreau's plowing prepares the ground for seeding, for the insemination and grafting of his craft; but it also performs a preliminary function that obsesses him throughout his writings—it turns up arrowheads, almost magically. Hawthorne, among others, remarked with some astonishment the way in which arrowheads seemed to gravitate about Thoreau, as though Indian "spirits [had] willed him to be the inheritor of their simple wealth." Be this as it may, Thoreau's Indian relics are his pervasive signs of originality and primitivism, though it cannot be ignored that they are most often turned up by the violence of the plow, that, as Thoreau notes in his journal of 1842, "in planting my corn in the same furrow which yielded its increase to [the Indian's] support so long, I displace some memorial of him." An 1859 journal entry, late enough perhaps to be taken as Thoreau's definitive statement on arrowheads, clarifies the problem he encountered in his attempt to uncover an American foundation. The arrowheads, "sown like a grain that is slow to germinate . . . bear crops of philosophers and poets," says Thoreau, "and the same seed is just as good to plant again. It is a stone fruit." These seedy relics are guaranteed to be planted again and again, because those collected a hundred years ago "have been dispersed again" and one "cannot tell the third-hand ones (for they are all second-hand) from the others." Indeed, "they were chiefly made to be lost." Thoreau's Indian pun is rather pathetic, but he is exact about the archeology of arrowheads. It is precisely because the arrowhead is always "second-hand" that it does not matter how often it has been retrieved: it is never original, never the first, for when "you do plow and hoe amid them . . . [and] turn up one layer you bury another so much the more securely." Thoreau's integration of the cultural artifact with nature—the arrowhead as "seed" and "fruit"—accentuates the limitless regression in which the sign of the primitive becomes involved. Making the arrowhead *natural* ensures that it will always remain the ghost of an artifact that can never be properly measured or understood. The degree to which Thoreau was played upon by this paradox of domestication and evidence shows up clearly when he finally can revolve the issue no further and lets the arrowhead speak for itself: "Eh, you think you have got me, do you? But I shall wear a hole in your pocket at last, or if you put me in your cabinet, your heir or great-grandson will forget me or throw me out the window directly, or when the house falls I shall drop into the cellar, and there I shall be quite at home again. Ready to be *found* again, eh?"

Like Thoreau himself, the arrowhead is most at home when lost; or more accurately, it "cannot be said to be lost or found." Because what is uncovered is certainly never first-hand and not even demonstrably second-hand, it can never be identified as part of the original foundation. Edwin Fussell has remarked that the plowing up of relics and bones provided Thoreau "the necessary reassurance that he was currently at home where other men had made themselves at home." This is no doubt the case, but that disturbed Thoreau at first, though in the end probably just bemused him, was that he could not get to the bottom of his search for the Indian, and *Indian* itself came finally to be almost an empty label for whatever phenomena, artifactual or fantastic, were presently missing from the landscape. Although James would still complain in 1879 that history "has left in the United States but so thin and impalpable a deposit that we very soon touch the hard substratum of nature; and nature herself, in the Western World, has the pecularity of seeming rather crude and immature," Thoreau found that the ease with which the substratum of nature could be reached was a monumental deception, an American con game played on native grounds. "Let us settle ourselves," he advises in *Walden,* "and work and wedge our feet downward through the mud and slush of opinion, and prejudice, and tradition, and delusion, and appearance, that alluvion which covers the globe . . . till we come to a hard bottom and rocks in place, which we call *reality,* and say, This is, and no mistake; and then begin, having a *point d'appui* . . . a place where you might found a wall or a state." But that wall or state can be no more securely *founded* than the arrowhead of primitive America can be *found.* For Thoreau, the act of locating a foundation is like the first chapter of *Walden* on "Economy"— a ritual of stripping down to the bare minimum; yet as he discovers in that chapter's shifting miasma of clothes metaphors, the bare minimum is always hidden under one more layer of convention's garments. The *point d'appui* would ideally be stripped bare, a ground prepared for building, whether the edifice stands on the edge of a pond or at the edge of the mind. The "bottom," like the first arrowhead, is a projection which acts as a hypothetical gauge, the very foundation of culture; but once the Indian is granted a culture of his own, the bottom of Nature drops out once more. The inherent conflict of this situation is what leads Thoreau to say that the arrowhead is a "stone fruit" and that it "cannot be lost or found." Like Rousseau's hypothetical "state of Nature," in which the very phrase embodies the contradiction, Thoreau's un*found* arrowheads come in and out of focus like Walden Pond's alternately solid and limitless bottom; the *point d'appui* remains finally unfathomed.

Still, as Thoreau asks in *Cape Cod,* "of what use is a bottom if it is out of sight, if it is two or three miles from the surface, and you are to be drowned so long before you get to it, though it were made of the same stuff with your native soil?" There is a practical value to instituting such terms as *bottom, foundation,* and *Nature;* like Rousseau's state that may never have existed or never will exist, Thoreau's Nature makes measurement possible at the same time it clouds its accuracy, or rather, at the same time it makes questionable what accuracy might mean in what is an abstrusely theoretical kind of archeology. As a label for that which seems to recede along with the edge of the frontier, or which is signified always by the next, deeper layer of arrowheads, Thoreau's Nature is a self-emptying term that works as a constant in his unending attempt to balance the equation of wilderness and civilization. The theorizer always in arrears because

of the constant addition to the facts of human knowledge is thus in a doubly bound position when he purports to be sifting through the strata of
the past: the very act of shedding the impediments of antiquity may only
restrengthen their power to elude, so that the further one seeks the foundation, the home of Nature, the further away it is.

The swirl of terms in which Thoreau becomes trapped is as baffling
as Cooper's quagmire of imitation, and one can easily sympathize with
John Seelye's conclusion that for Thoreau, "The Maine Woods, the Indian,
the Primitive Past, all seem to have proved nothing more than a *pokelogan*,
a cul-de-sac, ending at the blank wall of Ktaadn." To a certain extent this
is necessarily the case; for as Thoreau continues in the passage cited above,
the arrowhead is "no digusting mummy, but a clean stone, the best symbol
or letter that could have been transmitted to me . . . It is no single inscription on a particular rock, but a footprint—rather a mindprint—left everywhere, and altogether illegible." The statement is telling: that the arrowhead can pass at all for part of Nature, for part of what is truly primitive,
depends on its being illegible, in effect unable to be correctly interpreted.
Thoreau is reduced in his account to simply presenting the fact of the arrowhead by illustration, thus:

The Red Man, his mark

Thoreau's suspicion of the mediatory negotiations that attach to trade and
economic bargaining is evident throughout his career, even if his stance is
often more a rhetorical pose than a staunch conviction. But the question
of commercial mediation has a deeper vein than is first evident, one that
runs at the base of his theories of language. In an 1841 journal entry
Thoreau remarks, "we should communicate our wealth, and not purchase
that which does not belong to us for a sign. Why give each other a sign to
keep? If we gave the thing itself, there would be no need of a sign." The
outcome of such a theory is, of course, something akin to Swift's Grand
Academy of Lagado, where the abolition of all words is "urged as a great
advantage in point of health as well as brevity," and where it is thus determined "that since words are only names for *things*, it would be more convenient for all men to carry about them such *things* as were necessary to
express the particular business they are to discourse on."

Thoreau's desire to eliminate the mediating symbol of money is
closely aligned with his desire to denude language of similar encumbrances, though both end at similarly embarrassing impasses. His need to
define the arrowhead simply by reproducing it in a picture springs from a
desire, however often or drastically qualified, to locate the point at which

language stops being multiplicitous and slippery, the *point d'appui* where word and thing are yoked. Yet that desire has all the trappings of an impossible Swiftian fantasy, for when Thoreau complains in *Walden* that "the very language of our parlors" threatens to "lose all its nerve and degenerate into *parlaver*" because "our lives pass at such remoteness from its symbols, and its metaphors and tropes are necessarily far fetched, through slides and dumbwaiters," as though "only the savage dwelt near enough to Nature and Truth to borrow a trope from them," he not only fetches his own metaphors from afar but also undermines the hypothetical proximity of savage life and symbol by turning Nature itself into a "trope" which must be "borrowed." Like the "fresh fruits" of the savage, yet another trope, Nature is transformed into a *figure* by the mediating process of trade which seeks it out; and as figure, the prized conjunction of word and thing splinters. If Thoreau, as it seems, is leaning on Emerson when he addresses this problem, it is no wonder he can reach only a paradoxical conclusion, since Emerson's essay on language in "Nature" (1836) veers off into a similar cul-de-sac. In a state where "the corruption of man is followed by the corruption of language" and "a paper currency is employed, when there is no bullion in the vaults," Emerson advises "wise men [to] pierce this rotten diction and fasten words again to visible things"; yet this reversion toward a historical moment when "language becomes more picturesque, until its infancy, when it is all poetry," also finds its Eden among "savages, who have only what is necessary, [and thus] converse in figures." Emerson's *figure,* even more pointedly than Thoreau's *trope,* accentuates the paradox of their desire to regain the infancy of language: *figure* is at once a picture, an emblem of one-to-one correspondence like Thoreau's arrowhead; yet as figure, as metaphor, it thrusts the projected correspondence into indirection and displacement, turning representation into re-presentation. The tension in the term between illustration and *re*presentation, between transparency and trope, leaves its status finally unsettled; Emerson's *figure* must also be "borrowed," even at the risk of that overextension of credit it hopes to avoid.

Thoreau's view of Indian language is thus no simple one, though in its hypothetical moment it is similar to the ritualistic theory held by Natty Bumppo: names and thing should have a necessary relation—"Deerslayer," for example. Yet the illustration of the arrowhead indicates that Thoreau spotted the absurd limitations of such a theory. Word and thing, if not irremediably divorced by the introduction of the term *figure,* eventually come so close that "word" vanishes into "thing," or vice versa; the word becomes unintelligible, and the thing can be conveyed only by its own repetition. Thus Thoreau, unable to say what the arrowhead means, merely *re*presents it, partly as though that act were sufficient, but partly in despair too. He can no more successfully define the arrowhead than he can be sure he has found the earliest American one; like the currency of any system of exchange, linguistic or monetary, the arrowhead is "illegible" outside its system, while inside it, it is destined to remain a *figure* in an unfathomable account. Moreover, the system itself, if it masks itself as part of Nature, is likewise illegible. In this regard, the Red Man and his mark *are* virtually the same, mere signs of one another. The choice is between the instability and frustration of mediation, upon which the act of definition depends, and that sure stasis which resides only in a Swiftian utopia. No more, Thoreau laments in an important journal passage of 1838, "do we live a quiet, free life, such as Adam's, but are enveloped in an invisible network of speculations. . . . Could we for a moment drop this by-play, and simply wonder, without reference or inference." But "simply wonder" is exactly right; the absence of reference or inference would issue in a dumb, blank stare, a thoroughly "natural" state. While Thoreau remarks in *The Maine Woods* that Indian language is a "wild and primitive American sound," he is quick to add that "we may suspect change and deteriorization in almost every other particular but the language which is so wholly unintelligible to us." The qualification is hardly too fine: lack of deterioration is consequent only upon unintelligibility; that is, only a language which renders nothing intelligible is undefiled by the speculations of reference. Any intelligibility drawn from that *ur*-language involves a necessary falling away from a pure "sound," which in its concurrent desirability and impracticality corresponds to the pure figure of the arrowhead, both presumably free from the commerce of mediation.

"Pure sound" and "pure figure," since they are tropes of a fantasized moment, an Eden at the outset of the history of rhetoric, name a condition which is ultimately mystical or totemic in dimension, one which *must not* yet *can only,* be figurative, like the speech of a lost god. The unintelligibility of the arrowhead and the sound of savage language endow them with magical resonance, with what Lévi-Strauss has called *mana,* an overabundance of signifier in relation to what is signified: they mean more than can be known. As symbols "in the pure state," they inhabit and define an Eden of signification verging on the mystical and, since they can be filled with whatever content is desired, possess "symbolic value zero." The zero value of the arrowhead suggests not that it is worthless, but rather that it performs a function that cannot be accurately defined and hence cannot be assigned a specific *value* in a linguistic economy: its worth is at once null and limitless. Thoreau provides an acute explication of the coincidence of forces both sacred and psychological that are at play in the drama of the pure figure, when he remarks at one point in the *Week* that "poetry is the mysticism of mankind," that "if you can speak what you will never hear, if you can write what you will never read, you have done rare things," for "the unconsciousness of man is the consciousness of God." He then sets down an example of such poetry that amounts to a kind of primitive Rorschach test and illuminates the power latent in the pure figure of the arrowhead: "What is produced by a free stroke charms us. . . . Draw a blunt quill filled with ink over a sheet of paper, and fold the paper before the ink is dry, transversely to this line, and a delicately shaded and regular figure will be produced, in some respects more pleasing than an elaborate drawing." I will want to return to the question of the violence implicit in Thoreau's "free stroke" (for he goes on to compare it to the taking of a scalp), but want now only to point out that there is an economic rhetoric at work here, that it is a "free" stroke that is required to produce the pure figure, the figure which virtually represents nothing and hence has zero value, but which nonetheless contains limitless meaning by the very token of its ambiguous purity. Such a figure, then, belongs at once to the unconscious and to the mystical realm of the primitive, and Thoreau's whole project is directed at working out the conjunction of the two.

Yet this project is no simple one, for if the freedom and purity of the primitive figure depend upon its unintelligibility, Thoreau's penetration of the sacred abode must risk turning the treasure into plunder and profaning the very Eden he would investigate. Thoreau's paradoxical burden corresponds to that voiced by Lévi-Strauss in *Tristes Tropiques*—that since "man is inseparable from language and language implies society," the privileged state of Nature is destined to remain but a fantasy, an alluring cul-de-sac. Lévi-Strauss records that his search for specimens of the nonexistent Rousseauvian state led him finally, at the "extreme limits of the savage," to a tribe, the Munde, who were totally unintelligible to him, a circumstance that thwarts the very foundation of his professional interests and prompts an outcry worthy of Thoreau's sense of predicament:

> There they were, all ready to teach me their customs and beliefs, and I did not know their language. They were as close to me as a reflection in a mirror; I could touch them, but I could not understand them. I had been given, at one and the same time, my reward and my punishment. . . . I had only to succeed in guessing what they were like for them to be deprived of their

strangeness: in which case, I might just as well have stayed in my village. Or if, as was the case here, they retained their strangeness, I could make no use of it, since I was incapable of even grasping what it consisted of. Between these two extremes, what ambiguous instances provide us with the excuses by which we live? Who, in the last resort, is the real dupe of the confusion created in the reader's mind by observations which are carried just far enough to be intelligible and then are stopped in mid-career, because they cause surprise in human beings so similar to those who take such customs as a matter of course? Is it the reader who believes in us, or we ourselves who have no right to be satisfied until we have succeeded in dissipating a residue which serves as a pretext for our vanity?

Thoreau rarely took so dark a view of his own activities, but that can perhaps be ascribed to the fact that he hardly ever dealt with "real" Indians, or at least with any which could even tentatively have been called "savage." Yet his awareness of the paradoxical hinge upon which anthropology turns is just as pressing. To discover a state of Nature and its inhabitants would mean to find something that was, in effect, incommunicable. Lévi-Strauss's figuring of the savage as an ungraspable "reflection in a mirror" summons up a narcissistic stupefaction like that Thoreau indulges in when he lies on his belly and stares into Walden Pond, searching in vain for its true bottom. Completely savage language would for all practical purposes be mute, and the explorer (like Adam, or guesses) could but "simply wonder." Thoreau's admission that the arrowhead can only be known by the mark of its outline or that the only Indian language that is pure is the one that is uintelligible, points up his blunt recognition that his own enterprise fails sooner or later, almost by definition. Such an admission dissipates the residue of the "natural"; what it does for Thoreau's vanity is unclear, though it seems unlikely to have decreased it.

II

Since man, language, and society are inseparable, the only avenue to Nature lies in a merciless retreat away from the speculative web of reference and inference. This is why late in the *Week* Thoreau must take the position that "the most excellent speech falls finally into Silence. . . . Creation has not displaced her, but is her visible framework and foil. All sounds are her servants, and purveyors, proclaiming not only that their mistress is, but is a rare mistress, and earnestly to be sought after. . . . Silence is the universal refuge . . . ever our inviolable asylum, where no indignity can assail, no personality disturb us." Thoreau's Silence is an Adamic state, a sacred enclosure cut free from the commerce of language, yet teasingly purveyed by every sound. Silence is *figure* in its purest state—the virtual absence of figure, the true symbolic value zero; yet Thoreau's sexual rhetoric again impinges upon the commercial, and his mistress becomes a seductress on whose behalf mere sounds, not to mention speech, engage in a bargaining which at once flaunts her charms and denies her possession. Because "speech is fractional, [and] silence is integral," as Thoreau notes in his journal of 1840, the encroachment of language can only disfigure the integrity and purity of Silence. If Silence is the inviting refuge, the metaphysical equivalent of the pure primitive, it is nevertheless at the constant mercy of language, the equivalent of the cultural. A journal entry of 1853 invokes some familiar terms and makes clear the role of Thoreau's purest figure: "Silence is of various depth and fertility, like soil. Now it is a mere Sahara, where men perish of hunger and thirst, now a fertile bottom, or prairie of the West." But like Walden's curious bottom, the bottom of Silence may be a trap, an insidious enticement. "I have been breaking silence these twenty-three years," Thoreau writes in his 1841 journal, "and have hardly made a rent in it. Silence has no end; speech is but the beginning of it." The rhetorics of ownership and violence contained in the word *rent* further link the figure of Silence with the fertile soil of Nature, the unspoiled virgin who "by one bait or another . . . allures inhabitants into all her recesses." That Silence and Nature are West is relatively clear, but another passage in the *Week* confirms the association. After recording a Hindu proverb which runs, "As a dancer, having exhibited herself to the spectator, desists from the dance, so does Nature desist, having manifested herself to soul," Thoreau continues:

> It is easier to discover another such world as Columbus did, than to go within one fold of this which we appear to know so well; the land is lost sight of, the compass varies, and mankind mutiny; and still history accumulates like rubbish before the portals of nature. But there is only necessary a moment's sanity and sound senses, to teach us that there is a nature behind the ordinary, in which we have only some vague pre-emption right and western reserve as yet. We live on the outskirts of that region. . . . Let us wait a little, and not purchase any clearing here, trusting that richer bottoms will soon be put up.

Nature, Silence, and West are Thoreau's baits; yet as the passage suggests, and as Thoreau often insists, West is a state of mind, rather than a geographical location. West is a remote region buried within the mind, an unconscious region captured only by a "free stroke"; the language of history is denied entrance to that region and accumulates like rubbish at its portals. Purer than language is sheer sound or music, "the flower of language, thought colored and curved, fluent and flexible," which to the senses is "farthest from us" because it "addresses the greatest depth within us." Yet deeper still and more pure, virginally pure, must be perfect Silence, for "our finest relations are not simply kept silent about, but buried under a positive depth of silence never to be revealed." That Thoreau's Silence also corresponds to the source of the river as a sanctuary of purity and originality is suggested in a journal passage of 1842, where he notes that "the best intercourse and communion [men] would have is in silence above and behind their speech."

Despite Thoreau's persistent attempts to remain *outside* of something—town, society, commerce, and so forth—there is an overwhelming counter-sense of his need to get *inside* a shelter of one kind or another. This can, as in *Walden,* take the form of indulging in that "pleasure of construction" Thoreau enjoys when building his house about himself with boards or with words; or it can appear as a more primeval urge to crawl into the womb of nature, that mysterious region that is both interior and exterior. Thoreau's belief that his solitude weaves about him "a silken web or *chrysalis,*" from which he, "nymph-like, shall ere long burst forth a more perfect creature," yokes together his reverence for the mind as a kind of *"sanctum sanctorum"* with a similar description in "Walking" of his restorative pilgrimage into nature: "When I would recreate myself, I seek the darkest wood, the thickest and most interminable and, to the citizen, most dismal swamp. I enter a swamp as a sacred place, a *sanctum sanctorum.* There is the strength, the marrow of Nature." Yet it would seem that the kind of blessedness offered here could turn quickly into another *pokelogan.* Since what Thoreau would like to be or become is always over the western horizon—"Let us migrate interiorly with intermission, and pitch our tent each day nearer the western horizon," he records in his journal of 1840—it is nearly useless to define it in terms that always fracture as soon as they are invoked or which lead only to Ktaadn's blank wall of Silence. Thoreau's respect for the immobilization induced by the metaphysics of wilderness sublimity is certainly not so highly charged as, say, that in Poe's *Narrative of A. Gordon Pym,* where at the edge of a frontier nightmare the story's namesake careens off into a chasm guarded by a monstrous white figure, or even in *Pierre,* in which Melville warns "that it is not for man to follow the trail of truth too far, since by doing so he entirely loses the directing compass of his mind; for arrived at the Pole, to whose barrenness only it points, there, the needle indifferently respects all points of the horizon alike." Yet more than anything else, Thoreau's West is "our own interior white on the chart," as he puts it in *Walden;* but to fully enter such a region, the chamber of the pure figure of Silence, would mean reaching a place where one's compass ceases to function and all modes of reference blow apart.

Going West for Thoreau entails entering a spiritual domain in which he tracks himself like an animal in deep brush. His fascination with the raw violence and strategies of the hunt energizes his writing, for thought itself is a kind of game to be raised and captured. To succeed in the hunt one must live as though in constant preparation for it, for the hunter, of whatever kind, "will not bag any [game] if he does not already know its seasons and haunts and the color of its wing,—if he has not dreamed of it, so that he can *anticipate* it." Thoreau's spiritual exercises in the woods confirm Kenneth Burke's observation that "mystic *silence* has its roots" in the hunt, since "in the quest one is naturally silent, be it as the animal stalking its quarry or as the thinker meditating upon an idea. Thus, even the utterance of the question begins in the silence of the quest." Burke would even seem to have been reading Thoreau, who records in his 1851 journal, "the longest silence is the most pertinent question most pertinently put. Emphatically silent." The silent cavern entered by Thoreau is the wilderness of himself and of America, both pertinent and emphatic questions. For Cooper, as we noted, only *Home as Found*'s haunting Silent Pine, symbol of a paternity whose voice is wholly in question, is a true "American antiquity"; and for Melville's Pierre, silence is the very voice of god and of the literary craft, which in the end are for him very much the same. Thoreau's silence also reverberates with the question of American authority, but for him the quarry is an object of search like *Walden*'s raw woodchuck, whose attributes he takes by devouring, a feast which John Seelye finds to symbolize Thoreau's appropriation of "the spiritual landscape by turning it inside out, putting the furside inside and the skinside out, by internalizing the wildness." For Thoreau the hunter, the earth "spread out like a map around [him] is but the lining of [his] inmost soul exposed," much as in *Moby-Dick* Ahab's wrinkles finally come into enigmatic correspondence with the map by which he plans his revenge, "as if some invisible pencil was also tracing lines and courses upon the deeply marked chart of his forehead."

Thoreau enacts both roles in Ortega's apt hunting analogy: "Like the hunter in the absolute *outside* of the countryside, the philosopher is the alert man in the absolute *inside* of ideas, which are also an unconquerable and dangerous jungle." Yet Ortega points out another aspect of the hunt that is perhaps even more relevant for Thoreau, who is always on guard against snares in his path, a soft-bottomed bog in Nature's sanctuary, or an unintelligible Indian relic. *"It is not essential to the hunt that it be successful,"* says Ortega. "On the contrary were the hunter's efforts always and inevitably successful it would not be the effort we call hunting, it would be something else. Corresponding to the eventuality or chance of the prey's escaping is the eventuality of the hunter's *rentrer bredouille* [going home empty-handed]. The beauty of hunting lies in the fact that it is always problematic." Likewise, of course, "meditation always runs the risk of returning home empty-handed." This is the risk Thoreau continually runs; but to repeat, there would be no hunt without the risk, and one could almost push as far in Thoreau's case as to say there would be no hunt if he did not *always* go home empty handed, or nearly so. Indeed it is hard to guess what it might mean for Thoreau to succeed, to snag his prey, which is so vaporous and flees on so many fronts at once. Thoreau remarks in his journal entry concerning his search for arrowheads, "I would fain know that I am treading in the tracks of human game,—that I am on the trail of mind." The reason his tracking never ceases is that the trail of mind he is on is his own. But if it is also the case that the talent of composition is comparable to the taking of a scalp, Thoreau may, failing other game, at least go home with his head in his hands.

Nietzsche writes in *Beyond Good and Evil* that "in the writings of a hermit one always hears something of the echo of the desolate regions, something of the whispered tones and the furtive look of solitude; in his strongest words, even in his cry, there still vibrates a new and dangerous kind of silence—of burying something in silence." Consequently, the hermit will be suspicious of the writings of any philosopher, will doubt "whether behind every one of his caves there is not, must not be, another deeper cave—a more comprehensive, stranger, richer world beyond the surface, an abysmally deep ground behind every ground, under every attempt to furnish 'grounds.'" The hermit will claim that "there is something arbitrary in [the philosopher's] stopping *here* to look back and look around, in his not digging deeper *here* but laying his spade aside." Thoreau, of course, is both hermit and philosopher, and his writings continually scrutinize themselves with the suspicious eye of the hermit, one which finds its finest relations buried beneath a positive depth of silence and its richest bottoms yet outstanding. Thoreau keeps his West—that place which would furnish a true American *ground*—forever in abeyance, since to achieve it would mean to obliterate it. Yet such frustrating self-awareness does not prevent him from setting up shop and declaring himself at home. Thoreau, perhaps more than any American writer, has an uncanny sense of *place,* of actually being situated on a certain tract of land at a certain time. And just as there is in the end something ludicrous about raging after an ever-receding frontier, so Thoreau also finds something particularly relentless about the place one is at: "Think of the consummate folly of attempting to go away from *here!* When the constant endeavor should be to get nearer and nearer *here.* . . . A man dwells in his native valley like a corolla in its calyx, like an acorn in its cup. *Here,* of course, is all that you love, all that you expect, all that you are. Here is your bride elect, as close to you as she can be got." At times Thoreau could almost convince one that his persistent lamentations are all a ruse, that Nature is no mystery at all and that "travellers generally exaggerate the difficulties of the way." "If a person lost would conclude that after all he is not lost," the *Week* continues, "but standing in his own shoes on the very spot where he is, and that for the time being he will live there; but the places that have known him, *they* are lost,—how much anxiety and danger would vanish." But since his anxiety will not vanish sheerly on command, the best way for Thoreau to keep his project going is to keep it dangerous.

Neither can that anxiety be disconnected from the eroticism implicit in Thoreau's figuring of *here* as his "bride elect." As in the case of so many American writers, the question of sexuality in Thoreau is continually refracted into the lust of exploration and the hunt, even when those enterprises go under the banner of a chaste disavowal of intimacy or matrimony. Thoreau's *here* echoes Natty Bumppo's final declaration, a haunting utterance of "Here!" spoken into the fading sunset of the West. Natty's cry is the dying warrior's password, a last affirmation of natural right and heroic asceticism. Like Natty, who with the exception of a momentary lapse in *The Pathfinder* always chose Nature over woman, or like Ike Mc-Caslin in *The Bear,* who repudiates his marriage and finally can take only the woods for "his mistress and his wife," Thoreau simply declares, "all nature is my bride." Given such a remark, the nature of Thoreau's sanctum sanctorum, his wilderness chasm, begins to shape up differently. It is even clearer, if a little vulgar, in this spirited remark from the *Week:* "If we look into the heavens they are concave, and if we look into a gulf as bottomless, it would be concave also. The sky is curved downward to the earth in the horizon . . . I draw down its skirts." Thoreau draws down its skirts—with himself inside. Getting inside—inside of Nature, of Silence, of *here*—is at once an advance toward the Eden of the West and a return to a primitive paradise, the womb of America. Thoreau's insurgent vocabulary of invagination—whether flower, folds, buried depths, portals, recesses, and even bottoms, which take on a lurid tone at times—reinforces his figure of Nature as a virginal mistress or bride. But the status of Nature as a virgin land corresponds as well to the elusive mistress of Silence: her enticement depends upon remaining inviolate, which in turn excludes cultivation.

Richard Poirier has remarked that the greatest American writings "are alive with the effort to stabilize certain feelings and attitudes that have, as it were, no place in the world, no place at all except where a writer's style can give them one." This is evident enough in Thoreau's case, and all the more an accurate way of putting it since, as Thoreau says in his essay on Carlyle, "literally and really, the style is no more than the *stylus,* the pen [one] writes with." Thoreau wields his own *stylus* as a tool of cultivation, a literary plow which is at once a brutal weapon of incision and an instrument of insemination. His interest in the alignment of writing and cultivation situates Thoreau in the line of American narratives that link eroticism and regeneration with acts of totemic violence. If the question of violence in Thoreau is often channeled off into moments of sheer spectacle—his Trojan war with weeds in his bean field, say, or his lurid delight in the mock civil war fought by red and black ants enclosed in the theater of a glass tumbler—we must nevertheless be attuned to the way in which the same violence, however sublimated or diffused, underlies the transactions which engender the drama of his own settlement. To do so, we must follow out a peculiar detour on his map of the primitive.

Thoreau's insertion of himself into the feminized landscape of America is marked by the imperialistic eroticism which Annette Kolodny has observed throughout American literature and so accurately summed up in the commonplace phrase, "the lay of the land." But as in the case of *Pierre,* where a mother and a sister are converted into the receptacles of Melville's tortured version of manifest destiny, or *Home as Found,* where Cooper builds an enclosed garden around his American Eve and fosters an incestuous marriage in hopes of retrieving the shattered Edenic dream, so Thoreau's intimacy with his mistress Nature has its own ties to family romance. Thoreau's early life in a household that included a mother, two sisters, and two aunts, and his Leatherstocking-like avoidance of intimacy with women may have no small bearing on the sensuality with which he charged the accounts of his various pioneering enterprises. Yet if Thoreau enforced his own chastity with rituals of purification and so saved his higher energies for the sacred role of hunter and explorer, it is even clearer in his case than in Natty Bumppo's that the penetration of the wilderness is at least in part a sublimated return to the Mother. "Woman is a nature older than I," Thoreau writes in 1849, "and commanding from me a vast amount of veneration, like Nature. She is my mother at the same time that she is my sister. I cannot imagine a woman no older than I." Thoreau's positioning of "Nature" in the context of a discussion of his enigmatic relationship with women is by no means an accident, for his writings continually make a fetish of troubling the distinction between the two. He goes on to say that his "most intimate acquaintance with woman has been a sisterly relation, or at most a catholic-mother relation," one in which "she has exerted the influence of a goddess over me; cultivating my gentler humane nature; cultivating and preserving purity, innocence, and truth." We will need to reconsider the striking reversal of roles that has occurred—the woman now becoming the cultivator of Thoreau's nature—but should add here that in the ellipsis of the quotation Thoreau remarks of his sister-virgin-mother relationship, "—not that it has always been free from the suspicion of a lower sympathy." What amounts to a "lower sympathy" in Thoreau's eyes is not entirely clear, but we are forced to share his suspicion of it.

Although Thoreau's gardening does not impinge so nearly upon the sordid and the demonic as Cooper's in *Home as Found,* Hawthorne's in *The House of the Seven Gables,* or Melville's in *Pierre,* it is no less overtly mythological and personal. Emerson might have been projecting a career for Thoreau when he wrote in "Nature" that "in the woods . . . a man casts off his years, as the snake his slough, and at what period soever in his life, is always a child." Becoming a child in the garden of Nature is a transfiguration hardly peculiar to Thoreau, and both he and Emerson have a healthy tradition, running at least from Virgil to Wordsworth, to draw on for such sentiments. But one of Thoreau's particular gardens, his bean field at Walden, stands out with enchanting power:

> When I was four years old, as I well remember, I was brought
> from Boston to this my native town, through these very woods
> and this field, to the pond. It is one of the oldest scenes stamped
> on my memory. And now to-night my flute has waked the ech-
> oes over that very water. The pines still stand here older than
> I; or, if some have fallen, I have cooked my supper with their
> stumps, and a new growth is rising all around, preparing an-

other aspect for new infant eyes. Almost the same johnswort
springs from the same perennial root in this pasture, and even
I have at length helped to clothe that fabulous landscape of my
infant dreams, and one of the results of my presence and influence is seen in these bean leaves, corn blades, and potato vines.

While Thoreau's prose is as carefully cultivated as his garden and laden
with the conventions of pastoral, his description of the landscape of his
"infant dreams" as "fabulous" locates his garden in a topography halfway
between fable and fantasy, between historical and personal memory. His
gardening is at once an invocation of eclogic archetypes and a return to
the childhood of his own dreams. When he adds in the next paragraph that
the arrowheads turned up by his hoe prove "that an extinct nation had
anciently dwelt here and planted corn and beans ere white men came to
clear the land," Thoreau ironizes the violence of his own wars in the bean
field at the same time he turns his cultivation, whether by hoe or by pen,
into an elegy for a lost moment in American history, a moment which has
become analogous for him to a lost scene in his own life.

Perhaps the violence of Thoreau's gardening is not merely a theatrical
exhibition, though, but a crucial part of his remembrance of things past.
In what may be the most striking episode in the *Week,* Thoreau's rendition
of Cotton Mather's capitivity narrative of Hannah Dustan, an act of violent revenge provides him a convenient entrance into American mythology
and subtly annotates his own attempted recovery of the fantasized state of
Nature. For Mather, the Dustan captives' slaughter and scalping of the Indians who had seized them provides a lesson in just retribution and the
occasion for a sermon on Christian perseverance in the satanic wilderness.
Thoreau's account, though free from ecclesiastical baggage, follows the details of Mather's narrative fairly closely, except for two remarkable variations. Mather's version of the murder of Dustan's infant child by the Indians is relatively simple: "they dash'd out the Brains of the Infant, against
a tree"; but in Thoreau's rendering Hannah sees "her infant's brains
dashed out against an apple tree." The significance of Thoreau's addition
is clarified at the end of his account when, repeating himself for good measure, he notes that the Dustan family is "assembled alive once more, except
for the infant whose brains were dashed out against the apple tree" and
fixes the lesson of *his* narrative by adding "there have been many who in
later times have lived to say that they have eaten the fruit of that apple
tree. This seems a long while ago, and yet it happened since Milton wrote
his Paradise Lost." That Thoreau intends both himself and his readers to

be numbered among those who have eaten of the fruit is supported by his subtle conversion to the present tense midway in his story, as though to recreate the scene of violence as one in which we are directly participating—as indeed we are. Richard Slotkin has described Thoreau's fruit as "a kind of Indian-cannibal Eucharist" that "serves to link the present dwellers in the land to the reality of that bloody revelation of wilderness by means of a sacrament in which the symbolic fruit is perceived as a scant covering, an insignificant palliation or sublimation, of the reality of infant blood and torment." Even if Thoreau's narrative does not have quite the eschatological thrust Slotkin finds, it nevertheless points up the fact that the seizure of the American paradise is a complicated second performance of the fall of man, an act of grim violence that goes hand in hand with settlement. Yet as Thoreau recognizes, one way to account or atone for the incursion of white civilization and the violence it provoked is to render it the source of a fortunate fall, one that produces a fruit of communion with the past, a communion in which atonement is never complete and in which the participant, like the mythographer, is always "in arrears," yet one in which a repeated memorial incident will allow us "to say" we have eaten of the fruit and thus settled and naturalized the act.

That "saying" is of critical importance to Thoreau, and it is not to be disconnected from his anxiety about his complicity as a writer in the ravishing of the American Eden. The second important variation he works on Mather's account is concerned precisely with the act of violence that is presumably being commemorated as sacrament. While Mather describes the murder of the Indians as a typological imitation of "the Action of Jael upon Sisera" (Judg. 4), he turns the scalping into a simple act of practicality, by which the avengers "Received Fifty Pounds from the General Assembly of the Province, as a Recompence of their Action," and also "a very generous Token of his Favour" from "Colonel Nicholson, the Governour of Maryland." Although Thoreau takes note of the bounty paid for the Indian "trophies," he not only drops the biblical sanction for the murder, thus making *it* a simple act of practicality, but also severely complicates the motive for the scalping when he reports that the captives took the scalps and put them "into a bag as proofs of what they had done" because Hannah feared "that her story would not be believed if she should escape to tell it." Immediately after these remarks Thoreau switches to present tense in his narration, bringing the deed home to the reader and mounting the suspense of the captives' escape.

But we must wonder still why Thoreau feels compelled to raise the question of the integrity of Hannah's story, unless perhaps it is a reflection of his fear that his own accounts will not be believed without similar acts of regenerative violence. What proof of his own struggle with the primitive might amount to in Thoreau's case is open to question; certainly when he notes a few pages later that "the talent of composition is very danger- ous,—the striking out the heart of life at a blow, as the Indian takes off a scalp," we suspect Thoreau once more of indulgence in the spectacle of his own invention. Yet we might say as well that Thoreau has replicated the captivity narrative he borrows from Mather, that his variations at once constitute an act of violence against Mather's account yet reap the rewards attendant upon an improved story, one that places the episode in a more valuable context of American mythology and buttresses its sacramental power. The talent of composition *is* dangerous for Thoreau; wielding his pen as a plow or an axe, he burdens the pristine territory under investiga- tion with a "load of thought" analogous to those "superfluous commodi- ties" with which the white man has swindled the savage under the guise of trading for his "fresh fruits." The apple tree in Thoreau's account of Han- nah Dustan is all the more an interesting addition to the story in that it stands at once as a sign of the Edenic state Thoreau hopes to discover on his travels and conversely as a sign of the shattering of that Eden. The ap- ple tree is the trophy which Thoreau's violent foray into Mather produces; it is proof of his imaginative venture and the regenerative reward of his communion with a scene which has threatened to become lost from Ameri- can memory.

Thoreau employs the "trophy"—indeed, the "trope"—of the apple in a number of writings, and we will want to return to its role again; but it is necessary first to consider another aspect of Thoreau's Edenic mytholo- gizing of the captivity tale. That the slaughtered infant of Hannah Dustan may be echoing in Thoreau's mind an incident or threat from his own childhood, we can only speculate; yet that Thoreau's cultivation of the landscape of America's infancy and that of his own "infant dreams" are strangely interfused, seems further evident when he goes on from his invo- cation of Milton to chart the historical distance from Adam and Eve to the settlement of America and remarks that "the lives of but sixty old women, such as live under the hill, say of a century each, strung together, are suffi- cient to reach over the whole ground. Taking hold of hands they would span the interval from Eve to my own mother." We might take this to be merely a rhetorical flourish were it not for the strong identification Thoreau continually makes between the primitive and the infantile, and between Nature and the Mother (or, as we have seen, the older sister). Thoreau alternates spasmodically in his assessment of Nature, and for every instance in which he finds to be his mysteriously enfolding bride or mother, a home warm and safe wherever he is when he is *here,* he finds a counterfigure of significant aspect: "Man cannot afford to be a naturalist, to look at Nature directly, but only with the side of his eye. He must look through and beyond her. To look at her is [as] fatal as to look at the head of Medusa." Corresponding to the ambivalence surrounding the trope of the apple, then, is an ambivalence in Thoreau's attitude toward the Mother of Nature. Just as the apple is both the sign of Eden and the sign of its dispersal, so Nature is both comfort and threat; or rather, the fantasized return to Nature is both dream and nightmare. We will have to look to *Pierre* for a full-scale exploitation of this tension in the American topography; but Thoreau forecasts the vague region between incestuous eroticism and the threat of castration Melville will explore when he remarks of his voyage in the *Week* that the traveler who is "born again on the road" will "experience at last that old threat of his mother fulfilled, that he shall be skinned alive. His sores shall gradually deepen themselves that they may heal inwardly." Thoreau's being skinned alive parallels his devouring of the raw woodchuck as an act of totemic internalization, but the suggestion seems to be that his own ritual rebirth entails being inversely devoured by Nature, that in his erotic return to the landscape of his infant dreams he must run the risk of mutilation at the hands of that Mother he so cherishes as a virgin goddess. It is as though the "violence of love" which Thoreau speaks of in the famous pages on friendship were composed equally of the violence of his own cultivating penetration and of a countering violence of revenge dealt by the Nature he would possess.

It would be a mistake to read these episodes in the *Week* too psychoanalytically, in the vain hope of determining Thoreau's mental condition. Even if that were possible, it would be beside the point, which is to lay out Thoreau's use of figures that are ambiguously psychological and mythic in his narrative. The question of the imaginative rebirth Thoreau undergoes in the course of his voyage, and the way it is accomplished, it completely relevant in this respect, and there is a passage late in the *Week* that suggests the nature of this rebirth and hauntingly echoes the threat of the Mother, which that experience entails. It is "as if our birth had at first sundered things," Thoreau says of the literal birth that his voyage has figuratively reenacted, "and we had been thrust up through into nature like a wedge, and not till the wound heals and the scar disappears do we begin to discover where we are, and that nature is one and continuous everywhere." By the point in the *Week* at which this passage occurs, Thoreau has become considerably involved in an overt attempt to cover up the incursion of his voyage and heal the wound *it* has made by turning it into part of a natural process. What is of interest here, however, is that when juxtaposed to the earlier passage in which Thoreau is "born again" on the road by reliving the Mother's threat, his remarks not only encompass the rude violence carried out in the act of birth but also trouble our identification of the wounded. Is it, in fact, the child (Thoreau) or the Mother (Nature) who is wounded at birth and whose scar must heal? And who, then, is wounded by the reenactment of birth Thoreau attempts to perform by his voyage into Nature? The question is complex, and all the more so in that the figures it summons up are so startlingly reminiscent of the opening of Whitman's "Song of the Broad-Axe":

> Weapon shapely, naked, wan,
> Head from the mother's bowels drawn,
> Wooded flesh and metal bone, limb only one and lip only one,
> Gray-blue leaf by red-heat grown, helve produced from a
>   little seed sown.

Whitman's lines, among the best in American poetry, brilliantly explicate the tension in Thoreau's narrative. Like Thoreau's "wedge," Whitman's axe is at once child and phallus, the product of birth and the weapon turned back against the Mother Nature that bore it. Both narratives describe a release from captivity and an act of revenge that, whatever its intention, turns back in violence upon its source. Though Whitman's poem breaks into a celebration of the deeds performed by the American axe, his overt eroticism brings the actions of the weapon closer to a drama of incest than is comfortable.

If Thoreau's narrative is not as economically constructed as Whitman's packed lines, his sense of the ironies of that drama seems clearer; for perhaps more poignantly than Whitman, he recognized that his own pen was a weapon that, however much it celebrated the settlement of America, aligned itself unnervingly with the destruction of the new Eden. Thoreau's birth "up through into" Nature like a wedge is inversely repeated in the repenetration of Nature undertaken in his traveling, plowing, and writing. He might well have recalled, though repressing it in his own account, that Mather described the revenging wounds inflicted by the Dustan captives as "Home Blow, [struck] upon the Heads of their Sleeping Oppressors," for his return to the home of Nature, the primitive landscape of the Mother, is a liberation that also exercises a certin violence against a figure who rules over the home of his infant dreams. The interval between Thoreau's first and second sunderings of Nature, his two births, corres-

ponds to that "memorable interval" between the spoken and the written
he elaborates in the chapter on "Reading" in *Walden*. The spoken "is commonly transitory, a sound, a tongue, a dialect merely, almost brutish, and
we learn it unconsciously, like the brutes, of our mothers," while the written "is the maturity and experience of that; if [the spoken] is our mother
tongue, this is our father tongue, a reserved and select expression, too significant to be heard by the ear, which we must be born again in order to
speak." Against the feminine primacy of the spoken Thoreau shares with
Emerson and Rousseau, among others, he places the power of the written,
the father tongue whose *stylus* registers an advance in cultivation and necessarily joins forces with the masculine domination civilization inflicts
upon the primitive, the first home of Nature and Mother violently "rent"
by the inscriptions of plow and pen.

III

In his attempt to naturalize his traveling and his writing, then,
Thoreau's employment of the trope of cultivation is more than a literary
convention; rather, it is an exact index of the psychological and mythological motives of his frontier enterprise. But if Thoreau plays out the intimate
connection between *grafting* and *graphein,* he does so in full awareness of
the risk that his *grafting* may introduce a corrupt economy that issues
either in mutation and disease or in illicit profit gained by violence and
double-dealing. Thoreau's cultivation of Nature yokes literal seeding with
insemination by the letter in a precise way, for his whole project involves
implanting himself in the midst of Nature while at the same time conceal-
ing the injury generated by that act. When Thoreau notes in the discussion
of friendship in the *Week* that "speech . . . follows after silence" at a long
remove, just as "the buds in the graft do not put forth into leaves till long
after the graft has taken," he calls attention to the way in which language
grows round the enfolded recess of silence by grafting itself on to Nature's
void. Writing for Thoreau, even more pointedly than speech, is an act of
implanting, incubation, and labor; and as a "home-staying, laborious native of the soil," he claims in *Walden* that he would work his bean field
"if only for the sake of tropes and expressions, to serve a parable-maker
one day." One constantly feels, in fact, that Thoreau would not undertake
half his projects if he did not have before him the prospect of writing
about them, or, like Hannah Dustan, bringing home proof of his enterprise, the "trope" and "trophy" of his writing and scalping.

Yet the graft of writing is also a kind of rehabilitation for Thoreau, a cure of the ground which is also the disease itself. To accentuate this aspect of his own mythology, Thoreau continually reverts to the figure of the apple, at once a token of the primitive, innocent paradise, but likewise its most culturally burdened symbol. In the midst of the wilderness of the *Week,* Thoreau strikingly amends the "free aspect of the wild apple-trees" he has just praised, by reporting that in fact they are "not poison, but New English," their "ancestors" imported by his own; these "gentle trees," Thoreau adds, "imparted a half-civilized and twilight aspect to the otherwise barbarian land." In "Wild Apples," Thoreau links the apple's role to his own craft even more pointedly when he remarks that "*our* wild apple is wild only like myself, perchance, who belong not to the aboriginal race here, but have strayed into the woods from the cultivated stock." More naked yet is his observation in *The Maine Woods* that a particular "orchard of healthy and well-grown apple-trees" unfortunately bears "all natural fruit" and is thus "comparatively worthless for want of a grafter." He goes on to propose, in an open display of his own motives, that "it would be a good speculation, as well as a favor conferred on the settlers, for a Massachusetts boy to go down there with a trunk full of scions, and his grafting apparatus, in the spring." Placed against his earlier lamentation that ever since Adam man has been trapped in a "web of speculations" spun from inference and reference, this American apple orchard stops somewhat short of Eden's bliss and brings the "Massachusetts boy" even closer to Thoreau's own *grafting.* The paradise of the natural he keeps projecting as a desirable state shrivels and goes rotten on closer inspection, as though Thoreau had to guarantee his own fall and complicity in the act of settlement which makes its way by graft and trade. In order to obtain the savage's "fresh fruits" Thoreau must enter into trade himself; but since "no *trade* is simple, but artificial and complex," and since that which "commerce seizes is always the very coarsest part of the fruit,—the mere husk and rind," his search necessarily profanes its object in the very act of obtaining it. Or, in what is at once a more practical but also more disturbing alternative, it may prove to be the case that the wild, untouched fruit is *too* natural to be of use, that only a grafter can make it fit for consumption. In either case Thoreau is in danger: he either engages in an activity which he must continually admit is illicit, or he renounces the tangible proof of an American paradise.

Also subject to the paradox of settlement is the *too* natural Silence that waits like the untouched land or the blank page to be penetrated and engrafted, for it is the act of insemination, the graft of writing or speech, which both domesticates and obliterates Silence, removing it farther West or further within. Like the arrowhead or the blank wall of Ktaadn, unencumbered by interpretation, Silence is that which is always in refuge, most in recess. Of the words which parade and pander about Thoreau's mistress, those which come nearest must be written "exactly at the right crisis," for "poetry . . . is not recoverable thought, but a hue caught from a vaster *receding* thought" (my emphasis). If "the most excellent speech finally falls into Silence," however, one approach to the "right crisis" is to place it at the very edge of this *falling*. The writing act catches Nature, or the primitive past it represents, on the brink of Silence; yet in holding that Silence in reverence, Thoreau's writing marks itself as an inadequate deterioration and falling away from that which it sets up as unavailable to appropriation. Obviously, *fall* is a word with a razor edge, and we will see eventually how crucial its ambiguity is to the lesson of "Friday" in the *Week*. What is important to note here is that *fall* may connote a natural cycle, like that of the river itself, "falling all the way" to the sea according to "the law of its birth" and "an ancient, ineradicable inclination"; or it may indicate a plunge into the virtual abyss of Silence, a wholesale eradication of intelligibility. On the one hand, language stops short of the abyss and rescues intelligibility; on the other, language is in fact already *fallen*, the perversion of pure and sacred Silence, and thus the very condition of man's trangression and violation of an American Eden. These are the choices Thoreau juggles, but in either case writing becomes subject to the speculative web of reference; its *graft* creates meaning by instituting an economy of reference yet continually retreats defeated into its own silence to await the next "crisis" when the arrowhead, the foundation, the bottom, or whatever relic at the moment represents Nature, threatens to fall into too deep a *recession*.

Recede may be the most loaded word in Thoreau's magazine of puns, having a duplicity as paradoxical as that attached to his notion of the frontier as the place where facts are "fronted." The true wilderness, the home of the Indian, is the "Unappropriated Land" which Thoreau seeks to appropriate, but the very act unfortunately dissolves the wilderness and forces it constantly to recede, its "free" space usurped for profit and speculation by the agricultural wave whose limit forms the frontier between the savage and the civilized. That which Thoreau seeks *recedes* into the future, and its economic *recession* is paradoxically its most valuable attribute: it remains unprofaned by the commerce necessarily introduced by the tilling of the soil, or by the telling of the story. Since language and possession are inextricably entwined, it is entirely appropriate that the West is a place of recession, a pocket of virginal Silence; the West across the frontier must be

Adamic and free from the structures of value introduced by the mediating agencies of language and commerce. But again, because Thoreau is investigating a presumably *natural* American state that has been disrupted by the white man's entrance, that which recedes—the "vaster receding thought," for example—is also what fades into a silent past. What Thoreau pursues is both past and future, paradise lost and, since "there is an orientalism in the most restless pioneer, and the farthest west is but the farthest east," paradise still outstanding; yet both may prove to be beyond the frontier of the intelligible.

Thoreau's Indian, his version of Rousseauvian man, is thus both past and future, a wraithlike embodiment of Thoreau's projected ideal simultaneously lost in history and still waiting over the horizon; yet his language is unintelligible and his relationship with Nature troubling. "The Indian's intercourse with Nature," says Thoreau, "is at least such as admits of the greatest independence of each. If he is somewhat of a stranger in her midst, the gardener is too much of a familiar. There is something vulgar and foul in the latter's closeness to his mistress, something noble and cleanly in the former's distance." The white gardener's settlement and cultivation of the land penetrates and befouls it, and provokes a virtual enslavement by appropriation and ownership. Thus when Thoreau remarks further on that "man tames Nature only that he may make her more free than he found her, though he may never yet have succeeded," his "free" is at once wildly ironic and accurate: the taming of agriculture initiates a form of prostitution which erases freedom, but it may at the same time make Nature sexually freer, more fertile. Just so, Silence, verbally chaste, when inseminated by the white man's "load of thought" becomes productive, but in doing so loses its seductive charm. Clearly enough, Thoreau's penetration of Nature has two sides. On the one hand, it is a rude despoiling, but on the other, it represents a fathering and impregnation, the necessary cultivation entailed by settlement.

Thoreau has a number of strategies to account for his entrance into Nature, but one he returns to again and again in the journals is the metaphor of the gall. At a local level, Thoreau finds it "remarkable that a mere gall, which at first we are inclined to regard as something abnormal, should be made so beautiful, as if it were the *flower* of the tree; that a disease, an excrescence, should prove, perchance, the greatest beauty,—as the tear of the pearl. Beautiful scarlet sins they may be. . . . This gall is the tree's 'Ode to Dejection.' " While Thoreau claims in *Walden*, of course, that he does "not propose to write an ode to dejection," his career is exactly that, at least in the sense ascribed to the tree's gall. An 1854 journal entry is more exact on this subject: "Is not Art itself a gall? Nature is stung by God and the seed of man planted in her. The artist changes the direction of Nature and makes her grow according to his idea. If the gall was anticipated when the oak was made, so was the canoe when the birch was made. Genius stings Nature, and she grows according to its idea." Yet another journal passage, of just a year earlier, records that "Nature [itself] is a kind of gall . . . the Creator stung her and man is the grub she is destined to house and feed." Thoreau's indecision as to whether it is Art or Nature which forms the gall is important, since his whole enterprise is directed at troubling the distinction between the two. Perhaps more revealing, though, is his attempt to make the wounding and impregnating act part of a natural process, thus domesticating its violence and fitting it into a chain fathered finally by God. In the end, Thoreau's metaphor is all encompassing; since man becomes a center of civilization wherever he is, housed like a grub in the flesh of Nature, his every attempt to make a home must heal the wound made and nurse the scar of settlement.

A more classical instance of this confrontation between Art and Nature, and one which retains the figure of a wounding inscription so important to Thoreau, is Marvell's "The Garden." Thoreau quotes two lines from the poem—"Two paradises 'twere in one / To live in paradise alone"—at the outset of his journals as a beacon to his solitude, but the third stanza must also have struck home for him:

> No white nor red was ever seen
> So am'rous as this lovely green.
> Fond lovers, cruel as their flame,
> Cut in these trees their mistress' name.
> Little, alas, they know, or heed.
> How far these beauties hers exceed!
> Fair trees! wheres'e'er your barks I wound,
> No name shall but your own be found.

All told, Thoreau's work does just as efficient a job as Marvell's poem of "Annihilating all that's made / To a green thought in a green shade," and the wound he makes in Nature is as handily covered up by a healing gall; the action both satisfies the lust for violation and saves Nature by reconstituting it at a further remove, some realm presently beyond the reach of domestication. Thoreau's journal of 1851 records that "a surveyor must be curious in studying the wounds of trees, to distinguish a natural disease or scar from the 'blazing' of an axe." Sincere as this may be, it is nevertheless part of Thoreau's purpose to get to the point where the two scars are indistinguishable, where he can enter Nature undetected and without tell-tale trace. His writing itself performs this function while it at the same time betrays it. Like the "well-built sentence" that a journal entry of 1842 compares "to a modern corn-planter, which furrows out, drops the seed, and covers it up at one movement," Thoreau's own writing gouges out a clearing in the wilderness, implants itself, and attempts to cover up its violation by apology and oration. Yet that *re*covery has another side too: since the prize of the wilderness, the Eden of Nature, is automatically buried beneath the "load" of writing at the very moment its appearance is proclaimed, the writer necessarily covers up what he has exposed whether he wants to or not. Thoreau can neither keep his name succinctly carved in the bark of Nature nor ever find out what, if anything, lies beneath that bark.

The gall of writing ultimately becomes a surrogate for the "fresh fruits" of Nature that Thoreau has gone in search of, the most valuable product of his act of violation. As the central figure in a melodrama of naturalization, the gall represents the union of the savage and the civilized, of the feminine Nature and the fathering Art; and since it enacts both a rebirth and an erotic if violent coupling, the gall is the perfect emblem of Thoreau's ambivalence. We should recall at this point the journal passage quoted earlier in which Thoreau projects the figure of the woman as one who cultivates *his* nature, thus reversing the usual roles; this troubling of the distinction corresponds to the erosion of the frontier between Nature and Art, for as Thoreau remarks in his 1858 journal, "genius is inspired by its own works; it is hermaphroditic." As for Whitman, Thoreau's frontier between Nature and Art is the site of androgynous self-generation. The violence of the masculine is countered by the commanding comfort of the feminine, and in many respects Thoreau, like Whitman, finds the artist the perfect union of the two. "The practice of giving the feminine gender—to all ideal excellence personified," Thoreau writes in his 1840 journal, "is a mark of refinement, observable, in the mythologies even of the most barbarous nations. . . . Man is masculine, but his manliness is feminine. It is the inclination of brute force to moral power." And in the *Week*, Thoreau says of Chaucer that "his genius was feminine, not masculine. It was such a feminineness, however, as is . . . not to be found at all in woman, but is only the feminine in man. Such pure and genuine and childlike love of Nature is hardly to be found in any poet." If Thoreau's own "childlike" relationship with Nature borders on a fantasy of incest, it nonetheless provides an apt figure for the feminization he found necessary to his craft. "There must be the copulating and generating force of love behind every effort

destined to be successful," he writes in 1852. "The poet's relation to his
theme is the relation of lovers." That relation applies equally to Thoreau's
cultivation as a pioneer and his cultivation as a writer; and if his galls of
writing come at times to resemble the "bunch" that Whitman onanistically
"pluck'd at random from myself" in "Spontaneous Me"—a "bunch" that
is at once his sexual seed and the flower of his writing—it is because Thoreau shares with Whitman a tendency to channel off erotic excitement into
the act of writing. We might well compare his penetration of Nature's
frontier and his admonition that the words which come nearest to Silence
be written "exactly at the right crisis" to a rather extravagantly sublimated
sexual act, for both may be marked by an exhilaration of conquest and a
consequent shame for the befoulment, however great the rewards of the
completed cultivation. Thoreau's self-imposed chastity seems in fact designed to further the creative powers of his writing, for he notes in what
is, ironically enough, a wedding letter of 1852 to Harrison Blake that
"there is to be attributed to sensuality the loss to language of how many
pregnant symbols." Whatever loss Thoreau himself suffered at the hands
of sensuality, it was apparently too little to stifle the insemination he chose
to practice in his gardening and his writing.

IV

Because Thoreau's pen is wielded as an axe or a plow, his activity as
a writer reflects and endorses, while at the same time attempting to assuage, his actions as a pioneer and settler. "Homeliness is almost as great
a merit in a book as in a house," Thoreau writes in the *Week;* this is not
only because, as critics of Thoreau have often recognized, his books are
laboriously constructed, but also because writing and cultivation, whether
of himself or his property, are almost inseparable. That Thoreau is unable
or unwilling to free himself from the "load of thought" inherited even by
America is evident in his prodigious learning; and for all his rituals of
stripping down, he is just as oppressed by quotation as Cooper. Perry
Miller accurately characterizes the manic addiction to collecting his own
thoughts and those of others that marks the whole of Thoreau's work,
when he notes "the niggardly way [Thoreau] scrapes his mind," perserving
every scrap and husbanding his energies in anticipation of the day when
he can "construct an edifice. His problem was not, as was Emerson's, to
check a stream of expression, but to keep the crevices from showing after
he laid one brick on top of another. His existence was an anticipation that
the miracle would happen—that the inert bones would join together and

become flesh, that the resurrection would come." But the other side of Thoreau's vision of his solitary enclosure as a kind of chrysalis preparing him for a higher life is his constant fretting, as in *Walden*, that his dwelling will become "a workhouse, a labyrinth without a clue, a museum, an alms-house, a prison, or a splendid mausoleum instead."

While Thoreau is the essential American *bricoleur*, a skilled builder of hypotheses and spiritual playgrounds, the ingeniously practical collector and constructor who makes do with what is at hand and convinces one that nothing else is necessary, he is equally rabid in his consumption and merchandizing of the materials of the country about him, and is exceeded only by Whitman in his desire to get America *written down* and indexed like a list of native commodities. If he would have concurred with Emerson's remark in the chapter of *The Conduct of Life* (1860) entitled "Wealth," that "a garden is like those pernicious machineries we read of . . . which catch a man's coat-skirt or his hand, and draw in his arm, his leg, and his whole body to irresistible destruction." Thoreau would also have had to agree that "wealth has its source in applications of the mind to nature, from the rudest strokes of spade and axe up to the last secrets of art." He seems to have directly anticipated Emerson's further observation that the "craft of the merchant" lies in "bringing a thing from where it abounds to where it is costly," when he writes in 1841 about the act of journalizing: "If I make a huge effort to expose my innermost and richest wares to light, my counter seems cluttered with the meanest homemade stuffs; but after months or years I may discover the wealth of India . . . in that confused heap, and what perhaps seemed a festoon of dried apple or pumpkin will prove a string of Brazilian diamonds, or pearls from Core-mandel." That the farthest West is but the farthest East surfaces even in the imperialism of Thoreau's ransacking of his own mind.

More characteristic of Thoreau's attempt to domesticate his writing enterprise is his handiness at treating Nature as a book, a font of type, a hieroglyphic text, and even, finally, a virtual library. Along with Hawthorne, Melville, and Whitman, Thoreau inherited the Puritan fascination with the interpretation of Nature's text, and he comments over and over in his journal on various aspects of his reading of the landscape. Animal tracks are of particular interest, not only since they are a kind of natural writing but also because they represent the most persistent form of Thoreau's search for identity. "Every man," he writes in his journal of 1860, "thus *tracks himself* through life, in all his hearing and reading and observation and traveling. His observations make a chain." Tracking is a recuperation of what has been lost or denied at the outset; to track oneself is to return toward the origin, by going up river or deep into the woods, say, or by plowing up some arrowheads. Tracking is a form of reading and vice versa, yet both threaten to become lost, to trail off into the underbrush, or become absorbed in a welter of other tracks. Fast on the heels of the *Walden* passage in which Thoreau clamors for a *point d'appui* upon which to found his wall or state, he adds, among a series of epigrammatic statements, "I know not the first letter of the alphabet." Thoreau is not Hawthorne, but his anxiety about the alpha of language is just as pressingly tied to his reading of Nature's text. This is why the arrowhead, which Thoreau can only explain by drawing a picture, is in one respect an ideal symbol, though in another it is totally useless. It is also why Thoreau spends so much time elaborating the hieroglyphic leaves on the melting sand back in *Walden*, a beautiful mural in Nature produced by the "Deep Cut" of the railroad, a heroically magnified version of the regenerative gall. As John Irwin has pointed out, Thoreau's exercise at the sand bank "connects the attempt to find a basic unifying form beneath the multiplicity of natural forms with the attempt to penetrate the language of convention and discover within the original language of nature, that basic verbal form with its emblematic relationship between words and things." If the languages of convention and nature are fused by virtue of their hypothetical mirror relationship, though, Thoreau still has to hedge the rhetorical power of their capacity to be differentiated. For however persistent his attempts, Thoreau's desire to root out the emblematic relationship continually shows itself as a snare for the unwary tracker, one in which the pure *figure* of Nature—the illustration of the arrowhead, for example—remains a figure, a trope that ideally represents an unintelligible Eden free from the economy of language and its speculative web of reference, but as figure, is also a coin deposited in the sand *bank* he exploits in his commerce with Nature.

How seriously Thoreau pursued this paradox is revealed in an almost hallucinatory journal passage of 1851, one worthy of Borges, which binds together the rhetorics of archeology and hunting, the archive and the lair:

> I have sometimes imagined a library, *i.e.* a collection of the works of true poets, philosophers, naturalists, etc., deposited not in a brick or marble edifice in a crowded and dusty city, guarded by cold-blooded and methodical officials and preyed on by bookworms, in which you own no share, and are not likely to, but rather far away in the depths of a primitive forest, like the ruins of Central America, where you can trace a series

of crumbling alcoves, the older books protecting the most modern from the elements, partially buried by the luxuriance of nature, which the heroic student could reach only after adventures in the wilderness amid wild beasts and wild men.

Only *Moby-Dick*'s "Bower in the Arsacides" more insistently ties together the natural and the cultural in an inextricable knot; the churning, smoking textile mill seated inside the vine-covered whale skeleton is the industrial correlative of Thoreau's more respectably learned, but equally exotic, trope for imperialism.

Whether it ventures into landscape or library, however, Thoreau's journey is far from safe. Like writing, "travelling is no pastime," but is "as serious as the grave" and "requires a long probation to be broken into it." The restlessness of traveling "is a prevalent disease," Thoreau notes, one "which attacks Americans especially," and though it is "the opposite of nostalgia," still it "does not differ much from nostalgia." The *Week*'s rivers are the "guides" and the "constant lure" that urge him to "explore at their invitation the interior of continents," and the Merrimack is "the only key which could unlock [New Hampshire's] maze." Yet that maze may well issue in a cul-de-sac, a trap whose bait continues to recede on two fronts, whether as buried origin or manifest destiny. At the limit of the voyage Thoreau and his brother pitch their tent near Hooksett Pinnacle, "on the very spot which a few summers before had been occupied by a party of Penobscots." This is as close as they come to recapturing the lost primitive state in any physical sense; but in fact they are hardly away from home at all, for directly below the Pinnacle lies "Concord"—Concord, New Hampshire, that is—and almost the very port they left now seems magically to have appeared at the end of the line. Thoreau resorts to a similar sleight of hand when he returns home, but the irony of the doubled name is more than a simple joke here. For what Thoreau finds at the far limit of the journey is "that the frontiers were not this way any longer. This generation has come into the world fatally late for some enterprises. Go where we will on the *surface* of things, men have been there before us. We cannot now have the pleasure of erecting the *last* house"—the pleasure, that is, of taking the first step of conquest and cultivation.

Rudely baffled in his attempt to repossess the primitive, Thoreau blurts out his famous exclamation that internalizes the frontier and by that token even further and more maddeningly obliterates its mark: "The frontiers are not east or west, north or south, but wherever a man *fronts* a fact, though that fact be his neighbor, there is an unsettled wilderness between him and Canada, between him and the setting sun, or, farther still, between him and *it*. Let him build himself a log-house with the bark on where he is, *fronting* IT, and wage there an Old French war for seven or seventy years, with the Indians and Rangers, or whatever else may come between him and the reality, and save his scalp if he can." Almost absurdly, the frontier, or whatever it hides, is both there and not there; precisely because Thoreau finds he is there too late and the frontier is gone, he can declare IT still available to possession by an act of imagination or narration. Here the "fact" fronted is "it," a neutral, even neutered, object—if it is an object at all—at once concrete and abstract, like the arrowhead, an exact token of the unintelligible. Writing posits "it" as unassailable but violently takes "its" place and forces "it" into further recession. If, as Walter Michaels has claimed, *Walden's* search for a *point d'appui* is "a kind of ontological scavenger-hunt" in which "the prize is reality," it would be equally appropriate to find in this passage from the *Week* a bottom as treacherous as any in *Walden*. In view of the labyrinthine quality of the declaration, Thoreau's remark in *Walden*, that he went to the woods in order "to front only the essential facts of life," almost brings one to despair over its complexity. Fussell notes of this passage that Thoreau's "starting point is the frontier metaphor compressed in a single word," that " 'front,' normally a trasitive verb, under the impact of American conditions quietly turns into a copulative." This is exactly to the point, for since the frontier, like the *point d'appui,* is unfathomable, it may well be located always at one's fingertips: "it" is "here," where one "is," and this is why Thoreau is everywhere at home but nowhere settled. And just as everywhere is a frontier, so each moment constitutes an origin. Because "all biography is the life of Adam," as Thoreau writes in the Carlyle essay, his remark in *Walden* that "it is, after all, always the first person that is speaking" is optimistically accurate. The first person speaks as Adam did when creating himself at the beginning, the *point d'appui*. But *Walden* is not the *Week,* and Thoreau had tricked out his metaphysics more punningly by the second book; for the first, his *fronting* of IT stopped him cold, like the blank wall of Ktaadn. He knew the fact of the wilderness was there, but he could not grab hold of it, not to save his scalp. The *Week's* frontiers, like the many "realities" in *Walden,* threaten to "all go to pieces in [the] account of them."

The paradise of IT, a place or moment free from reference where one's compass points everywhere at once and one could, like Adam, "simply wonder," is a *pokelogan.* It is what writing and traveling strive for but in so doing vanquish. Like Lévi-Strauss, Thoreau finds that his "load of

thought" so engulfs the undefiled objects of his inspection that he can
reach bottom only by metaphoric ruse. Edward Said's characterization of
Lévi-Strauss's predicament is in this regard directly applicable to Thoreau:
"Because the observing ethnologist is a product of literate society, and because anthropology itself is subject to the enslaving laws of literacy, the
zero state [of Nature] is a forbidden paradise which literacy penetrates
only at the critical moment that the paradise is being obliterated." Since
the zero state's paradise is lost at the very moment it is *found,* it cannot
be successfully written, not even at "exactly the right crisis." It remains a
fantasized projection in the topography of a dream, a state which, like the
arrowhead, has symbolic value zero and thus a meaning both null and limitless. In his attempted recovery of that state, Thoreau might well have
come to the same conclusion as Lévi-Strauss—that "travelling was a snare
and a delusion," that "every effort to understand [the specimens of Na-
ture] destroys the object studied in favor of another object of a different
nature; this second requires from us a new effort which destroys it in favour of a third, and so on and so forth until we reach the one lasting presence, the point at which the distinction between meaning and the absence
of meaning disappears: the same point from which we began." This is the
irony endorsed by Thoreau's finding himself, at the limit of his voyage in
the *Week,* once again at "Concord." The very point at which he began has
become his point of termination, its name almost a mocking repetition of
his inability to escape one home and search out another, and moreover a
sharp signal that the language of civilization has coincided with, if not preceded, his assault on Nature.

At the same time, "we are clearing the forest in our westward progress," Thoreau writes in his journal of 1851, "we are accumulating a forest
of books in our rear, as wild and unexploited as any of nature's primitive
wilderness." This forest of books matches by obverse reflection the hallucinatory library in the middle of a wild jungle Thoreau imagines, while at
the same time it provides a further *naturalization* of his craft. Going forward for Thoreau means going away from history; but it also means digging back through the accumulated strata of what Whitman called in
"Slang in America," "the infinite go-before of the present" to reach a primitive past, though the account of such a project only adds to the accumulating facts to which the theorizer is in "arrears." Even "our brave new
poets," Thoreau complains in his journal of 1841, "are [as] secondary as
[Saxon translators], and refer the eye that reads them and their poetry, too,
back and backward without end." Since it is precisely the *recovery* of the
relics of the past that renders their authenticity suspect, Thoreau's histori-

cal task in the *Week* and elsewhere paradoxically affirms the observation made by Rousseau in his attempt to account for the ruptured transaction between the savage and the civilized: "What is even crueler is that, as all the progress of the human species continually moves it farther away from its primitive state, the more new knowledge we accumulate, the more we deprive ourselves of the means of acquiring the most important knowledge of all; so that it is, in a sense, by dint of studying man that we have made ourselves incapable of knowing him." Because Thoreau's journey leads back and forth at the same time, back toward the unfallen garden, forth to the new Eden of the West, it is no wonder that he declares in the 1842 journal, "Our eye splits on every object, and we can as well take one path as the other. If I consider its history, it is old; if its destiny, it is new."

Since history accumulates like rubbish about the portals of Nature and surrounds the figure of Silence like the gall about a wound in Nature's flesh, Thoreau must further naturalize his pursuit by prophesying that "when out of history the truth shall be extracted, it will have shed its dates like withered leaves." Yet as in Wallace Steven's "The Rock," where "The fiction of the leaves in the icon/Of the poem, the figuration of blessedness . . . a cure of the ground and of ourselves,/In the predicate that there is nothing else," the suspicion arises in Thoreau's case too that the ground of truth is perpetually a fiction. To protect that truth, though, Thoreau turns it into mythology, which he can affirm to be more true than history—and more *natural*. Although he admits that "mythology is only the most ancient history and biography," he yet maintains that "in the history of the human mind, these glowing and ruddy fables precede the noonday thoughts of men, as Aurora the sun's rays. The matutine intellect of the poet, keeping in advance of the glare of philosophy, always dwells in the auroral atmosphere." This well-known passage from the *Week* fully dramatizes Thoreau's almost comically paradoxical position. While he aligns himself with an auroral atmosphere, he must move west to keep in advance of the philosophical "glare" of noon—presumably the facts of history which succeed the ruddy fables of noon—must follow a westward course to the frontier, but one which cannot sustain its own retreat before the facts that his own narrative generates, that increasing "load of thought" that will itself one day become mythology. Such a "retreat" is the only kind Thoreau, wittily playing with Emerson's "Circles," found of merit—"an orderly advance in the face of circumstances."

A retreat that advances to the frontier at the same time it moves back through history is in either case the victim of its own project. "Men seem anxious to accomplish an orderly retreat through the centuries," Thoreau writes in the *Week,* "earnestly rebuilding the works behind, as they are battered down by the encroachments of time; but while they loiter, they and their works both fall prey to the arch enemy." Whether retreating to the rear or forward, the pioneer who brings his load to bear upon the savage accordingly finds himself in the position of Natty Bumppo—"*particeps criminis,*" as Thoreau says of the satiric poet. Indeed, Thoreau's account is itself a kind of satire on American settlement, at least on his own role in it; for while he pursues the unravished and the wild, and plunges ever more deeply because driven behind by a profane commerce, he cannot but be himself a harbinger of that white glare. The "fruit" he would seize characterizes his frustrating enterprise; it is the fresh reward and unblemished sign of paradise, yet the record of its possession, as a figure of literary mythology, is a dialogue between enslavement and nostalgia, a narrative in which the writer's performance erodes the paradise he would achieve. Capitalistic and imperalistic, Thoreau's *grafting* disfigures the figure of the landscape and enters it in an account which his speculation generates and tries to close out at the same time.

V

But perhaps I spoke too soon in designating Thoreau's termination at Concord, New Hampshire, the ironically thwarted goal in his search for the frontier. In fact, Thoreau's journey up into the White Mountains pushes the frontier farther, to a point where the travelers breathe "the free air of Unappropriated Land." As though unsatisfied with this ambiguous label, Thoreau goes on to explain how they "had traced up the river to which our native stream is a tributary, until from Merrimack it became the Pemigewasset that leaped by our side, and when we had passed its fountainhead, the Wild Amonoosuck, whose puny channel was crossed at a stride, guiding us toward its distant source in the mountains, and at length, without its guidance, we were enabled to reach the summit of AGIOCO-CHOOK." Here Thoreau's account stops. The next remark tells us that they returned from the mountain trip one week later. The truncation of the narrative is entirely appropriate, though somewhat surprising. One would expect at least a brief eulogy like the one in *The Maine Woods,* where Thoreau declares that farther upstream than one can penetrate, the Indian "is lost to my sight, as a more distant and misty cloud is seen flitting by behind a nearer, and is lost in space. So he goes about his destiny, the red face of man." But in the *Week* Thoreau halts at a strange Indian name displayed in full caps, a name which seems to absorb his accomplishments into it as the landscape has done, draining away its power of articulation, almost as though he has undergone, as his journal of 1851 records, one of those "revolutions which create an interval impassable to memory." AGIO-COCHOOK balks interpretation as stringently as the arrowhead; it is as if Thoreau staked his claim to the frontier, but by putting up a sign of that claim dissolved the possibility of its being understood or communicated, the possibility of its taking on negotiable value. For this reason, Thoreau's consummative trip is essentially *silent,* a pretended if not actual penetration into the heart of darkness, the zero state of Nature which cannot be written. At a certain point, though no identifiably necessary one, Thoreau can only renounce his narrative and stammer out a name or, as in *The Maine Woods,* a nearly mad flurry of inadequate words: "Talk of mysteries!—Think of our life in nature,—daily to be shown matter, to come in contact with it,—rocks, trees, wind on our cheeks! the *solid* earth! the *actual* world! the *common sense! Contact! Contact! Who* are we? *where* are we?" Writing stops at the frontier which it itself is; the rest is silence.

It is no mistake that Thoreau delimits the penetration of his journey and his literacy by erecting a forbidding Indian name in our path. For when he somewhat jokingly finds, in a story of the Pilgrim's purchase of Indian land in *Cape Cod,* that "Not Any seems to have been [the name of] the sole proprietor of all America before the Yankees," he not only hits on the sad truth of an imperialism that rode roughshod over a land proclaimed free for the taking but also accentuates the cul-de-sac where his attempted tracing of the American garden ends. "Not Any" encompasses both "not any" *owner* and "not any" *name:* the questions of commerce and language cannot be separated, for it is the conjunction of the two that most defines the American fall, that nick of time in which ownership replaced simple wonderment, and in which the American "web of speculations" can be *said* to have begun. Thoreau is not one to squander his sentiment, though, and even the Indian, because his "memory is in harmony with the russet hue of the fall of the year," means most to him as a replica of Rousseauvian man, an occasion for mythologizing the American discovery and labor of its garden: he is the finest trope that Thoreau's cultivation yields.

But the elegance of that trope does not mitigate the violence that it conceals. Thoreau's writing enterprise must bear the shame of this violence even while it transforms the American settlement by a mythic model of domestication and regeneration. Like Lévi-Strauss, Thoreau is "the less able to ignore his own civilization and to dissociate himself from its faults in that his very existence is incomprehensible except as an attempt at redemption: he is the symbol of atonement." As an elegy to the American Indian, the *Week* poses in part as a cure for the disease of white commerce and involves a dredging up of past affliction in order to cleanse it in confrontation, in order to assuage any doubt that "our bold ancestors who settled this land" struggled not with "a copper-colored race of men," but with "vapors, fever and ague of the unsettled woods." The act of writing entails working through what now seems "shadowy and unreal" in order to reach, if only by a recuperative projection, an assertion of the struggle as original and the settlement as a real appropriation, an event that can be documented. Thoreau needs the guarantee of a violent seizure in order to mark a *fall,* a moment of America's beginning, though as continually proves to be the case, locating such a *point d'appui* is no easy matter. Since the frontier between now and paradise in America is at once past and future, both projection and nostalgia, the wilderness of natural man, while hailed as something toward which a journey is made, is equally at home within memory as the relic of a struggle. Fussell points out that "in his passion for Indian relics [Thoreau] desired to anticipate something altogether more wraith-like, the reemergence of the past, the imaginative return of the dead." One should add to this that Thoreau recognized his activity was problematic at best, one which could not generate the evidence of Nature's lost state without participating in its vanquishing. Always on the lookout for symptoms of America's origin and its initial possessors, Thoreau was more than aware that "inside the civilized man stand[s] the savage still in the place of honor," indeed, that "these aboriginal men cannot be repressed, but under some guise or other . . . survive and reappear continually." In this last remark from the journals, though, Thoreau delineates the way in which the repressed figure of the Indian, like the state of Nature, goes under various guises but is continually displaced into darker, more remote abodes. Because each recovery of the arrowhead only plows under a layer still more primitive and pure, Thoreau's account of that transaction by which the white gardener's intimacy with his mistress the land violently displaces the "innocence" of the Indian's silent intercourse with Nature results in no definitive possession but one which must be continually reenacted, as both as conquest over, and a commemoration of, the lost native fathers.

The act of writing the myth of America, whatever its value as a commemorative act, remains one more commercial incursion in which the white man's "load of thought" further buries that which it would recover. The success of the myth will depend upon its own repression of the telling symptoms of a disease that results from "the grazing of cattle and the rooting of swine" in the American garden, which has been "converted into a stye and hot-bed, where men for profit increase the ordinary decay of nature." The health of the commercial labor, even the labor of writing, that inflicts itself on the primitive, hides within itself an illness that the poet uproots and domesticates while he at the same time confirms it as incurable by constantly relocating the site of its origin. Yet even in this case Thoreau is able to convert trauma into restoration by making disease the condition of an empowering ritual. Disease "is one of the permanent conditions of life," Channing records from Thoreau, for "life is a warfare, a struggle, and the diseases of the body answer to the trouble and defects of the spirit. Man begins by quarreling with the animal in him, and the result is immediate disease. In proportion as the spirit is more ambitious and persevering, the more obstacles it will meet with. It is as a seer that man asserts his disease to be exceptional." It is one thing if the animal Thoreau quarrels with is a woodchuck that he can devour raw; but if the animal is the repressed spirit of the aboriginal Indian, Thoreau's cure must wage a more pitched battle with internalization.

Although Thoreau's cultivation of his anxieties yields fruit, the gall of writing, it also breeds a profane trade without making proper restitution to that which has been uprooted and displaced, however shadowy and unreal. The reward of cultivation's "cure," the innocent fruit, remains outstanding, either plowed under by the advancing front of civilization, or recessed beyond the frontier of the intelligible or negotiable, too free to be fertile. Thoreau's plow reemploys the shadows it would disperse and uncovers the Red Man's "mark" only to *re*cover it. Thus he can say that "every sentence is the result of a long probation," that indeed, "the word which is best said came nearest to not being spoken at all, for it is cousin to a deed which the speaker could better have done. Nay, almost it must have taken the place of the deed by some urgent necessity, even by some misfortune, so that the truest writer will be some captive knight after all" —the Hannah Dustan of his own narrative. It is the "truest writer" who recognizes the necessary "misfortune" of being a fallen "captive" of his own myth, who knows that what he "says" is but a displacement of an act he can never rectify but only dramatically repeat in the interests of his own seizure of power and as a communal sacrifice. Like the Indian's, then, Thoreau's memory is in harmony with the fall of the year. In his ongoing melodrama of America's fall from a paradise it probably never knew nor will know, writing is perpetual elegy. It is "because we naturally look most into the west, as forward into the day," Thoreau notes in the *Week,* that we "in the forenoon see the sunny side of things, but in the afternoon [see]

the shadow of every tree." Because the fabled future of the West is paradoxically a land of nostalgia, Thoreau's auroras, like those of Wallace Stevens, are of autumn. The *Week,* balked in its recovery of paradise, though
not unexpectedly, is a book that elaborates the poetics of afternoon and
autumn, a moment in which writing takes account of its own fall. It is this
continual conjunction of fate and violence in the *Week,* as Walter Hesford
points out, that makes us feel throughout "that we are enjoying a golden
moment on the edge of fall." This is the exact message of the book—that
Thoreau's America, hardly unsettled but not yet settled, *founded* but not
very securely, exists at least temporarily, and perhaps perpetually, in such
a moment.

On "Friday" Thoreau "awoke in autumn," the season having changed
"in some unimaginable point of time, like the turning of a leaf," and com-
menced the swift downstream journey, the return home from the incursion
into the wilderness, falling away from the *point* of penetration at which
his probe ended. This mapping of the journey while Nature is "composing
her poem Autumn," is only the most obvious and suitable closure for a
book which deals with *falling* as a poetic. If Thoreau sets up continual categories of innocence, "pure discoveries, glimpses of *terra firma,*" he knows
with a keen reflection that these are available only to "shipwrecked mariners," only to one who knows himself to be a violator always in arrears
to his own project. Only by the end of the *Week* does one see exactly what
Thoreau meant when he said even before the voyage began that "the lapse
of the current" is "an emblem of all progress." That "lapse"—of the river's
"current" and whatever else is "current"—has all the resonance which
Thoreau assigns it in *Walden* when he derives *lobe* (leaf), *labium* (lip), *labor,* and *lapse* from the same etymological roots, thus implicating autumn,
his own pioneering labor, the fall of his birth, the language that falls from
his lips (or his pen), and the declivity of the river in a panoramic melodrama embracing the loss of Eden, the settlement of America, and the seasonal cycle of nature. Thoreau had written, in a series of translations from
the laws of Menu published in *The Dial* in 1843, that "*if* [the Brahmin]
has any incurable disease, let him advance in a straight path, towards the
invincible *north-eastern* point, feeding on water and air, till his mortal
frame totally decay, and his soul become united with the Supreme." If
Thoreau's voyage in the *Week* was such a spiritual pilgrimage (though
once he reached the Merrimack, of course, his journey veered to the north-
west), one in which his spirit, as he says of the *Week*'s style, "rise[s] from
the page like an exhilaration, and wash[es] away our critical brains like
burr millstones, flowing to higher levels above and behind ourselves," the
journey of recuperation had still to account for the *lapse* that instigated

Thoreau's disease and hung like an afternoon shadow over his every attempt to reach the sanctuary of purity. Though the style of the *Week* is that of "great prose," which "commands our respect more than great verse, since it implies a more permanent and level height, a life more pervaded with the grandeur of thought," that grandeur has its own hand in the disease (the dis-ease or labor) of America; for "the prose writer [who] has conquered, like a Roman, and settled colonies" is one who has wielded his own *stylus* with the violence that settlement requires. Thoreau could not be more aware of his own implication in the white gardener's violent and profane closeness to his mistress than when he calls the downstream voyage a "plowing homeward." The pen that aligns itself with the plow in a laborious enterprise must abide by its own violation, must, even if it sets up as an innocent sign the untouched fruit, locate its own property in that fruit's fall.

What Thoreau awoke from on Friday was the dream in which the return to a silent American wilderness was accomplished, if only with an ironic measure of success. But since "the heroic spirit will not fail to dream of remoter retirements and more rugged paths," and since the marks of the past in their purest form are unintelligible, the completion of the return is incident upon a trick turned by the tools of memory. The Thoreau who had at birth, as we noted earlier, been thrust like a wedge into Nature has replicated the experience, turning the violence of delivery back on itself in order to be "born again on the road," in order that his wounds heal and the scar disappear. As traveler or writer, he cures himself by finding that Nature is "one and continuous everywhere" and by declaring his own craft part of Nature, even its improvement. The wedge, like the point of pen or plow, cultivates its own healing gall about that silent chasm of Nature, but because it is only a *graft,* Thoreau concludes at the end of the *Week,* his account cannot write Silence itself:

> It were vain for me to endeavor to interpret the Silence. She cannot be done into English. For six thousand years men have translated her with what fidelity belonged to each, and still she is little better than a sealed book. A man may run on confidently for a time, thinking he has her under his thumb, and shall one day exhaust her, but he too must at last be silent, and men remark only how brave a beginning he has made; for when he at length dives into her, so vast is the disproportion of the told to the untold, that the former will seem but the bubble on the surface where he disappeared.

That Silence has in the end become the river itself should not be surprising;

for the traveler who had at the outset "resolved to launch myself on [the river's] bosom and float whither it would bear me" has dived into the Mother of Nature and been born again on the journey, if only by domesticating the violence of the act and having failed to translate the Silence accurately.

Thoreau's figuring of Silence as both a woman and a book only further underlies the paradox in his interpretive enterprise. "She" remains pure *figure*, what cannot be interpreted, but yet, as figure, can only be interpreted, that is, subjected to the violence of translation. But "is not Nature, rightly read," Thoreau asks, "that of which she is commonly taken to be the symbol merely?" Because Nature is a self-emptying term endowed with sacred and feminine mystery, Thoreau can domesticate it endlessly and still leave it untouched. He knows with a vengeance the frontiers beyond which his *telling* and *tilling* of the story cannot go. The *Week* is a text whose power lies in its admission that, as Thoreau would put it in *Walden*, "the volatile truth of our words should continually betray the inadequacy of the residual statement" and leave behind the "literal monument alone," as though struck to stone by the Medusa of Nature. In such a narrative it is the "unwritten sequel" that can be held out as the "most indispensible part. It should be the author's aim to say once and emphatically, 'He said,' ἔφηέ. This is the most the bookmaker can attain to. If he make his volume a mole whereon the waves of Silence may break, it is well." It is an autumnal poetic which can *say* it has eaten of the communal fruit and told its story, yet still hold forth the silent and seductive fruit at a further remove in the wilderness dream.

Yet "all our life," Thoreau remarks in his journal of 1859, "is a persistent dreaming awake. The boy does not camp in his father's yard. That would not be adventurous enough, there are too many sights and sounds to disturb the illusion; so he marches off twenty or thirty miles and there pitches his tent, where stranger inhabitants are tamely sleeping in their beds, just like his father at home, and camps in their yard perchance. But then he dreams uninterruptedly that he is anywhere but where he is." Thoreau could never escape camping in his own or someone else's yard, not that it would have mattered much; for as he suggests in the journal entry with which we began, "it is vain to dream of a wilderness distant from ourselves. There is none such." Even in our dreams, Thoreau discovers in the *Week*, "we but act a part which must have been learned and rehearsed in our waking hours, and no doubt could discover some waking consent thereto. . . . In dreams we see ourselves naked and acting out our real characters" and have a "juster apprehension of things, unconstrained by habit, which is then in some measure put off, and divested of memory, which we call history." But the contradictions and ambiguity here are also of note, for it is not clear whether Thoreau's dreams are rehearsed or unconstrained by habit, nor whether dreams are divested of memory, and hence of history, or must be divested of memory in order to *become* history. This confusion, however, is in perfect keeping with an enterprise that finds its dream of Eden stuck in an endless historical regression and even finds itself rehearsing the violations it seeks to be shed of. Thoreau's enactment of a return to Nature ends without having clearly succeeded, though it is difficult to say exactly what might constitute success for one who finds, as he writes in *Walden*, that "the wildest scenes" continually become "unaccountably familiar" and whose every satisfaction of desire at once estranges him from yet another scene lost in the landscape of the West or that of his "infant dreams."

Thoreau's journey is problematic at best, but since "half the walk is but retracing our steps," as he puts it in "Walking," going away from home and returning to it are hardly different. Home, after all, is where one's dreams begin. By the end of the *Week*, the "wild apple-tree" of the American garden is in fact found to inhabit the "native port" to which Thoreau returns, its stem still marked by the wound which the boat's "chain had worn in the chafing of the spring freshets." By an exquisite sleight of hand, the regenerative tree is brought *home* from the wild, though its scar stays as a telling sign that the journey, like the writing labor, is a healing gall grown about its own wound. But after all, Thoreau asks earlier on, "where is the skilful swordsman who can give clean wounds, and not rip up his work with the other edge?" For the skilled writer faced with this challenge, his task is to be "not like a vine, which being cut in the spring bears no fruit, but bleeds to death in the endeavor to heal its wounds," but to be "as vigorous as a sugar maple, with sap enough to maintain his own verdure." Thoreau remarks in "Wild Apples" that he knows of "no trees which have more difficulties to contend with, and which more sturdily resist their foes. These are the ones whose story we have to tell." The wild itself sturdily resists Thoreau in his attempt to graft himself on by way of a story; but in the end, if the apple tree of the *Week* is proof, he succeeds in domesticating the violence of his act and settling his account with Nature, though perhaps only by a ruse like that which placed "Concord" at the opposite limit of the voyage. Like the figure of the beautiful bug born from the "old table of apple-tree wood" at the end of *Walden*, a sign of Thoreau's resurrection from the dead wood of society, the stage prop of the apple tree at the close of the *Week* is a sign that Thoreau's pen remains as double-edged as his plow. As a sacrificial trope—the trophy he has brought home—the apple tree counters his pioneering imperialism and justifies his inability to purify his craft, standing at once for that which is obliterated by his labor and for the atonement that his transgression entails. Guaranteeing that his plunder is neither complete nor in vain, it allows Thoreau to *say* he has pursued a home that could not be found but settled for one that can.

JOHN CARLOS ROWE

"The Being of Language:
The Language of Being"

To learn means: to become knowing. In Latin, knowing is qui vidit, *one who has seen, has caught sight of something, and who never again loses sight of what he has caught sight of. To learn means: to attain to such seeing. To this belongs our reaching it; namely, on the way, on a journey. To put oneself on a journey, to experience, means to learn.*

—HEIDEGGER, "Words," *On the Way to Language*

I have sought to re-name the things seen, now lost in chaos of borrowed titles, many of them inappropriate, under which the true character lies hid. In letters, in journals, in reports of happenings I have recognized new contours suggested by old words so that new names were constituted.

—WILLIAM CARLOS WILLIAMS, *In the American Grain*

W*alden* is Thoreau's perfect form; it has the mathematical precision of a musical composition. Thoreau certainly appears to demonstrate in this work the radically formalized truth he had foreseen in an earlier work: "The most distinct and beautiful statement of any truth must take at last the mathematical form." *Walden* is "addressed to poor students," who love to play its verbal games and diagram its architectonic order in the place of healthier sport. Such economy and control are rare in the literature of the American Renaissance, which seems better represented by the outwanderings of Whitman or the divine rage of Melville. There is little

---

From *Through the Custom-House: Nineteenth-Century American Fiction and Modern Theory.* © 1982 by the Johns Hopkins University Press.

voyaging here; this is a book of construction and possession: "In most books, the *I,* or first person, is omitted; in this it will be retained; that, in respect to egotism, is the main difference. We commonly do not remember that it is, after all, always the first person that is speaking." All radiates concentrically from this artifical "I," whose insistent presence organizes and determines what we might see. Thoreau has much to say against ownership, but in this book he appropriates nature and brings it within his compass. The writing defines and encloses a Transcendental fiefdom; *Walden* legalizes the everlasting wholeness of natural creation. All seasons speak the same truth in but varied manifestations, so that the poet need only lift the corners of his veils to disclose the divinity in things.

This is a book of discovery, but not of creation. Perhaps it is no accident that the most extended literary discussion concentrates on "Reading" rather than on writing. Of course, Thoreau emphasizes the intimate bond between the two activities: "Books must be read as deliberately and reservedly as they were written." Yet, *Walden* is primarily intended as a Baedeker to the order of nature, the primacy of which remains unquestioned. Writing is sacred and mystical in its universal appeal and endurance, but nonetheless secondary to the literal text of nature: "It is the work of art nearest to life itself." "Reading" quickly gives way to "Sounds" more basic to "the language which all things and events speak without metaphor, which alone is copious and standard." William Drake writes, "The step from 'Reading' to 'Sounds' is that from the language of men to the 'language' of things, from what can be said *about* nature, to nature itself." The classics play an important role throughout *Walden,* but they must be put aside in the early stages of Thoreau's ritualized self-purification: "I did not read books the first summer; I hoed beans."

Walden betrays the desire for an established metaphysical center to determine human behavior and organize knowledge. The metaphors of building and clothing appear to offer human beings the freedom of a creative imagination, but such activities are themselves merely techniques for discovering and obeying the dictates of an authoritative Being. Fishing, diving, and mining are basic to this work of reconnaissance: "My instinct tells me that my head is an organ for burrowing, as some creatures use their snout and fore-paws, and with it I would mine and burrow my way through these hills. I think that the richest vein is somewhere hereabouts; so by the divining rod and thin vapors I judge; and here I will begin to mine." Such deep diving intends to bring to light what is hidden, freeing what has been imprisoned in humans by their faulty methods of perception and cognition. *Awakening* is the avowed aim of *Walden,* and it means the *arising* of truth into consciousness by means of a systematic removal of barriers in order to open a path. For Thoreau, to awaken is to "come into being" rather than to "bring into being." Language facilitates such discovery only to the extent that it serves a prior perception and thus may be made "pertinent" to reality. Metaphor is employed ironically to reveal the "commonsensical" in everyday speech and thus to free us to receive the tangible, literal spirituality that only nature presents. As Drake remarks, "To say that nature has a language, is itself a metaphor. Metaphor as Thoreau speaks of it always defines human experience, *within human bounds*." Thus, in a work that is nothing but metaphor, Thoreau struggles to destroy the metaphorical in order to allow the presence of the indwelling god to emerge.

The achievement of *Walden* is the result of this confidence that the natural origin of language escapes the symbolism of words and remains eternally and creatively present. In such a bookish work there is remarkably little reflection upon language itself, as if the natural facts were sufficient for the grammar of our lives. There is something disturbingly evasive in such passages as the following from "Higher Laws": "Every man is the builder of a temple, called his body, to the god he worships, after a style purely his own, nor can he get off by hammering marble instead. We are all sculptors and painters, and our material is our own flesh and blood and bones. Any nobleness begins at once to refine a man's features, any meanness or sensuality to imbrute them." Substituting the body for the materials of the sculptor, Thoreau disparages the symbolic mode of the traditional artist. True art speaks directly in and through natural existence, spontaneously manifesting itself in the life of the artist.

And yet, such sophistry is purchased only by means of an elaborate metaphoric structure yoking temple and body, style and behavior. Thoreau is able to elide the conventional distinctions between body and soul, substance and spirit, only by means of a language that operates by syntagmatic associations and paradigmatic substitutions essential to figurative language. Thoreau may employ language in *Walden* more cleverly than in any of his other works, but he scrupulously avoids the problematic of language itself. Emerson insists that "Nature is the symbol of spirit," thus suggesting a correspondence between the production of words as "signs of natural facts" and the recognition of "natural facts" as the "symbols of particular spiritual facts." Emerson's view involves a rich and varied language coordinated with natural symbolism; Thoreau's insistence on the ultimate literality of natural facts reduces language to a secondary representation.

There are, of course, many ways in which *Walden* can be read as an extended meditation on the use and abuse of language. In *The Senses of*

Walden, Stanley Cavell employs Wittgenstein to interpret *Walden* as the discovery of "what writing is and, in particular, what writing *Walden* is." *Walden* certainly abounds with evidence that self-knowledge is as much a linguistic process as a purely natural one; in fact, the entire work turns on the doubling of the place of Walden in its textual realization. The awakening promised in the epigraph and the spring that concludes the work's seasonal cycles are metaphors for the composition of the text; the dwelling that Thoreau builds is ultimately a house of words. Yet, the aim of this "wording of the world" is a simplicity and clarity that result in the resolution of true self-knowledge.

The discipline of Thoreau's deliberation is equivalent to Wittgenstein's goal of learning how what we say is what we mean. Thoreau relies, however, on his confidence in a fundamental language of Nature from which human speech derives; Wittgenstein's problems are compounded by the fact that his investigations must remain totally within the domain of ordinary language. Wittgenstein must repeat the basic Kantian move of bracketing the thing-in-itself as unknowable, thus shifting the concern of understanding to the development of such internal linguistic distinctions as literal and figurative, grammatical and performative, conventional and original. In *Walden*, Thoreau decidedly does not bracket the thing-in-itself, even though he acknowledges the difficulty of expressing it. Cavell brilliantly suggests that Thoreau provides in *Walden* that "deduction of the thing-in-itself" that Kant "ought to have provided" as "an essential feature (category) of objectivity itself, viz., that of *a world apart from me in which* objects are met." Transcendental deduction, however, can be performed only on a system of representation; Thoreau's ability to offer such a deduction of objectivity depends upon his confidence in the "language" of Nature, on the possibility of an "objective" language. Thus, Thoreau can assert in *Walden* what Kant in the three critiques only subjunctively "wished" for: that the order of the mind has a structural identity with the order of Nature.

The objectivity of Nature in *Walden* thus secretly governs the subjectivity of human language, which eternally symbolizes that literal origin. Cavell argues that "the externality of the world is articulated by Thoreau as its nextness to me." This idea of the proximity of man and Nature determines Cavell's understanding of philosophical unity in Thoreau: "Unity between these aspects is viewed not as a mutual absorption, but as perpetual nextness, an act of neighboring or befriending." I shall develop a similar notion of metaphysical difference in my Heideggerian reading of *A Week on the Concord and Merrimack Rivers,* which draws, as Cavell's reading of *Walden* does, on Thoreau's paradoxical "friendship" (itself a metaphor for self-consciousness) as a complex of proximity and distance. However, I employ Heidegger's metaphor of the "between" (of earth and sky, of man and nature, of beings and Being), which differs crucially from "nextness."

The "neighborhood" of man and Nature is made possible by the authority of the language of Nature, whose objective and literal presence always exceeds human speech. When we say what we mean, when we speak deliberately, we approach the simplicity of such natural language, and words become facts. But the "between" of man and Nature describes a different space of human dwelling, because this between constitutes a relation that does not exist as a possibility prior to human language. In *Walden*, the language of Nature makes possible human speech, but the human language of *A Week* invents the idea of Nature as part of the measurement of our being. The grounding of human language in an inexpressible natural presence is symbolized in *Walden* in terms of building: a house, a self, a neighborhood with what *is*. The displacement of natural presence into the "difference" of human language in *A Week* is expressed in metaphors of voyaging, of traveling the between of beings and Being that is measured only by such movement. This "bridging" and "crossing" is the essential activity of metaphor. The text of *Walden* celebrates its departure from Walden as the realization of the natural experiment; the text of *A Week* celebrates the return to Concord as a "fall" into that language that has forever displaced the Nature it set out to discover.

In this description of the spring thaw flowing down the railroad cut, Thoreau offers one of the most extended and self-conscious verbal plays in *Walden*. The intricate blending of natural energies is a metaphor for the act of composition as an interpretation of specific phenomena in Nature: "As it flows it takes the forms of sappy leaves or vines, making heaps of pulpy sprays a foot or more in depth, and resembling, as you look down on them, the laciniated lobed and imbricated thalluses of some lichens; or you are reminded of coral, of leopards' paws or birds' feet, of brains or lungs or bowels, and excrements of all kinds." At such a moment language appears to call forth not only the intricate relations of the natural scene but also the pure metaphorics of such relations. Such poetry seems to constitute the truth of Nature by means of an integrated verbal display that challenges the self-sufficiency of natural phenomena. Everything observed seems to contribute to the production of signs that announce their metaphorical powers. Such technical descriptions as "laciniated lobed and imbricated thalluses of some lichens" signify through poetic complexes of alliteration, assonance, consonance, condensation, and syllabic rhythm. Yet, at such a critical moment Thoreau hesitates and then retreats, insisting that the true "artistry" remains external and divine: "I am affected as if in a peculiar sense I stood in the laboratory of the Artist who made the world and me,—had come to where he was still at work, sporting on this bank, and with an excess of energy strewing his fresh designs about."

Metaphor has made such vision possible, but it is quickly rejected in favor of "such a foliaceous mass as the vitals of the animal body." And as if checking the dangerous excess implied in the verbal dance, Thoreau insists on dissecting words themselves to reveal their natural grounding, effectively emptying them of their autonomous powers:

> No wonder that the earth expresses itself outwardly in leaves, it so labors with the idea inwardly. The atoms have already learned this law, and are pregnant by it. The overhanging leaf sees here its prototype. *Internally,* whether in the globe or animal body, it is a moist thick *lobe,* a word especially applicable to the liver and lungs and the *leaves* of fat (λειβω, labor, lapsus, to flow or flow or slip downward, a lapsing; λοβος, globus, lobe, globe; also lap, flap, and many other words,) *externally* a dry thin *leaf,* even as the *f* and *v* are a pressed and dried *b.* The radicals of lobe are *lb,* the soft mass of the *b* (single lobed, or B, the double lobed,) with a liquid *l* behind it pressing it forward. In globe, *glb,* the gutteral *g* adds to the meaning the capacity of the throat.

Thoreau's phonemic, phonetic, and etymological analyses serve to restrain the flight of metaphor and situate the imagination within the "facts" of nature. Language is reduced to the physical associations of words and things that reveal a hidden natural form. *Walden* clearly argues for a natural principle of growth and unfolding that denies any sense of completion or closure, but language imitates that organic development only by means of a formal precision with respect to external facts that restricts imaginative play by narrowing the range of authentic (or pertinent) meanings. Emerson avoids some of these dangers by insisting that art is "a nature passed through the alembic of man. Thus in art does Nature work through the will of a man filled with the beauty of her first works." For Emerson, both natural and linguistic symbolisms require a reciprocal interpretation, whereas Thoreau insists on the *presence* of unmediated truth in the earth's "living poetry."

Thus, in *Walden* every impulse to discuss poetics is quickly diverted back to the controlling meditation on the permanence and variety of natural forms. The mastery of this work relies largely on Thoreau's insistence that language and thought would be indistinguishable from natural phenomena if we fully understood our being. In his study of Thoreau, James McIntosh argues that the principal drama in *Walden* is the struggle of the "I" to sustain his integrity in the face of an encompassing natural order. Revisions made between 1847 and 1852 seem to indicate that in the process of composition Thoreau grew "less anxious to write of himself as a part of nature, more intent on asserting his intelligent separateness." But the very diversity and activity that individualize the narrator and his style merely confirm the determining power of the underlying natural forms. The anxiety of alienation is neatly resolved as the *illusion* of separation that properly honed senses may see beyond. Every verbal strategy seems designed to measure and refine the a priori ground of being in nature.

A Week on the Concord and Merrimack Rivers (1849) is wilder and less "homely" than *Walden*. There is an authentic conflict between poetic expression and a determining natural order. Although *A Week* prefigures most of the basic tenets of the Transcendentalism formalized by *Walden*, it leads Thoreau in certain directions that threaten to subvert his subsequent confidence in a metaphysics of natural presence. Appropriately, much of his doubt and equivocation concerns the relation of human discourse to natural form. *A Week* supplies the lack felt in *Walden* concerning the function and identity of the poet. As Robert Evans notes, "Thoreau left us no manifesto or defense of poetry—only the *Week,* in which he drew together most of his ideas concerning poetry and the function of the poet." Thoreau may foreshadow the more rigorous naturalism of *Walden* when he writes that "the works of man are everywhere swallowed up in the immensity of nature," but he introduces a more problematic conception of art when he suggests: "Art is not tame, and Nature is not wild, in the ordinary sense. A perfect work of man's art would also be wild or natural in a good sense. *Man tames Nature only that he may at last make her more free even than he found her, though he may never yet have succeeded*" (my italics). This reflection allows the possibility of a human poetry that would supplement the natural process, actively contributing to the unfolding of Being itself. Thoreau's modernity is best expressed in the notion that nature might be liberated and opened to its own being through human language. Thoreau's sentiment in this passage seems to combine two basic tenets of Emerson's radicalized version of romanticism: that the "poets are thus liberating gods" and by virtue of such imaginative freedom entreat us to "participate the invention of nature."

A Week is a quest for the origins of poetry in both humanity and nature. The genetic critics are certainly correct in arguing that *Walden* refines the motley form of *A Week* by employing fewer literary digressions and quotations in order to center the subject of natural experience. Yet, the balance and control of *Walden* are achieved only by repressing basic questions about human discourse that surface in the discursive voyage of *A Week*. This distinction between the organization of these works affects other areas of concentration as well. *Walden* involves a withdrawal from social life designed to enable the "I" ultimately to achieve a higher form of communal existence. Although Thoreau writes repeatedly about the need to substitute more authentic communication for the conventional social "parlaver," there is less direct confrontation with the question of social intercourse than we might expect. "Life in the woods" remains a lonely experiment between two worlds. However, the entire narrative of *A Week* is controlled by the mutual voyage of the brothers, which figures variously as the relation between writer and reader as well as among individuals in society. Although the voyage is a departure from Concord, the brothers bear the essence of social intercourse with them. Simplified as a fraternal microcosm, social organization becomes a primary subject for continuing meditation. The extended essay on friendship that appears in "Wednesday" serves to organize Thoreau's related concerns with literary and interpersonal communication.

At first glance, *A Week* appears to be a cruder version of the same spiritual quest that organizes the form of *Walden*. Joyce Holland summarizes the accepted interpretation of the voyage motif: "Hence the upstream voyage becomes a voyage backwards through history to the pure and primal state, and the enduring moment of existence is shown by counterpointing the two symbolic motions 'up' and 'down.' " Yet, the process of reducing "life to its lowest terms" in preparation for a new, spiritualized Concord spring is increasingly a literary task. The actual journey achieves greater naturalness as it is symbolized through a complex of poetical and historical references and allusions. As Robert Evans writes, "So often does he deal with poetry and poetics that these subjects become the major themes, or subject matter, of the book, while the journey down the Concord and Merrimack Rivers gently recedes from the reader's view until it is quite lost from focus." Thoreau may argue in anticipation of *Walden* that the Transcendentalist's "process of discovery is very simple. An unwearied and systematic application of known laws to nature causes the unknown to reveal themselves," but language in *A Week* is not merely a tool like "a plumb line, a level, a surveyor's compass, a thermometer, or a barometer!" If language opens the path to universal knowledge, it also uncovers unconscious desires, dreams, fears, and passions. More directly than in *Walden,* Thoreau questions the adequacy of an immediate, sensuous communion with nature.

Every schoolchild knows that *Walden* is about innocence, the auroral Adam bathed in the primal light of nature. Writing that work is a formal attempt to preserve the meaning and truth discovered in the woods. In this sense, *Walden* displays a mode of writing that is fundamentally journalistic, not in the sense of recording events in linear sequence but in the close correlation of writing and experience. Although apparently but a short step from the formlessness of the *Journal, A Week* depends upon a fundamental difference between the experience of the voyage in 1839 and the writing of the text. John's death (1842) figures pervasively in the work as the unspoken sign of an irrecoverable companionship. The more general dilemma of the historian reflects some of the personal anxiety Thoreau must have felt: "Critical acumen is exerted in vain to uncover the past; the *past* cannot be *presented;* we cannot know what we are not." Thoreau may continue in this same passage to claim that "one veil hangs over past, present, and future, and it is the province of the historian to find out, not what was, but what is." However, such a conception of natural duration is complicated by the immediacy of the brother's absence, which continues to raise questions about the relation of experience and language, presence and representation. This anxiety concerning the dualities of transience and endurance governs Thoreau's discourse on friendship, thus extending the personal dilemma to the broader domain of social relations and human brotherhood.

A Week directly confronts our alienation from nature by attempting to reflect on the essence of language. The work is full of references to the Fall, all of which are closely associated in Thoreau's effort to analyze the origins of the modern American fall. The Indian's primal participation in nature must be reconstructed from the fragments of a vanishing culture: arrowheads, bits of pottery, the buried brands of a hunter's campfire. "Sunday" carefully subverts Christian orthodoxy by arguing that Christ's doctrinal "conformity to tradition" initiated a systematic metaphysics that violates the infinite variety of natural creation. The Christian's "cut and dried" ideology is explicitly related to the American colonist's clearing of the wilderness. Thoreau's American Adam *plants* "the civil apple tree," whose "perfume" invades the wilderness: "Some spring the white man came, built him a house, and made a clearing here, letting in the sun, dried up a farm, piled up the old gray stones in fences, cut down the pines around his dwelling, planted orchard seeds brought from the old country, and persuaded the civil apple tree to blossom next to the wild pine and the juniper, shedding its perfume in the wilderness." Throughout the narrative, the apple tree functions as an emblem of this American fall. It is the tree against whose trunk the brains of Hannah Dustan's infant child are dashed by Indians and yet from which "many . . . in later times have lived to say that they have eaten of the fruit." Only at the very end of the voyage does the poet transform it back into "the wild apple-tree" to which the brothers may fasten their craft.

The corruption of the white colonists and the indiscriminate progress of the modern age compel Thoreau to substitute a spiritual frontier for the vanishing physical wilderness. History has generated a split between the spiritual and the actual that violates the wholeness of divine creation and signifies nineteenth-century Americans' falling away from their true being. The superficiality of Thoreau's generation is the result of the incapacity to relate apparent oppositions, to see the spiritual depth blossoming in the actual surface of things. Being is not merely concealed from man, but divided and fragmented by Thoreau's contemporaries themselves, who have purchased their own fall. The poet must be more than an inspired explorer who discovers what is present; the poet must also be a visionary who will redeem Being by restoring the active relation of surface and depth, time and eternity, the particular and the universal:

> The frontiers are not east or west, north or south, but wherever a man *fronts* a fact, though that fact be his neighbor, there is an unsettled wilderness between him and Canada, between him and the setting sun, or, farther still, between him and *it*. Let him build himself a log house with the bark on where he is, *fronting* IT, and wage there an old French war for seven or seventy years, with Indians and Rangers, or whatever else may come between him and the reality, and save his scalp if he can.

"Building" is dramatized in the language of the passive itself, which allows the unnameable Being ("IT") to be "fronted" through language. If direct participation in the language of nature is no longer possible for the fallen nineteenth-century American, Thoreau attempts to open a path homeward by reflecting on the nature of language.

The literary form of *A Week* appears to be modeled after the natural flow of the river journey. Thoreau seems to elide any basic distinction between writing and experience by elaborately developing the voyage as a metaphor for composition. I have already suggested how his brother's death disrupts the easy equation of literary form and natural order. But there is other evidence to indicate that the experience of the voyage is inadequate to capture the presence of Being. The ecstatic moment of transcendental vision atop Saddleback Mountain is interpolated into the narrative from a later excursion, which Thoreau had made to the Berkshires and Catskills in 1844. The addition is motivated by the writer's description of the morning mists that obscure the sunrise for the brothers in the opening paragraphs of "Tuesday": "Though we were enveloped in mist as usual, we trusted that there was a bright day behind it." Thoreau tells the Saddleback anecdote in order to demonstrate the limits of such "fogs," which in the given context must be taken figuratively for the obscurity in which we ordinarily live. Thoreau even playfully suggests that the narrative itself has been obscured by such fog: "As we cannot distinguish objects through this dense fog, let me tell this story more at length."

These contextual clues indicate the story's importance as a supplement to the voyage, which at this moment at least leaves the poet in obscurity rather than offering him clear vision. Once the solitary traveler has experienced "the gracious god" rising above fog and mists of temporal existence, he must descend Saddleback "in the region of cloud and drizzling rain." This emblematic reentrance into time provides an appropriate transition for the writer back to the original "Tuesday" morning: "But now we must make haste back before the fog disperse the blithe Merrimack water." Brought together in the poet's composition of *A Week,* the foggy morning in 1839 and the excursion to Saddleback in 1844 offer an integrated presentation of the relation of temporal illusion and obscurity to eternal reality and clarity. Yet, it is an eminently "literary" achievement, which Thoreau makes no effort to disguise. Nature may be sufficient unto itself, but Thoreau suggests here the need for a poetic composition that will allow us entrance into the complex structure of the natural order. The Saddleback episode argues against the ability of any immediate experience to bring the truth of nature into proximity with man.

The poetic form of *A Week* is also made explicit by the week that Thoreau deletes from his narrative of the 1839 voyage. This omission is especially significant because it occurs at the precise end of the outward voyage, at the moment when the literal and metaphorical origin of the rivers is anticipated. "Thus, in fair days as well as foul, we had traced up the river to which our native stream is a tributary, until from Merrimack it became the Pemigewasset that leaped by our side, and when we had passed its fountainhead, the Wild Amonoosuck, whose puny channel was crossed at a stride, guiding us toward its distant source among the mountains, at length, without its guidance, we were enabled to reach the summit of AGI-OCOCHOOK." The "fountainhead" is "crossed at a stride" and the "guidance" of the rivers is left behind as the travelers head for yet another "summit."

This casual reference to both the source of the rivers "among the mountains" and the summit of Agiocochook undercuts the relation between the actual and spiritual voyages Thoreau has developed so carefully in the preceding narrative. Whatever the brothers "discover" in the mountains is deleted from the text. One suspects that this is the same kind of temporal condensation to be found in the *Walden,* the single week offering a more unified structure for Thoreau's philosophic reflections and his parody of measured time. Historically, the second week's journey was conducted "alternately by foot and stage," which may have caused Thoreau to omit the week as disruptive of the purer and simpler fluvial excursion. These formal and biographical explanations are certainly acceptable enough to account for the deletion.

However, within the context of Thoreau's philosophic and poetic aims, this omission is as significant and literary as the interpretation of the Saddleback episode, which has attracted such extended critical attention. In fact, the content of the "Tuesday" vision may tell us something about Thoreau's reasons for omitting the significant approach to the origin in "Thursday." On Saddleback, the full vision of the sun-god at his fullest radiance is denied the lonely traveler:

> But, alas, owing, as I think, to some unworthiness in myself, my
> private sun did stain himself, and
> > "Anon permit the basest clouds to ride
> > With ugly wrack on his celestial face,"—
> for before the god had reached the zenith the heavenly pave-
> ment rose and embraced my wavering virtue, or rather I sank
> down again into that "forlorn world," from which the celestial
> sun had hid his visage.

In this passage the distinction between "my private sun" and the "celestial face" of the eternal god is caused by an "unworthiness" in the mortal who yearns for divine vision. Thoreau's "unworthiness" appears to be a conventional reference to his limited mortal capacity for apprehending the universal. Yet, in the preceding paragraph he offers a clue to a precise notion of this "stain" that obscures his vision. The dawn itself is a full, untranslatable presence: "As there was wanting the symbol, so there was not the substance of impurity, *no spot nor stain.* It was a favor for which to be forever silent to be shown this vision" (my italics). Thoreau is clearly incapable of remaining silent, however, especially during the literary moment in which he reconstructs his experience on the mountain. Purity is associated with the absence of symbolism in the spiritual "fact" of divine presence. Even so, such mystery can only be recaptured through language, and Thoreau offers a gaudy panoply of rhetorical figures and classical references to approximate his vision. He concludes such "unworthy" literary flights by qualifying what the reader has been allowed to see: "But my muse would fail to convey an impression of the gorgeous tapestry by which I was surrounded, such as men see faintly reflected afar off in the chambers of the east." The verbal effort to "front" the unspeakable purity of "IT" ends by dividing and obscuring its presence. Writing becomes an act of displacing the god in the very struggle to awaken us to his Being.

Thoreau's "unworthiness" in this moment need not, however, be taken as an indication of the essential inadequacy of language. His "stain" is caused by a particular mode of expression that distorts the true poeticality of nature and thus of language itself. William Bysshe Stein sees Thoreau's response to the vision on Saddleback as flawed by the style it employs: "Instead of responding spiritually to the sight, he affects an aesthetic enthusiasm, even as the trite verbal expression of his emotion implies. . . . The pedantry of a bookworm underscores the insincerity of the rapture." In fact, the dominant presence in Thoreau's account is not the concealed divinity arising to view, but the central "I" imposing its will on all that it sees. The moment of vision is transformed into a self-conscious paean: "As the light in the east steadily increased, it revealed to me more clearly the new world into which I had risen in the night, the new terra firma perchance of my future life." The "snowy pastures" spread out "all around beneath me," and the vain "I" sees divinity as a guarantee of immortality: "As I had climbed above storm and cloud, so by successive days' journeys I might reach the region of eternal day, beyond the tapering shadow of the earth." Thus, "*my private sun* did stain *himself*" marks the failure of such inauthenic poetizing. Because his muse failed, the traveler is condemned to return to the rain and mist surrounding the mountain.

Throughout *A Week* Thoreau insists on a poetry inspired by the divinity in nature and bearing the traces of the god. This is not a simple theory of inspiration, but a complex notion of the play between one's temporal being and the concealed immanence of the divine: "When the poet is most inspired, is stimulated by an *aura* which never even colors the afternoons of common men, then his talent is all gone, and he is no longer a poet. The gods do not grant him any skill more than another. They never put their gifts into his hands, but they encompass and sustain him with their breath." But what is the nature of such poetic saying? The effort of the poet to recollect the Saddleback experience fails when he attempts to transform the divine into his own private possession. Thoreau's "poetic description" is closely related to the technological impulse of the white colonial, who brings his fall into a New World:

> The white man comes, pale as the dawn, with a load of thought, with a slumbering intelligence as a fire raked up, knowing well what he knows, not guessing but calculating; . . . building a house that endures, a framed house. He buys the Indian's moccasins and baskets, then buys his hunting-grounds, and at length forgets where he is buried and ploughs up his bones. And here town records, old, tattered, time-worn, weather-stained chronicles, contain the Indian sachem's mark perchance, an arrow or a beaver, and the few fatal words by which he deeded his hunting grounds away. He comes with a list of ancient Saxon, Norman, and Celtic names, and strews them up and down this river.

Like the white man's "load of thought" and "framed house," his very "names" represent a desire to possess and control the wilderness. In a similar sense, the poet's insistence on naming the divine reflects his own participation in the original sin of the white settlers. True poetic saying ought to be that language in which the divine is made to abide in its own proper dwelling, not displaced either by the "commonsensical" truths of reason or the "egotistical sublime" of the vain poet.

The failure to recollect the full presence of the divine on Saddleback helps explain the omission of the week's journey to the source in the mountains. In his essays on Hölderlin, which investigate the proximity of poetry and thinking, Heidegger refers to the poetic "measure" whereby man is enabled to span the dimension of "the between of sky and earth": "Man exists as mortal. He is called mortal because he can die. To be able to die means: to be capable of death as death. Only man dies—and indeed continually, so long as he stays on this earth, so long as he dwells. His dwelling, however, rests in the poetic. Hölderlin sees the nature of the 'poetic' in taking of the measure by which the measure-taking of human being is accomplished."

For Heidegger, this measure is both an assertion of man's mortality and a way of thinking of that mortality as man's relation to Being. Poetry constitutes the difference whereby Being is disclosed as the Being of beings. It is a relation that allows Being to appear in its nature, rather than in the form of what we desire from or impose on it. And this nature is disclosed only as the concealment of Being, which is fundamental to the difference constituting Being and beings:

> The measure consists in the way in which the god who remains unknown, is revealed *as* such by the sky. God's appearance through the sky consists in a disclosing that lets us see what conceals itself, but lets us see it not by seeking to wrest what is concealed out of its concealedness, but only by guarding the concealed in its self-concealment. Thus the unknown god appears as the unknown by way of the sky's manifestness. This appearance is the measure against which man measures himself.

The language that insists on disclosure falsifies the nature of language for both Thoreau and Heidegger. The origin of the rivers (and thus the "goal" of the voyage) is not simply *omitted* from the narrative; the text itself becomes a way of disclosing the concealedness of the origin as its very nature. The authentic philosophic origin—Being-in-itself—is allowed to emerge only in the narrative of the journey itself, which preserves the mystery in the production of its signs.

The subsequent discussion of Thoreau's poetics will attempt to demonstrate that this apparently paradoxical manner of "fronting" Being is an essentially poetic activity. It is the aim of such poetry to open the way to an authentic human dwelling: the establishment of human being-in-common in the world. Perhaps this is why Thoreau selects the first stanza from George Herbert's "Vertue" to open the section immediately following the deferred week in "Thursday."

> Sweet days, so cool, so calm, so bright,
> The bridal of the earth and sky,
> Sweet dews shall weep thy fall to-night,
>   For thou must die.

Herbert's lament about the transcience of nature and its association with the inevitability of man's death effects the narrative entrance back into time. But the lines of the poem resonate with other associations in *A Week* to suggest a spiritualized human temporality that differs from the measured time of "common men" or meaningless seasonal repetition. The days are "sweet" because they are the "bridal of the earth and sky." And yet this marriage of earthly and divine is the result of the days' relation to the night. Thoreau's misquotations, "Sweet days" and "Sweet dews," are telling, because they make more explicit the subtler equation in Herbert's alliteration of "Sweet day" with "The dew." The metaphysical pun "to-night" and "to [unto] night" suggests how the dews fulfill their nature by bringing the "days" into relation to the night. The concealed divine, in the form of the night, brings the nature of the day into its own by virtue of the divine's self-concealedness. Time and nature are made "bright" by the measure that relates them to their own temporality. Herbert's "Vertue" minimizes the emphasis I have placed on "day[s]" by adding stanzas concerning the same evanescence in the "Sweet rose" and "Sweet spring," only to end with lines that superficially would seem more appropriate for the conventional interpretation of Thoreau's transcendentalism:

> Onely a sweet and vertuous soul,
> Like season'd timber, never gives;
> But though the whole world turn to coal,
>   Then chiefly lives.

The origin in the mountains is displaced by the poetic voyage itself, whose source is to be discovered in this ever-renewed "fronting" of time and eternity, beings and Being, being in the world and death. My emphasis on these lines from Herbert would be excessive were it not that they are so clearly associated with Thoreau's own conception of spiritual voyaging. One recalls that the brothers' boat has been artfully constructed with an eye to "The bridal of the earth and sky." It is "painted green below, with a border of blue, with reference to the two elements in which it was to spend its existence." As Thoreau interprets such iconography: "If rightly made, a boat would be a sort of amphibious animal, a creature of two elements, related by one half its structure to some swift and shapely fish, and by the other to some strong-winged and graceful bird." Yet, this boat is merely a painted symbol, whose true "art is all . . . but the wood." The vehicle of spiritual voyaging—of human dwelling in time—is what the paint only crudely represents: the poetry of being that is the essential subject of the writer's journey. Perhaps this conjunction of voyaging and dwelling, transcience and endurance, openness and concealment is closer to the true architecture of the "House Beautiful" Thoreau had built in his dreams at Walden.

In both *A Week* and *Walden*, "wildness" is the word Thoreau uses to indicate the unnameable in nature that the modern American has forgotten. Critics frequently refer to the "wild" as the element of nature's potential energy: the possibility of regeneration and transformation. This inner-structuring principle of nature cannot be itself measured or named; it is the presence of the divine which is forever absent, like the elusive loon in *Walden*. In *A Week* the Indian epitomizes the individual who can dwell by "fronting" this wildness, and thus it is the life of the Indian that gives us some further hint of the nature of poetry. When Thoreau writes that "gardening is civil and social, but it wants the vigor and freedom of the forest and the outlaw," there seems to be a clear distinction between the conventional polarities of city and frontier, form and openness, law and freedom. But these oppositions are resolved in the Indian's mode of being, itself an "intercourse with Nature": "We would not always be soothing and taming nature, breaking the horse and the ox, but sometimes ride the horse wild and chase the buffalo. The Indian's intercourse with Nature is at least such as admits of the greatest independence of each. If he is somewhat of a stranger in her midst, the gardener is too much of a familiar."

The savage is not closer to nature in a conventional Romantic sense, but rather is "somewhat of a stranger." I am reminded of how Thoreau's familiarity with the divine on Saddleback quickly turned into a desire for possession. Instead, the Indian or the poet participates in nature by virtue of a certain strangeness, which is in the nature of each person's relation to Being as the disclosure of what is concealed *as* concealment. This reciprocal difference—self-recognition through strangeness—is what makes possible being-in-common and human dwelling. It is not alienation in an existential sense, but an "intercourse" that "admits of the greatest independence of each." In such a manner man "fronts" his own strangeness as the measure of his relation to the "wildness" of Being. What appears to be a polar opposition ought to be considered the ontological difference (in the Heideggerean terms I have employed) in which man takes up his poetic vocation on earth. True poetry speaks endlessly this difference, because it is the enduring saying of the measure taking of being human.

Most would agree that for Thoreau history is not the mere crudity of what happened, but the natural emergence and evolution of Being. It would seem to be a simple step to assert that Being in its essence is its "coming into being," but much is lost by such shortcuts of thought. Being is what endures in its own withholding and is disclosed as such by thinking. *Understanding* as the "possession" of Being in ideas or words is a falsification, indeed *the* violation perpetuated by "white men" and their Christian theology. In *A Week* Thoreau searches the classics in an effort to retrieve the original wholeness of the relation of Being and beings, Being and thought, as the essence of history:

> The fable, which is naturally and truly composed, so as to satisfy the imagination ere it addresses the understanding, beautiful though strange as a wildflower, is to the wise man an apothegm and admits of his most generous interpretation. When we read that Bacchus made the Tyrrhenian mariners mad, so

that they leapt into the sea, mistaking it for a meadow full of flowers, and so became dolphins, we are not concerned about the historical truth of this, but rather a higher poetical truth. We seem to hear the music of a thought, and care not if the understanding be not gratified.

The fable makes possible a thinking prior to ordinary cognition, a thinking that is able to step outside the concern for understanding "literal" distinctions. By establishing a primary relationship between Being and thinking, *mythus* (of which fable is but a part) is the authentic saying: the opening of the way to the conversation of Being among men.

Heidegger puts the problem in the following terms in "Hölderlin and the Essence of Poetry": "The poet himself stands between the former—the gods, and the latter—the people. He is one who has been cast out—out into that *Between,* between gods and men. But only and for the first time in this Between is it decided, who man is and where he is settling his existence. 'Poetically, dwells man on this earth.' " As I have already suggested, this is not simply "mediation" but what I have chosen to call "fronting," which in Thoreau's own usage retains the sense of the frontier. For Heidegger, this is the place of *emergence* of the measure of the between of earth and sky, of Being and beings in the world. Thoreau's conception of *mythus* establishes a similar site for human dwelling:

> The hidden significance of these fables which is sometimes thought to have been detected, the ethics running parallel to the poetry and history, are not so remarkable as the readiness with which they may be made to express a variety of truths. As if they were the skeletons of still older and more universal truths than any whose flesh and blood they are for the time made to wear. It is like striving to make the sun, or the wind, or the sea symbols to signify exclusively the particular thoughts and dreams of men as its hieroglyphics to address men unborn. In the history of the human mind these glowing and ruddy fables precede the noonday thoughts of men, as Aurora the sun's rays. The matutine intellect of the poet, keeping in advance of the glare of philosophy always dwells in this auroral atmosphere.

Mythus, "authentic poetry," is itself the facilitation of the language of Being, not a mere symbolic product or representation. *Mythus* endures only through change and transformation, by the perpetual renewal of the reciprocal difference that makes the project of human dwelling possible and necessary. An "ancient fable" achieves its "completeness and roundness" only by means of a ceaseless history of interpretation, in itself the essence of the historical situation of one's being as temporal:

> By such slow aggregation has mythology grown from the first. The very nursery takes of this generation were the nursery tales of primeval races. They migrate from east to west, and again from west to east; now expanded into the "tale divine" of bards, now shrunk into a popular rhyme. This is an approach to that universal language which men have sought in vain. This fond reiteration of the oldest expressions of truth by the latest posterity, content with slightly and religiously retouching the old material, is the most impressive proof of a common humanity.

Thoreau underscores the transcience of contemporary values by suggesting how mythology endures through diverse migrations and cultural appropriations. If ancient poetry has "now shrunk into a popular rhyme," it reflects the destitution of our age. But Thoreau's characteristic verbal play implies a rebirth in the "nursery" that would bring about the "popularity" of true poetic saying as that which relates the social self to being. In this way poetry informs the ontological movement of beings in time as historical. This process suggests that the realization of *mythus* is the project of human dwelling on earth, the realization of being with others, not only the "proof" but the *constitution* of a "common humanity." Poetry as an entrance into man's being in time establishes the foundation on which Thoreau bases his subsequent attacks on the expectations of "common men" for "heaven": "What is this heaven which they expect, if it is no better than they expect? Are they prepared for a better than they can now imagine? Where is the heaven of him who dies on a stage, in a theatre? Here or nowhere is our heaven."

"We have need to be earth-born as well as heaven-born, γηγενεις, as was said of the Titans of old, or in a sense than they," Thoreau warns those who long for an eternal life out of time. And this "earth we till and love" is more truly cultivated through our "music," which allows us to constitute ourselves as other than the mere animal: "With our music we would fain challenge transiently another and finer sort of intercourse than our daily toil permits. The strains come back to us amended in the echo, as when a friend reads our verse. Why have they so painted the fruits, and freighted them with such fragrance as to satisfy a more than animal appetite?" This is a remarkable passage, bringing together poetry and friendship as well as suggesting a contradiction of Thoreau's earlier remarks about the inferiority of word to deed. Such epigrammatic saws as "A sentence should read as if its author, had he held a plough instead of a pen, could have drawn a furrow straight and deep to the end" seem to imply that writing is a mere representation of what could have been more authentically lived. Yet, the distinction between the immediacy of experience and the secondary mediation of words is part of the modern fall—the misinterpretation of Being and beings—that Thoreau has outlined in *A Week*. "The poet sings how the blood flows in his veins" is neither metaphorical nor representational, but a saying that is simultaneous with human action. Authentic poetry *is* action, in itself what constitutes action as such. Modern "civilization" has degraded the Muse:

> We cannot escape the impression that the Muse has stooped a little in her flight, when we come to the literature of civilized eras. Now first we hear of various ages and styles of poetry; it is pastoral, and lyric, and narrative, and didactic; but the poetry of runic monuments is of one style, and for every age. The bard has in great measure lost the dignity and sacredness of his office. Formerly he was called a *seer,* but now it is thought that one man sees as much as another. He has no longer the bardic rage, and only conceives the deed, which he formerly stood ready to perform.

For both Heidegger and Thoreau, the divorce of word and deed is the subject of the true poet in "a destitute time." It is a separation that points toward a fundamental violence: the distinction between Being (*physis*) and thinking (*logos*) that is the target of Heidegger's destruction of Western metaphysics and Thoreau's more modest criticism of civilization and its discontents. Heidegger's attempt to recapture the original pre-Socratic meaning of the identity-in-difference of *physis* and *logos* has some remarkable affinities with the poetics outlined in *A Week*. In his analysis of the thought of Heraclitus and Parmenides, Heidegger attempts to restore the original bond between these two aspects of Being. In this originary sense, *physis* is the Being of nature as unfolding and emergence:

> *Physis* as emergence can be observed everywhere, e.g. in celestial phenomena (the rising of the sun), in the rolling of the sea, in the growth of the plants, in the coming forth of man and animal from the womb. But *physis,* the realm of that which arises, is not synonymous with these phenomena, which today we regard as part of "nature." This opening up and inward-jutting-

beyond-itself [in-sich-aus-sich-hinaus-stehen] must not be taken as a process among other processes that we observe in the realm of the essent. *Physis* is being itself, by virtue of which essents become and remain observable. . . .

. . . *Physis* means the power that emerges and the enduring realm under its sway. This power of emerging and enduring includes "becoming" as well as "being" in the restricted sense of inert duration. *Physis* is the process of a-rising, of emerging from the hidden, whereby the hidden is first made to stand.

Heidegger speaks of *physis* as "scattering" and "opening" in order to establish a functional relationship with *logos* as "gathering" and "bringing together," but only "in the sense of 'permanent gathering.' " Interpreted subsequently as "thinking," "word," "logic," "meaning," *logos* gradually drifted apart from its originary bond with *physis:* "In thus maintaining a bond, the *logos* has the character of permeating power, of *physis.* It does not let what it holds in its power dissolve into an empty freedom from opposition, but by uniting the opposites maintains the full sharpness of their tension." The reciprocal difference of *physis* and *logos* is falsified by substituting such terms as "object" and "subject," "nature" and "mind." Their originary bond depends upon the permeation of *physis* and *logos,* each of which finds its power in and through the other.

The conventional formulation of Thoreau's transcendentalism depends upon polarities—subject and object, individual and nature, time and eternity—that lead to the critical conclusion that "he is not a writer with settled or comfortable views but one committed to forcing together opposites in the hope they will mesh." Much of our literary criticism still relies on the traditional distinction between immediate experience and its secondary representation. In this view, any system of signs operates only in reference to a prior "reality": an object or event. In the originary sense that links *physis* and *logos,* however, action and word are integrally bound together. The event does not precede its representation, but is constituted as event only through the signs that situate the event in time. Writing about Sir Walter Raleigh, Thoreau remarks:

The word which is best said came nearest to not being spoken at all, for it is cousin to a deed which the speaker could have better done. Nay, almost it must have taken the place of a deed by some urgent necessity, even by some misfortune, so that the truest writer will be some captive knight, after all. And perhaps the fates had such a design, when, having stored Raleigh so

richly with the substance of life and experience, they made him
a fast prisoner, and compelled him to make his words his deeds,
and transfer to his expression the emphasis and sincerity of his
action.

Raleigh's natural and fluent style opened the possibility of a "new
world" of poetic dwelling, which ironically did not flower in the American
colony he never visited. When Thoreau refers to "some urgent necessity,
even some misfortune" by which one is compelled to substitute words for
deeds, he implies a more fundamental imprisonment than Raleigh's political captivity. He recalls the destitute time of America's origin, when the
white man arrived without the poetic vision of Raleigh. The transient and
ephemeral events of American history have not been constituted by that
poetry of being which "contains only enduring and essential truth." The
culture that distinguishes poet and hero, word and deed, undermines its
own history. Raleigh stands as the lost figure of the true New World discoverer, whose bonding of experience and word might have restored the
"new beginning," the "origin," violated by the actual white settlers long
before their arrival: "There have been some nations who could do nothing
but construct tombs, and these are the only traces which they have left.
They are the heathen."

A Week is an attempt to think poetically and thus retrieve this lost
origin: the ontological bond of man and nature, time and eternity, being
in the world and Being. The apparently discursive form of the work is designed to call forth this identity-in-difference that is approximated in Heidegger's interpretation of the pre-Socratic understanding of Being as physis
and logos. In its effort to come to terms with the fact of John Thoreau's
death, A Week both reflects upon and employs a poetry that opens the
possibility of a true dwelling on earth. Poetry discloses man's destitution
in order to "put him on the way" to the being of language: the language
of being. Attempts to analyze the unity of A Week are inevitably restricted
by the Western philosophic heritage that Thoreau attacks in this work.
"Examine your authority," Thoreau insists, "you did not invent it; it was
imposed on you. . . . Your scheme must be the framework of the universe;
all other schemes will soon be ruins." Do we imagine that our naive categories of thought could lead to anything but contradiction, confusion, and
paradox? We have lacked deliberate method all along.

In his introduction to the Rinehart edition of A Week, Walter Harding
casually remarks the diversity of subjects incorporated into the work:
"Thus he introduces into the text essays on fables, the Christian religion,

poetry, Sir Walter Raleigh, reform movements, history, friendship, Aulus Persius Flaccus, Goethe, cattle shows, and Chaucer, to name only a few of the more important ones. Each of these essays is basically independent and can stand alone."

Harding's list offers an appropriate contemporary example of what Thoreau argues the "modern" has done to the harmony of classical thought. I have already demonstrated how Thoreau's subversion of Christian theology opens the way for an originary poetry or *mythus* that might constitute our being in time. I have insisted with Thoreau that *mythus* is the inauguration of history in its nature, not merely the record of isolated events. The call for a renewed poetic saying is particularly urgent for Thoreau, who finds himself in an alienated time that has been created by modern American society. Mythology, Christianity, poetry, history, social reform, and friendship: these are the generic topics of Harding's list. They all have their places—are "situated"—in Thoreau's poetic thinking. "Friendship" alone remains to be accounted for, and it adds a final support to Thoreau's dynamic structuring of a "hypaethral" dwelling: "I thought that one peculiarity of my 'Week' was its hypaethral character, to use an epithet applied to those Egyptian temples which are open to the heavens above, under the ether. . . . I trust it does not smell so much of the study and library, even of the poet's attic, as of the fields and woods, that it is a hypaethral or unroofed book, lying open under the ether, and permeated by it, open to all weathers, not easy to be kept on a shelf."

Thoreau's discussion of friendship in "Wednesday" seems self-evident in terms of the conventional interpretation of his Transcendentalism: true friendship is a simulacrum of the Ideal for which human beings yearn. The relation of the brothers on the voyage is a microcosm of the social communality Thoreau desires. And yet, for many critics this episode remains one of the most troubling in his writings, betraying as it does an underlying anxiety concerning the transience of human relations and the inability of the individual to discover an enduring relation with others. A certain nostalgia and sense of loss dominate this section, and the importance of John's death as a controlling concern cannot be overemphasized. When Thoreau writes that "friendship is evanescent in every man's experience, and remembered like heat lightning in past summers," one senses that Thoreau's own identity has been threatened by his brother's absence.

What is most remarkable, however, is the extent to which friendship is related to the ideals of poetry discussed in the rest of the volume. Thoreau makes little attempt to relate friendship and poetry directly; in fact, there seems to be far less analysis of interpersonal communication than we might expect on such a subject. Emerson's "Friendship," however, does repeatedly stress the relation between poetry and friendship: "We seek our friend not sacredly, but with an adulterate passion which would appropriate him to ourselves. In vain. We are armed all over with subtle antagonisms, which, soon as we meet, begin to play, and translate all poetry into stale prose." Emerson stresses the ideal self-consciousness that is merely shadowed in the temporal friend: "Thou art not Being, as Truth is, as Justice is,—thou art not my soul, but a picture and effigy of that." Thoreau suggests that it is the longing for the Ideal that may corrupt authentic friendship, just as it had perverted his "poetry" on Saddleback: "When they say farewell, then indeed we begin to keep them company. How often we find ourselves turning our backs on our actual Friends, that we may go and meet their ideal cousins. I would that I were worthy to be any man's Friend."

In my analysis of Thoreau's poetics, I have argued that human dwelling depends upon the interdependence of *physis* and *logos,* the constitution of Being in and through the poetic saying of beings. Unlike *Walden,* the text of *A Week* is not merely a metaphor for a fuller, more immediate experience of the divine, but the "bringing-into-being" of the nature of such experience. The endurance of friendship shares this recollective or cognitive quality, for the words of love may be "few and rare indeed, but, like a strain of music, they are incessantly repeated and modulated by the memory." The truly universal friendship enters *mythus,* revealing and completing itself only in its temporal transformations. The "presence of loss" is a necessary aspect of the path that leads to an understanding of the essence of friendship; only in this way is the friend constituted as friend. Evanescence is not so much transcended as *related* to the enduring and universal aspects of human interrelation. In a curious monologue addressed to a hypothetical friend, Thoreau insists: "I love thee not as something private and personal, which is *your own,* but as something universal and worthy of love, *which I have found.* . . . I did not think that humanity was so rich. Give me an opportunity to live." Thoreau appears to establish a hierarchy of ideal love and secular friendship in the manner of Emerson, but he continues in the following way: "You are the fact in a fiction, you are the truth more strange and admirable than fiction. Consent only to be what you are. I alone will never stand in your way." The "fiction" refers to the desired ideal, which appears to be realized as a possibility through the "fact" of the secular friend, which revises the Emersonian apothegm: "Friends such as we desire are dreams and fables."

In this context we may recall the prose that prefaces "The Atlantides" in *A Week:* "The Friend is some fair floating isle of palms eluding the mariner in Pacific seas. Many are the dangers to be encountered, equinoctial gales and coral reefs, ere he may sail before the constant trades. But who would not sail through mutiny and storm, even over Atlantic waves, to reach the fabulous retreating shores of some continent man?" The quest may be governed by a transcendental ideal, but it is finally man in time who is the goal of such a journey. Thoreau recognizes that the elusive fiction of ideal friendship may be constructed only on the basis of human differences, which are essential to being in the world itself: "We must accept or refuse one another as we are. I could tame a hyena more easily than my Friend. He is a material no tool of mine will work."

This is more than a simple assertion of the radical individualism that Emerson reaffirms at the end of his essay: "I do then with my friends as I do with my books. I would have them where I can find them, but I seldom use them." The friend points toward the divine by virtue of his own self-preservation, thus disclosing the ground of human dwelling as the difference between Being and beings in the world and also between being and being. Like the poet who would appropriate the divine as a guarantee of his own identity or the white settlers who subordinate natural wildness to their Anglo-Saxon names, we violate our friends if we attempt to make them our property. In this regard, Thoreau does agree with Emerson, who writes, "Leave to girls and boys to regard a friend as property, and to suck a short and all-confounding pleasure, instead of the noblest benefit."

The ontological implications of friendship are constantly emphasized. As we have seen, ordinary language may suffice for the exchange of news or goods, but only poetry speaks of our spiritual situation in time. The ratio holds as well for mere neighbors and true friends: "We do not wish for Friends to feed and clothe our bodies,—neighbors are kind enough for that,—but to do the like office to our spirits." Like poetic saying, the language of friendship is universal to the extent that it makes individuality possible. The friend expresses the truth of man's being in the divine love that springs from human difference: "To his Friend a man's peculiar character appears in every feature and in every action, and it is thus drawn out and improved by him." Only by understanding this pervasive notion of "identity-in-difference" as the ontological basis of Thoreau's poetics may we begin to resolve the apparent contradictions in *A Week*. Critics have been too hasty in leaping to the conclusion of the essay on friendship to quote: "My Friend is not of some other race or family of men, but flesh of my flesh, bone of my bone. He is my real brother. I see his nature groping yonder like mine. We do not live far apart." This vision of human dwelling in common has been achieved poetically by the entire discourse on friendship. "Brotherhood" springs from the recognition of differences and the necessity of our social condition. Thoreau realizes in this essay the full implications of what Emerson had termed "a sort of paradox in nature": "I who alone am, I who see nothing in nature whose existence I can affirm with equal evidence to my own, behold now the semblance of my being, in all its height, variety and curiosity, reiterated in a foreign form."

As most commentators have noticed, the essay on friendship prefigures the more general social vision of *Walden*. Emerson privileges the "law of *one to one*" as the basis of a transcendental poetic, which seems to be at odds with social intercourse: "The high freedom of great conversation . . . requires an absolute running of two souls into one." By stressing the difference of self and other as the principle of friendship. Thoreau makes a more viable connection between brotherhood and wider social relations. The ideal of brotherly love achieved at the end of this digression is not merely a representation of the natural relation of John and Henry during the voyage, but a more enduring constitution of what eludes us in ordinary experience. *A Week* returns us to time by means of a journey into poetry, the language of which is itself a reflection on the nature of language and the social intercourse in initiates.

Walden mocks measured time by finding the signs of divinity in all seasons, in every weather. *A Week* demonstrates how Thoreau struggles not to transcend the temporal but to enter it more authentically than either clocks or unreflective experience allow. *A Week* is a way of thinking the being of poetry as the poetry of being. The experience of nature—of human nature, of nature in itself—is always on the way to language, to the poetic saying that constitutes it as human history. Much of this seems lacking in *Walden;* Thoreau seems to give up the reflection on language that organizes *A Week* for a more immediate dialogue with the sound of nature.

I have already suggested how *Walden* appears to suffer from the same dualistic mentality that is the source of modern alienation for the poet of *A Week*. Perhaps the failure of *A Week* made Thoreau impatient for clarity and understanding, and he sought a form and order that would permit his readers to see in more accustomed ways. Yet, such accommodation has its inevitable costs, and Thoreau has paid richly as the prophet of posters, the politician's poet, the soothsayer. The "rambling," "discursive," "disjointed," "contradictory" qualities of *A Week* tell us more about our criticism, our culture, and our language than they express the truth of Thoreau. What Heidegger says of Hölderlin's timeliness seems equally appropriate for the poet of *A Week on the Concord and Merrimack Rivers:* "It would thus be mistaken to believe that Hölderlin's time will come only on that day when 'everyman' will understand his poetry. It will never arrive in such a misshapen way; for it is its own destitution that endows the era with forces by which, unaware of what it is doing, it keeps Hölderlin's poetry from becoming timely."

BARRY WOOD

Thoreau's Narrative Art
in "Civil Disobedience"

Over thirty years ago Stanley Edgar Hyman wrote an essay called "Henry Thoreau in Our Time" which has since become a landmark study. "The first thing we should insist on," he wrote "is that Thoreau was a writer. . . . At his best Thoreau wrote the only really first-rate prose ever written by an American, with the possible exception of Abraham Lincoln. . . . [Thoreau was] a writer in the great stream of the American tradition, the mythic and nonrealist writers, Hawthorne and Melville, Twain and James, and, in our day . . . Hemingway and Faulkner" Along with F. O. Matthiessen's *American Renaissance* (1941) with its similar stress on Thoreau as artist and writer, Hyman's essay provided the direction for criticism in the following three decades: first in the study of *Walden* but more recently with the early excursions and *A Week on the Concord and Merrimack Rivers,* Hyman also pointed to Thoreau's most famous political essay to stress the literary Thoreau and made a crucial but largely ignored distinction: "As a political warrior, Thoreau was a comic little figure with a receding chin, and not enough high style to carry off a gesture. As a political writer, he was the most ringing and magnificent polemicist America has ever produced. Three years later he made an essay called 'Civil Disobedience' out of his prison experience, fusing the soft coal of his night in jail into solid diamond." No one has applied this emphasis on Thoreau's literary art to "Civil Disobedience"; at the same time, the exaggerated efforts to find a workable plan of political action from it have

From *Philological Quarterly* 60, no. 1 (Winter 1981). © 1982 by the University of Iowa.

not met with more than temporary approval. As Lawrence Bowling has said, writing about his social criticism: "Most of Thoreau's critics have advanced only as far as the discovery that he was not a great thinker and have not arrived at the realization that he made his major contribution in the realm of art."

The enormous influence of "Civil Disobedience," not only on thinkers like Tolstoy and Gandhi but also on the British Labor Movement and American life generally, is well known. Combined with a few other Thoreau essays—"Slavery in Massachusetts," "A Plea for Captain John Brown," and perhaps the "Economy" chapter of *Walden*—it has inspired commentary so extensive that a recent book appeared devoted solely to "Thoreau's political reputation in America." Yet the single-minded emphasis in commentary on "Civil Disobedience" to the political rather than the artistic suggests a virtual blind spot even among the most sensitive critics, while at the same time revealing more about the shifting political attitudes in our time than Thoreau's. The fact is that Thoreau's reputation (in other areas too, not simply political) is out of all proportion to the ideas he sets forth, or even to the experiences upon which these ideas are hung. He was not the first to live in a cabin by a pond near Concord, nor the first to travel in New Hampshire, Cape Code, or the Maine Woods, nor even the first to climb Wachusett, Saddleback, or Ktaadn. Before Thoreau withheld his poll tax Bronson Alcott had done the same. Even the ideas of "Civil Disobedience" had important forerunners: Emerson's "Politics" and Paley's *Moral and Political Philosophy* for instance. What accounts for Thoreau's influence, lies elsewhere—in the artistic power of his work and the sense of drama running through all his writings. In the major works this sense of drama approaches what Hyman calls "a vast rebirth ritual," but everywhere we find the use of a sustained narrative thread which leads the reader forward in anticipation of discovery. The speaking "I" is always present, as Thoreau himself notes with no apologies on the first page of *Walden,* and this leads to a mode of writing which demonstrates discovery, the achievement of perspective, the awakening of vision, and spiritual renewal. Whatever ideas appear are enfolded in a story, so much so that the narrative structure is often the key to the ideas.

If the narrative elements of Thoreau's writers have not been stressed, neither have they been missed. The relations between the works and specific events, excursions, or sojourns in Thoreau's life are well known. But these facts are often passed over as a biographical element less interesting than the presumed "message" being developed. Such an omission ignores what the narrative ordering of the work actually *accomplishes* in the unfolding and development of the ideas. In the case of "Civil Disobedience" it has not yet been shown how narrative order operates as a synthesizing device for the reconciliation of the two realms of experience—the real and the transcendent. I imagine that Thoreau is more generally linked with Emerson than Melville among writers of his time, but some perspective is gained by comparing him with both. Emerson typically engineered his transcendental philosophy through symbolism by using Nature as a "vehicle of thought" or a "symbol of spirit"; that is, he demonstrated that man lives simultaneously in two worlds which are joined in moments of "exhiliration" or, at times of creativity, when the scholar becomes Man Thinking or the poet becomes a "liberating god." Melville accomplished the same linkage of two worlds through his voyages during which his Tajis and Ishmaels find themselves literally travelling across the boundary from the real world into the transcendental. Symbol in Emerson and narrative in Melville both have a synthesizing capacity. Thoreau stands, as it were, midway: we find in him the same duality of worlds and we find him using both symbolism and narrative journeys to give a single account a double reference.

In "Civil Disobedience" there appear to be two rather different centers of interest. One derives from the political ideas set forth about which so much has been written. The other focuses on the story of Thoreau's night in jail, probably July 23 or 24, 1846. Reference to this story is made obliquely in *A Week,* but the version occurring later, in *Walden,* provides a fuller account:

> One afternoon, near the end of the first summer, when I went to the village to get a shoe from the cobbler's, I was seized and put into jail, because, as I have elsewhere related, I did not pay a tax to, or recognize the authority of, the state which buys and sells men, women, and children, like cattle at the door of its senate-house. I had gone down to the woods for other purposes. But, wherever a man goes, men will pursue and paw him with their dirty institutions, and, if they can, constrain him to belong to their desperate odd-fellow society. It is true, I might have resisted forcibly with more or less effect, might have run "amok" against society; but I preferred that society should run "amok" against me, it being the desperate party. However, I was released the next day, obtained my mended shoe, and returned to the woods in season to get my dinner of huckleberries on Fair-Haven Hill.

In "Civil Disobedience" this rather undramatic event is given considerable narrative scope, especially in the central paragraphs which are properly separated and set in reduced type in authoritative editions. This narrative effectively divides the essay into three parts. There is, in the two flanking sections, an important tonal difference, suggesting that the central narrative is operating as a bridge between the two sections of philosophical argument.

Thoreau says of his night in jail that "it was like travelling into a far country, such as I had never expected to behold, to lie there for one night. . . . It was to see my native village in the light of the middle ages, and our Concord [River] was turned into a Rhine stream, and visions of knights and castles passed before me." This vision of "a far country" and "a long journey," with imagery from Europe and the middle ages, is completed, as in the *Walden* account, by Thoreau's retreat from the village and ascent of "one of our highest hills, two miles off." Embedded in this account is a series of contrasts: most obviously, the village world of Concord and the natural world beyond it where the narrative begins and ends; the darkness of the night spent in jail and the sunlight of the days preceding and following it; the "medieval" quality of the Concord scene and the immediacy and spontaneity of the huckleberrying party moving up the high hill. The narrative movement—from the natural world into the village and back to the natural—sets forth in dramatic terms the dialectical progress of the larger essay: contrasts in the narrative suggest the contrasting views of the State set forth in the first and third sections; and the movement through the narrative middle, like Thoreau's own movement through the night in the Concord jail, provides a "before" and "after" polarity basic to the political idea of the essay. What *is* is seen against what *could be*. Indeed, if the Transcendentalist is understood as attempting to see *this* world in terms of *another*, the *real* as against the *ideal*, then the narrative center of "Civil Disobedience" can be seen as a powerful rhetorical strategy for linking the two views of the State. The narrative journey from one view to another, from one realm to another, makes possible a synthesis of the two in a higher third.

That Thoreau is operating within a polar view of things is everywhere apparent; it is part of his Transcendentalist heritage. In the first part of the essay his criticism of "standing government" links the ruling mechanism in America with "tradition . . . endeavoring to transmit itself unimpaired to posterity"; this is contrasted with the "vitality and force of a single living man." Here again is the Emersonian dilemma posed in the opening lines of *Nature*—the "retrospective" quality of American life with men desperately in need of their own "original relation to the universe"—recast in political terms. Repeatedly this dichotomy is observed: government is opposed by "character"; legislators with their tariff restrictions are contrasted with the "bounce" of a trade and commerce made of India rubber (a good example of what Bowling calls "social criticism as poetry"); government by "majority" is opposed by government by "conscience"; law is contrasted with "right"; machines are balanced by "men"; and the persistence of slavery in "a nation which has undertaken to be the refuge of liberty" is cited as grounds for "honest men to rebel and revolutionize." In Thoreau's view, the ideal possibilities of democracy are not realized because of "the opponents to a reform . . . who are more interested in commerce and agriculture than they are in humanity."

As Thoreau describes it, American life is full of contradictions and American policy is inconsistent with its stated values. Moreover, no *political* solution can eliminate these problems. At best a democratic society resorts to the vote—an artificial procedure for deciding who shall have their say by reducing right to might. The divisive tensions of society are thus left unresolved, precisely because "voting *for the right* is *doing* nothing for it." Doing *something* means, for Thoreau, resolving the polarities through action which carries dichotomies to a new level where they can be synthesized in a higher unity. "Action from principle,—the perception and the performance of right,—changes things and relations; it is essentially revolutionary." *Revolutionary:* the word is perfectly chosen, for it suggests that real action transfers political contradictions from the social world of stalemate to the cyclical, organic world of new creation. Here natural law, or what Thoreau terms "higher law," functions to resolve contradictions. Exactly this kind of organic resolution appears in Thoreau's final remarks before he describes his night in jail:

> I perceive that, when an acorn and a chestnut fall side by side, the one does not remain inert to make way for the other, but both obey their own laws, and spring and grow and flourish as best they can, till one, perchance, overshadows and destroys the other. If a plant cannot live according to its nature, it dies; and so a man.

The first long section of "Civil Disobedience" thus describes in symptomatic terms the basic problems of American political life, and sets a course for their solution. Tensions and polarities, Thoreau feels, may be overcome by "action from principle"; and the notion of *action* thus leads directly into Thoreau's account of his own actions. His narrative, then, is clearly the beginning of a process which will lead from the problematic politics described to the idealized vision at the end of the essay. Thoreau's action, of course, was that of not paying his poll tax, an act of resistance to civil government.

What the central narrative accomplishes is a transformation of the basic political dichotomies into a more dramatic form. The true nature of these dichotomies is rooted out, for Thoreau's actions force the State to make clear its generally unstated view of the truly self-reliant man. As Thoreau details his night in jail it becomes clear that physical incarceration is, short of capital punishment, the closest thing to death that the State can manage. Thoreau sees that the State's answer to opposition is tantamount to murder, as his imagery reveals. Thus, while he is literally put *in* jail, figuratively he is put well *below* the realm of ordinary society in a place of wood, stone, and iron where he says the window gratings "strained the light." The night spent in the dark cell, described as a journey into a far country, parallels Dante's night spent in a dark wood in canto 1 of *The Inferno* which was figuratively *his* journey into the far country of hell. Thoreau's night, like Dante's, is followed by an emergence at dawn and a renewed vision of the world. The night in prison is thus cast as a kind of mythic descent: Thoreau's remarks about the shedding and flowing of blood through the Mexican War—"I see this blood flowing now"—recall Dante's imagery of Phlegethon; and the view from his cell, leading him to "a closer view of my native town. I was fairly inside of it," suggests a descent into the belly of Leviathan so prominent in medieval mythology and iconography. Here indeed is Piers Plowman's harrowing of hell transferred to New England soil. Thoreau's descent, symbolically cast as a journey into death and hell, gives rise to a vision of his native town and the Concord River as locked in a kind of hellish death—ossified in a Massachusetts version of the middle ages, yet as unsubstantial as the old world "Rhine stream" into which it seems to turn as he looks on. This vision of death is followed by a symbolic rebirth at dawn when Thoreau is released from prison. Not only does he experience "a change" in his vision but he comes out of the darkness of his cell to ascend a hill, paralleling again Dante's ascent of Mount Purgatory in his climb toward the final haven of the *Paradiso*. That the hill Thoreau climbs is not only "one of our highest" but also named Fair-Haven completes the pattern of spiritual rebirth.

The narrative center of "Civil Disobedience," then, is more than a piece of biography thrown in the midst of a primarily political essay. It is instead the key to the dual vision of the essay. The entire section of the essay preceding the narrative middle is an expansion of that night's vision of death. From this very low level, symbolically entombed, the individual is bound to experience life in the State as a series of contradictions whose precise meaning is death for the moral and spiritual man. The journey through death followed by emergence and ascent effects a narrative synthesis: political contradictions are metaphorically carried up Fair-Haven Hill from which point a new perspective is gained, leading to the resolution of these contradictions in a "higher" view.

The third part of "Civil Disobedience," like the first, may be seen as an expansion of the central narrative, this time of his changed vision from Fair-Haven Hill. In place of the polarized world of the present (and past) America, Thoreau sets forth the "really free and enlightened State" he imagines for the future: a fusion of the individual and the State into mutual service. Here the individual will not be powerless, dominated by the "overwhelming brute force" of millions; instead the State will come to "recognize the individual as a higher and independent power, from which all its own power and authority are derived." Thoreau's vision here parallels Emerson's reconciliation of "society" and "solitude" whereby the greatest individual self-reliance derives from the fullest assimilation of society by the individual soul and the ideal society is constructed from completely self-reliant men. Thus, if "the last improvement possible in government"—considered without reference to the individual—is democracy with its domination of the man by the majority, "is it not possible to take a step further towards recognizing and organizing the rights of man?" This "step further" is metaphorically a step upward:

> Seen from a lower point of view, the Constitution, with all its faults, is very good ... but seen from a point of view a little higher, they [this State and this American government] are what I have described them; seen from a higher still, and the highest, who shall say what they are, or that they are worth looking at or thinking of at all?

Significantly, the essay rises and ends on a note of heavenly vision: "a still more perfect and glorious State, which also I have imagined, but not yet anywhere seen."

If we approach "Civil Disobedience" primarily as a political essay as thousands of readers have done, the two flanking views of the State inevitably receive a horizontal reading, the second functioning as a solution to problems presented in the first. Some dozens of commentators who find Thoreau politically naive or his strategies for reform unclear have obviously assumed this kind of structure. The central narrative suggests, however, something akin to renewed vision or imaginative rebirth for which a programmatic reading is inadequate. In the upward passage from night to day, bondage to freedom, Concord jail to Fair-Haven Hill, Thoreau builds a vertical narrative order which transcends political categories—which moves from the realm of understanding to the realm of imagination. We are reminded of a relevant remark about this in *Walden:* "When one man has reduced a fact of the imagination to be a fact to his understanding, I foresee that all men will at length establish their lives on that basis."

What Thoreau displays is a typically romantic perspective: a desire for a genuine metamorphosis in which the existing State is to die and an ideal state born in its place. From this standpoint, however, the ideal does not simply succeed or replace the real but is rather synthesized from it, as blossoming new life is synthesized from the materials of death. Thoreau's transcendental picture of the perfect State evolves from his death-vision of the present state and is in fact impossible without that death-vision. The narrative center of "Civil Disobedience" is therefore the vehicle for an imaginative synthesis, providing a mythic layering to his entry into and emergence from jail at dawn such that the reconciliation of opposites in this passage is a version of heroic triumph. Those commentators who have noted the considerable differences between the idealized account Thoreau gives and the event as reported by others are exactly right: it is precisely this displacement of the real event to the level of heroic narrative that validates the idealized vision of the essay. This is the essence of the artistry of "Civil Disobedience" and it is integral to interpretation.

This reading of the essay as narrative emphasizes its obvious similarities with Thoreau's other writings, especially *Walden*. Thoreau's passage from Concord jail to Fair-Haven Hill had already occurred in less dramatic form the previous summer (1845) with his move to Walden Pond, and his changed vision of Concord in the essay underlines the focus in the later book on renewal and rebirth. Like "Civil Disobedience," with its discussion of the contradictions in the existing State, *Walden* begins with a long discussion of economic contradictions—the development of industry that leads to waste, the abundance of things that crushes human freedom, the poverty of wealth, the institutional life of civilization that submerges the self-reliant soul. Like the essay with its vision at dawn, *Walden* is full of morning visions, culminating in the rebirth ritual of spring. Such images of metamorphosis in *Walden* as the bank of thawing clay on later winter morning or the resurrection of a "beautiful bug" from an old apple-wood table enhance and validate the archetype of death and rebirth at the center of the "Civil Disobedience" narrative.

In Thoreau's major excursions and books, it appears that he designed his art around a series of journeys which thus became passages from the real to the transcendent—symbolized in the frontier regions west of Concord ("Walking"), the upper reaches of the Merrimack (*A Week*), the heights of mountains ("A Walk to Wachusett"), the primitive depths of the forest (*The Maine Woods*), or the tranquil waters of the pond (*Walden*). "I went to the woods," he wrote in *Walden,* "because I wished to live deliberately." In "Civil Disobedience" we discover a similar passage, perhaps the only one that Thoreau did not deliberately plan: a walk to the cobbler's store to get a shoe interrupted, redirected, stalled for a dozen hours by a night in jail, then resumed the next morning. It is not surprising that the artistic account took on the shape of all the other passages in his works with their ascending movements toward morning, spring, hills, mountains, and the sun.

RICHARD BRIDGMAN

Rags and Meanness:
Journals, Early Essays,
Translations, and Poems

When we speak of a peculiarity in a man or a nation, we think to describe only one part, a mere mathematical point; but it is not so. It pervades all.

—Journal

Much of what Thoreau felt in his early years is concentrated in his poems and journals. They initiate the terms of his confusions and they help to explain both the violence and the evasions present in his writing. On the positive side, he idealized friendship and exulted in the diversity of nature. On the negative, he discovered little that was attractive in himself or in the social realities around him, and so dwelt obsessively on viciousness, destruction, and dissolution. Given these strained conditions, absorption in nature was a relief from quotidian irritations, not to say from himself. He once testified passionately: "I love Nature partly *because* she is not man, but a retreat from him. . . . In her midst I can be glad with an entire gladness." However, Thoreau suffered from the Transcendental dilemma: nature wore the colors of the spirit; the world could but reflect his moods. "Packed in my mind lie all the clothes / Which outward nature wears." And although he enjoyed periods of authentic happiness, he also suffered moments of the utmost grimness, when he believed that "Death cannot come too soon / Where it can come at all."

Thoreau often asserted his indifference to political argument, saying

---

From *Dark Thoreau.* © 1982 by the University of Nebraska Press.

that the brave man does not even hear the idle clashing of swords in the outer world, so "infinite" is the "din" within his spirit. "Is he not at war?" Thoreau was. Still, he rarely focused directly on that internal uproar, for, paradoxically, the inner self also constituted a central refuge for him. "For an impenetrable shield, stand inside yourself," he counseled, and did just that for a good part of his social life. Yet the tensions continued to harass him behind that shield. One can hear the anxiety in his question, "How shall I help myself?" The immediate answer was: "By withdrawing into the garret, and associating with spiders and mice, determining to meet myself face to face sooner or later." This curious (and unfulfilled) vow essentially repeated a declaration Thoreau had made at the opening of his journal three years earlier: "To be alone I find it necessary to escape the present,— I avoid myself. . . . I seek a garret. The spiders must not be disturbed, nor the floor swept, nor the lumber arranged." Thoreau was distracted by daily life and, moreover, he realized that this very distraction permitted him to evade himself. The solution conceived was a retreat. If in 1837 Thoreau's prescription for self-health was a solitary environment among other reclusive creatures, by 1840 he had realized that he was still avoiding himself and that, worse yet, he needed the shock of self-confrontation that he alone could provide. It would take him five years more, however, to find the appropriate retreat in the cabin at Walden Pond—and even then he would only go part way toward meeting himself "face to face."

Again and again in his life, Thoreau returned to this prescription of confronting or revealing himself, but always in secret. If the house is "the very haunt and lair of our vice," he also acknowledged it to be "a great relief when . . . we can retire to our chamber and be completely true to ourselves. . . . In that moment I will be nakedly as vicious as I am." Sometimes he felt that he did not understand himself, but that retirement would enable him to unveil the mystery. At other times, he felt that he knew all too well who he was, and sought the relief of confessing it in private. At yet others, he found solace in the idea that such candor would be the first step upward: "If we only see clearly enough how mean our lives are, they will be splendid enough." But to this he at once added a warning against excessive idealizing: "Let us remember not to strive upwards too long, but sometimes drop plumb down the other way, and wallow in meanness." All this speculative bravado yielded at last to ugly resignation: "At any rate, a carcass had better lie on the bottom than float an offense to all nostrils."

The affirmation that the rotting carcass is "an offense to all nostrils" clashes of course with the representation of the dead horse near his path as a "tonic of wildness." But Thoreau's imagination was ranging back and forth, trying to come to terms with the inadmissible. The root problem seemed to him his body proper, that unfortunate corporeal reality on which he had to depend. "I must confess there is nothing so strange to me as my own body. I love any other piece of nature, almost, better." And yet Thoreau realized that the full dimensions of his being were not to be found even in private. "The nearest approach to discovering what we are is in dreams." But if true, dreams were too unreliable, too sporadic and uncontrolled a source of knowledge for him. When he did manage to look within, what he saw forced him to ask himself: "Did you ever remember the moment when you were not mean?" The occasion for this particular question came during an especially dark mood. Two more somber questions followed: "Is it not a satire to say that life is organic?" And: "Where is my heart gone? They say men cannot part with it and live."

As for meanness, it was a condition Thoreau sometimes chose to praise as at least smacking of reality and, at other times, to curse in others and lament in himself. For Thoreau, the significance of certain key terms could shift radically, and not just over an extended period of time. Mutually exclusive ideas came to rest in words of special power for Thoreau. "Meanness" was one of them. Once Thoreau, for example, regarding himself as low and degraded, found the concept applicable to himself. "I am sure that my acquaintances mistake me," he told his journal in 1850. "I am not the man they take me for. On a little nearer view they would find me out.... If I should turn myself inside out, my rags and meanness would appear." In *Walden*, though, meanness was memorably offered as the possible essence of life. If so, then Thoreau intended to "get the whole and genuine meanness of it, and publish its meanness to the world." Such a salutary acknowledgment of the hardpan reality of existence was not possible for Thoreau for a long time, however, because he found himself incapable of giving full assent to those of his perceptions that failed to harmonize with the idealism he had learned, even when he felt their accuracy.

Thoreau's early journals furnish plentiful evidence of his dissatisfaction with himself. He lamented his physical being, his creative inadequacies, and the stunted condition of his heart. At age twenty-two, he was already sounding a mournful note of sterility in a poem: "The birds have sung their summer out, / But still my spring does not begin." That melancholy expression of thwarted growth was reflected in his vocational frustration. By 1840, aside from his journal, Thoreau had written only a few essays and poems, and, although just on the edge of being published in *The Dial*, he had absolutely no reputation as a writer. But the best he could do about his dissatisfaction was to persist in constructing in his journal an

ideal of behavior, accompanied by an undercurrent of doubt that indicated
his awareness of the warring elements in his nature.

Lacking human closeness outside his family, Thoreau felt frozen,
whereas the affectionate life of others seemed to flourish. "The days of tilts
and tournaments has gone by, but no herald summons us to the tourna-
ment of love." He turned his seasonal metaphor specifically to love. "Any
exhibition of affection—as an inadvertent word, or act, or look—seems
premature, as if the time were not ripe for it." Yet Thoreau felt he needed
human intimacy. "How insufficient is all wisdom without love! . . . Our
life without love is like coke and ashes,—like the cocoanut in which the
milk is dried up." But the question of where he might derive that needed
love was distinctly a problem for him. At a pitch of feeling, he remarked:
"Love is so delicate and fastidious that I see not how [it] can ever begin."
Then, as an indication of one way in which intercourse was blocked: "Did
I ask thee to love me who hate myself?" Thoreau's advice to his potential
lover was to share his enthusiasms: "No! Love that I love, and I will love
thee that lovest it." This was love by indirection. Thoreau could not express his yearnings in terms of a heterosexual union. The feminine was virtually a nonexistent gender for him, except when he was complaining
about its trivialities. When his hunger for companionship surged through
him, the best expression he could manage was a neutralized desire: "I
would live henceforth with some gentle soul such a life as may be conceived, double for variety, single for harmony." The desired state was ambiguous, as indeterminate as the gender.

In this connection, Thoreau's translation of the most famous of Anacreon's poems becomes significant. Anacreon had directed his sardonic
lyric toward a proud young woman who persisted in ignoring him. His
conceit was to address her as a young mare whom, if he wished, he could
master and ride. In a standard modern prose version:

> Pray, why do you look askance at me, my Thracian filly, and
> shun me so resolutely as though I knew nothing of my art? I
> would have you to know I could bridle you right well and take
> rein and ride you about the turning-post of the course. But in-
> stead you graze in the meadows and frisk and frolic to your
> heart's content; for you have not a clever breaker to ride you.

The poem has been translated many times. For our purposes the opening
is the crucial part. In the eighteenth century:

> Why with Scorn-reverting Eye,
> Pretty *Thracian Filley*, Why

> Me as skill-less and unwise
> Fly you

At the beginning of the nineteenth:

> Like some wanton filly sporting,
> Maid of Thrace! thou fly'st my courting,
> Wanton filly! tell me why

Now, the very fact that Thoreau should have selected a poem in which the voice asserts its superiority to a disdainful woman is certainly meaningful in itself. Moreover, the existence of a classical model freed him to be much bolder and more direct in his translation than he could ever bring himself to be in his own right. But consider *his* version of the opening lines:

> Thracian colt, why at me
> Looking aslant with thy eyes,
> Dost thou cruelly flee.

Thoreau has neutralized the gender of the filly. He knew Greek sufficiently well not to have made such a fundamental error in his translation. It is true that "colt" has been used elsewhere to designate a young mare, as in the *Oxford English Dictionary*'s citation of Tennyson writing in 1858: "She's yet a colt—Take, break her." But the *OED* also shows that since as early as 1400 "filly" had been the standard term used to distinguish the young female horse. Edith Seybold, in her study of Thoreau's engagement with the classics, has commented on his occasional willfulness in translation, contending that he sometimes "deliberately mistranslated, knowing quite well that the lines meant one thing as Horace and Persius wrote them but finding a second meaning more acceptable to himself." In this instance, Thoreau's transformation of the "filly" into a "colt" effectively muted the force of Anacreon's bridling and riding a woman.

The precise significance of this change for Thoreau's mind is of course impossible to determine. But the Anacreon translation seems to me related to a more general confusion of genders in Thoreau's writing, particularly that involving his well-known elegy, "Lately, alas, I knew a gentle boy." This poem laments Thoreau's estrangement from a boy "whose features all were cast in Virtue's mould." So smitten had he been with this boy that he "quite forgot my homage to confess." Because of this oversight, he was now "forced to know, though hard it is, / I might have loved him had I loved him less."

Thoreau's "gentle boy" probably was the eleven-year-old Edmund

Sewall, although we have no particular indication why Edmund should have inspired such a poem. In fact, the little evidence surviving runs in the contrary direction. The Sewall family remembered Edmund's being irritated at being referred to as "the gentle boy." Further, it is not clear why there was no Thoreauvian rhapsody when later, in March 1840, Edmund was not only enrolled in Thoreau's school but also came to live for the term in the Thoreau household. Perhaps the feelings had changed. In spite of these questions, Edmund remains the most likely candidate as the subject of the poem. He is certainly a more plausible identification than the assertions of Thoreau's contemporaries and early biographers that the poem referred to *Ellen* Sewall, apparently because they were unwilling to accept the idea that Thoreau's intensity could have been directed toward her barely adolescent brother.

Although H. S. Canby argued that inasmuch as Ellen did not arrive in Concord until a month after the poem was written, Edmund must have been its subject, he then assigned the poem "Nature doth have her dawn each day" to Ellen Sewall, even though in *it* the masculine pronoun is used in connection with "my mate." And, to construct the case that the poem "I'm guided in the darkest night" is also addressed to Ellen, the chronology of her visits to Concord, as well as the November 18 letter to Prudence Ward in which Ellen describes turning down "H. T.," have been used. Once this hypothesis of Thoreau's having wooed Ellen is established, it is then further used to interpret several of Thoreau's journal entries as also referring to her. What must again give us pause is that these interpretations, like that of the "gentle boy" poem, oblige one to change the gender of the pronouns in the journal entries. For example, Thoreau writes on October 17, 1840: "In the presence of my friend I am ashamed of my fingers and toes. I have no feature so fair as my love for him." But why should Thoreau disguise the pronoun in this entry? In what respect would he be more vulnerable if he referred to "my love for *her?*" In any case, were Thoreau infatuated with Ellen, those of his family or friends who might read his journal would presumably recognize its subject, despite the change in the pronoun's gender.

Next, an entry for October 19, 1840: "My friend dwells in the distant horizon as rich as an eastern city there." Even though the pronouns that follow are masculine, it has been argued that, because Ellen lived in Scituate, southeast of Concord, this entry also refers to her. It continues: "There he sails all lonely under the edge of the sky," but although eventually "he rides in my roadsted . . . never does he fairly come to anchor in my harbor. Perhaps I afford no good anchorage." Finally, Thoreau shifts to a sun image: "He seems to move in a burnished atmosphere, while I peer in upon him from surrouding spaces of Cimmerian darkness."

No matter how one judges the merits of these arguments based on biographical detail, what is significant is what generated them. The pattern in Thoreau's writing is that when he was driven to express passionate feelings, either a general ambiguity of reference obtained or males were the object of those feelings. This inevitably raises the issue of homosexuality, but not very usefully, I think. On the basis of several quotations illustrating the "theme of same-sex intimacy," Jonathan Katz has appropriated Thoreau for his anthology *Gay American History,* and one can see why, though at the same time feeling that the term limits our understanding of Thoreau. There are moments enough in his writing to be woven into such an interpretation. For example, on the water, Thoreau once noted that "There sits one by the shore who wishes to go with me, but I cannot think of it. I must be fancy-free. . . . I could better afford to take him into bed with me, for then I might, perhaps, abandon him in my dreams." The imagery is odd and not necessary to make the point that Thoreau seems to be making—that he wishes to remain independent, whereas even offering a boat-ride entails responsibilities. But even as with the journal entries discussed earlier, the possibility of sensual involvement pulsates in the background.

There is no evidence, however, that Thoreau was ever sexually intimate with a man. He did have youthful attractions to women, primarily older, maternal ones. But, on the whole, Thoreau was clearly unsettled by women, as he was in general by any close physical proximity. Other people's bodies troubled him as much as did his own. Further, it was clear to him that marriage would bring fleshly obligations such as he could not easily entertain, not to speak of dubious entanglements of material responsibility. But Thoreau's erotic feelings flared up from time to time in the presence of boys, men, and nature.

Throughout his life, Thoreau's remarks show that he almost invariably regarded sensual love with suspicion if not outright disgust. "Can love be in aught allied to dissipation," he asked. "Let us love by refusing not accepting one another." The reason? "There is a danger that we may stain and pollute one another." Accordingly, Thoreau's formula for marriage was a severe one. "If it is the result of a pure love, there can be nothing sensual in marriage. Chastity is something positive, not negative. It is the virtue of the married especially. All lusts or base pleasures must give place to loftier delights. They who meet as superior beings cannot perform the deeds of inferior ones."

Once Thoreau had more or less permanently established chastity for himself, he elevated it and imposed it imaginatively on his friends. To be sure, such repression was hardly unusual in Thoreau's century. Its concealments of sex were sufficient for him to have remarked that "one of the most interesting of all human facts is veiled more completely than any mystery." He himself had experienced an idealized but elusive version of it. "The intercourse of the sexes, I have dreamed, is incredibly beautiful, too fair to be remembered. I have had thoughts about it, but they are the most fleeting and irrecoverable in my experience." Still, Thoreau could fantasize that communion with one's beloved might involve bewitching threats to one's self-control: "What if the lover should learn that his beloved dealt in incantations and philters! What if he should hear that she consulted a clairvoyant!" And he could not countenance another's curiosity. Any questioning, even of the most innocent sort, seemed to violate his privacy. "I require that thou knowest everything without being told anything. I parted from my beloved because there was one thing which I had to tell her. She *questioned* me. She should have known all by sympathy." A decade later, in curious image, Thoreau reiterated that position, this time in respect to friends. "My friend is he who can make a good guess at me, hit me on the wing."

Given the power of his inhibitions, Thoreau had to suppose that his feelings could be intuited. As he put it in an unfortunate piece of doggerel:

> if the truth were known, Love cannot speak,
> But only thinks and does;
> Though surely out 'twill leak
> Without the help of Greek,
> Or any tongue.

Thoreau eventually reconciled himself to his bachelorhood. In 1851 he told his journal: "I am sure that the design of my maker when he has brought me nearest to woman was not the propagation, but rather the maturation, of the species. Man is capable of a love of woman quite transcending marriage." He became habituated to conceiving of love and friendship as if they were synonymous. Thoreau did have a number of intimate friendships of considerable depth and intensity, beginning in his family, but he commonly displayed such reticence that when he refers to "my friend" we do not necessarily know whether he means male or female, relative or close companion. In some few cases, this uncertainty may be the result of editorial discretion, observed, as an editor of the journals explained, "out of regard for the feelings of possible relatives or descendants of the persons mentioned." However, Thoreau normally observed a prudent distance in his references. Typically, we do not even know whether the famous opening question of the whole huge journal can be positively attributed to Emerson or not: " 'What are you doing now?' he asked. 'Do you keep a journal?' " And when Thoreau's brother John died of lockjaw, followed shortly by the death of the Emersons' son, Waldo, only an ellipsis of forty-one days appeared in Thoreau's journal, from January 9, 1842, to February 18. We know from other sources that Thoreau himself was ill with a psychosomatic case of sympathetic lockjaw during a portion of this period, so severe was his bereavement (and possibly guilt because of his having courted the same young woman his brother loved). The most Thoreau said was in a letter: "I have been confined to my chamber for a month with a prolonged shock of the same disorder." When he recommenced his journal, he made but a few perfunctory remarks to the effect that the death of "friends" should inspire us, since good can never disappear. He does admit that his "soul and body have tottered along together of late," but his only deep acknowledgment of the profundity of the trauma is the wonderful sentence: "I am like a feather floating in the atmosphere; on every side is depth unfathomable."

In the powerfully yearning days of his youth, Thoreau preferred to believe that friendships were fated and irresistible, "like air bubbles on water, hastening to flow together." And he asked why such classic friendships as those of Orestes and Pylades, or Damon and Pythias, should not be put to shame by a present-day community. But his imagery betrayed the insubstantiality of his conceptions, for air bubbles are doomed to burst, and he could not assert that modern friendships would be superior to classical ones, but could only question why they should not be.

In those days, Thoreau also chose to believe that the attitudes of one's friends were of no moment. One's idealizations and subjective extensions were the only reality. Temporal disagreements were of no consequence. "What matter a few words more or less with my friend,—with all mankind;—they will still be my friends in spite of themselves. Let them stand aloof if they can!" Ultimately these brave words proved of no practical value for Thoreau in subduing the anxiety of loneliness. Friendship remained a problem for him, even though, by 1842, he was dealing more complexly with its actualities. At the same time, he continued to rationalize away difficulties. "My friend is cold and reserved," he remarked, "because his love for me is waxing and not waning," a sanguine conclusion that would not normally be drawn from such chilly evidence. Thoreau then pursued a Stendhalian crystallization analogy: "These are the early processes; the particles are just beginning to shoot in crystals." Then, restlessly dropping this unpromising image, Thoreau turned to a declaration of the satisfaction that he took from withheld friendship: "If the mountains came to me, I should no longer go to the mountains. So soon as that consummation takes place which I wish, it will be past." Finally, Thoreau reverted briefly to his preference for postponed fulfillment: "Shall I not have a friend in reserve? Heaven is to come. I hope this is not it."

This sequence strikes me as an altogether representative instance of Thoreau's thinking, in that it presents a series of disconnected and not especially apt images in the service of explaining away disappointment. To look ahead a bit, by 1851 Thoreau had incorporated this generalized observation into a particular and positive truth about himself: "I find that I postpone all actual intercourse with my friends to a certain real intercourse which takes place commonly when we are actually at a distance from one another." In this formulation, fulfillment was not postponed and happily anticipated. Rather, the *imaginary* intercouse with the friend was now described as "real" compared to the crude actuality of their physical encounters.

Thoreau composed several poems on various aspects of friendship, some of them among his most intriguing. None is without interest, nor is any without its problems. When these poems have been noticed, it has primarily been to tease biographical revelations out of them, but they also confirm that Thoreau's vision of friendship almost invariably entailed separation. Early in his manhood, he was able to identify friendship as that condition in which one shared "a kindred nature" with another, so that "each may other help, and service do." But even in this 1838 poem, "Friendship," this familiar conception underwent revision. "Two sturdy oaks, I mean," Thoreau writes in clarification, which "barely touch." Only deep in the ground are "their roots . . . intertwined / Insep'rably." If this assertion of covert intimacy were not austere enough, even that much Thoreau could not long believe or accept. It was much more characteristic of him to envision friendship as "a double star" fixed in the heavens and revolving "about one centre." It is true that here, in 1839, he could still assert that the revolving was accompanied by "spheral song," but soon enough that harmony yielded to sterner realities about intimacy. Should he roll near the path of another, "with a pleased anxiety," he would feel the other's "purer influence on my opaque mass," yet he was always doomed to learn that ultimately he had "scarce changed its sidireal [sic] time." These feelings of inferiority and ineffectuality accurately reflected Thoreau's troubled condition.

The 1838 poem "Friendship" said that possession of the same "loves and hates" would prove that the two persons were "mates." If the needs of rhyme seem to have triumphed over psychological insight here, eventually Thoreau was obliged to assert that hate was the positive element in a relationship, so that he might justify his feelings, as well as those of his Concord neighbors. The central poem on this topic is "Let such pure hate still underprop." Its central and startling conceit appears in the opening stanza:

> Let such pure hate still underprop
> Our love, that we may be
> Each other's conscience,
> And have our sympathy
> Mainly from thence.

The balance of the poem expresses familiar Thoreauvian themes: that human beings, even when attracted by deep bonds of sympathy, remain solitary stars; that love does not communicate by words, for none is sufficient to bridge the "gulf of feeling," except by "decrees of fate"; that love shines serenely on above the clouds and is irresistible. Thoreau was ever trying to establish the imperial indifference of love toward temporary confusions and setbacks. Being all too well aware of the flaws and obstacles that threatened such friendships as he had experienced, he insisted all the more on friendship's austere and fated triumph.

Hanging over the whole argument was that harshly moralistic opening, "Let such pure hate still underprop / Our love." Having detected hate in his human relationships, or, if not hate, then some reduced versions of it—disapproval, envy, rancor—and finding himself incapable of purging himself (or the other) of that negative emotion, he sought to incorporate it into his model by idealizing it into a "pure" hate. That Thoreau possessed a plenitude of violent feelings cannot be doubted. One of the most famous incidents associated with him is normally recounted as an instance of his independence; it seems to me to tell quite another tale. It occurred after Thoreau was newly graduated from Harvard College and was teaching in the Concord Town School. Admonished by an observing committeeman and deacon to thrash his pupils, Thoreau at first refused, then took six of them ostensibly at random (including, disconcertingly enough, "the maidservant in his own house"), used the ferule on them, and resigned his position. A moment's thought will suggest that *six* of the innocent was a somewhat excessive number to punish so that Thoreau might prove his contempt for his judges. Evident in this episode is the explosive fury normally suppressed by Thoreau but sporadically appearing with alarming metaphoric force in his writing. He managed to control his furious resentments for the most part (or, by retiring from company, to reduce the potentiality for their exacerbation), but the strain on him was evident. His former, admiring pupil, Horace Hosmer, reported that "Henry was not loved. He was a conscientious teacher, but rigid." Another student, one of the six arbitrarily punished, was still alive in 1917 and, according to Edward Emerson, "all through life has cherished his grievance, not understanding the cause." Still, the younger Emerson, who knew Thoreau intimately, was anxious to make the point that "Thoreau, although brusque on occasions, was refined, courteous, kind and humane." This seems to have been the case, at least with people who made no serious demands on him, such as children and the old.

Others, though, even friends who were not readily inclined to judge him, proved more taxing. Over and over he insisted on the necessity of hate as a component of love. "I need thy hate as much as thy love. Thou wilt not repel me entirely when thou repellest what is evil in me." The responsibility was exigent: "Love is a severe critic. . . . They who aspire to love worthily, subject themselves to an ordeal more rigid than any other." And in a journal entry for December 31, 1840, after considering the alternative to this harsh, if elevated, conception of love, Thoreau dismissed it contemptuously: "This sickly preaching of love, and a sympathy that will be tender to our faults, is the dyspepsia of the soul."

The paradox is evident. Thoreau resented criticism but at the same time, privately charged with self-disgust, felt the need for it. But his championing of hate as an essential component of friendship reached such obsessive proportions at times as to become grotesque:

> Surely, surely, thou wilt trust me
> When I say thou dost disgust me.
> O, I hate thee with a hate
> That would fain annihilate.

These lines, intended altogether seriously, display the power of Thoreau's feeling, not against a bureaucratic state, nor a slaveholder, nor a businessman—all objects of Thoreau's wrath at one time or another—but against someone he designates in the poem as "my dear friend." "Yet sometimes against my will / My dear friend, I love thee still." But immediately following this confession of lingering susceptibility, Thoreau returns to underscore the obligatory nature of his disgust:

> It were treason to our love,

And a sin to God above,
One iota to abate
Of a pure impartial hate.

Hate also appears in a friendly letter Thoreau wrote to the Emersons during his absence on Staten Island in 1843. This was shortly after he had left their household after a stay of two years, at which time he had thanked them "for your long kindness to me." In the letter in question, Thoreau warmly recalled "sacred" walks in the woods with his sponsors, then continued:

> But know, my friends, that I a good deal hate you all in my most private thoughts—as the substratum of the little love I bear you. Though you are a rare band and do not make half use enough of one another.

From that quite unexpected remark, Thoreau then passed on without further comment to an analysis of the newest number of *The Dial*.

What are we to make of this passage, other than that in its abrupt candor it is altogether typical of Thoreau? The Emersons must have felt they knew how to take their protégé's words, since these remarks seem to have occasioned no concern. Emerson's next letter said that they "were all very glad to have such cordial greetings from you." It is true that the letter in question immediately followed the one containing Thoreau's soulful testimony to Lidian Emerson that "the thought of you will constantly elevate my life." It is also true that Thoreau's next letters were notably dampered, and it may be that he brought forth his testimony of hate as a means of laying to rest the indiscretion of his sentimental overreaction. The quantity of hate, we see, is "a good deal"; of love, "a little."

Since for Thoreau hate could be the expression of conscience and therefore operate in the service of the good, one might assume that the "higher" function of hate was operating in the paragraph from the letter to the Emersons. However, Thoreau also had reasons for being resentful toward them, especially toward Emerson himself. When he was absent, then Thoreau could play the attractive role of father to the Emerson family. He genuinely enjoyed their children and had inclinations toward imaginative appropriation. For example, in 1843 he wrote Emerson that his daughter Edith "says 'papa' less and less abstractedly every day, looking in *my* face." Some four years later, he again wrote to the absent breadwinner that his son Eddy "very seriously asked me, the other day, 'Mr. Thoreau, will you be my father?' . . . So you must come back soon, or you will be superseded." There is no little complacency in those reports.

But now Emerson had been the agent, however well-meaning, of exiling Thoreau in the inhospitable environment of Staten Island. And Lidian had evidently retreated from that original "trustful" mood expressed in the letter from her that had so stirred Thoreau's feelings. In his June 20, 1843, reply Thoreau admitted to Lidian that "I, perhaps, am more willing to deceive by appearances than you say you are; it would not be worth the while to tell how willing—but I have the power perhaps too much to forget my meanness as soon as seen, and not be incited by permanent sorrow. My actual life is unspeakably mean." I suspect that a component of the meanness Thoreau observed in himself was that rankling resentment he tried to elevate into a virtue. So, when Thoreau told the Emersons that he hated them a good deal "in my most private thoughts," he probably meant it, even though his designation of hate as the agent of conscience underpropping love would protect him should offense be taken.

For all his attempts at rationalization, Thoreau felt himself in most respects seriously out of phase with his world. His writings tell us that he often perceived no goal, no hope, and no inspiration in that world and, moreover, that the problem extended to the subjective level of existence. When he consulted his inner condition, he heard an "infinite din within," but he tried to convince himself that, even if he reproached himself for not actively engaging in the struggles with the outer world, for not allowing "the indignation which has so long rankled in his breast" to "take to horse and to the field," still, the true vocation of the brave man was in fact internal battle. "Is he not at war?" And in another journal entry he confirmed this sense of psychic strife by observing sternly: "I have a deep sympathy with war, it so apes the gait and bearing of the soul." Thus a change of scene or of occupation could not eliminate Thoreau's malaise. Residence at Walden Pond could perhaps clarify his ideas somewhat, but it could not still the internal uproar. Much of the distress of the young poet remains visible in *Walden,* even if that book's surface optimism has shone so brightly as to blind us to its caves of darkness.

Often impatient with his contemporaries, Thoreau gravitated to the classics for inspiration and guidance. One of his early projects was a translation of Aeschylus's *The Prometheus Bound.* Although Emerson had requested it, both the author and the subject attracted Thoreau. In a little sermon composed for his 1839 journal, he had reflected that Aeschylus was a man who had "lived his own healthy Attic life," who had disregarded rhetorical display to speak genuinely, and who "like every genius

. . . was a solitary liver and worker." Feeling a sympathetic relationship, then, Thoreau returned a few weeks later to expand on Aeschylus's greatness. He "had a clear eye for the commonnest things." Further, it seemed to Thoreau that "the social condition of genius is the same in all ages. Aeschylus was undoubtedly alone and without sympathy in his simple reverence for the mystery of the universe." So, already respectful of the poet, Thoreau turned willingly to his dramatization of a demigod sacrificed for helping man. The role of the stoic under sentence of perpetual torture for his good deeds supplied a certain appealing parallel to his own situation. "O revered Mother, O Ether / Revolving common light to all," reads Thoreau's version of the play's concluding lines, "You see me, how unjust things I endure!"

Thoreau readily identified with such figures as Prometheus who were noble and inspired but obliged to endure some torment or bondage. "The god Apollo (Wisdom, Wit, Poetry) condemned to serve, keep the sheep of *King* Admetus" constituted a favorite analogy in his mind. "Who is King Admetus? It is Business, with his four prime ministers Trade and Commerce and Manufactures and Agriculture. And this is what makes mythology true and interesting to us." Thoreau saw the social applicability, but he also identified directly with the subjugated Apollo. "I am thinking what an elysian day it is, and how I seem always to be keeping the flocks of Admetus such days—that is my luck."

Thoreau was trying to *make* himself, to construct a mode of life that would be both satisfying and defensible, while at the same time he suffered from guilt, loneliness, and despair. For example, although his essay "The Service" offers a rather complacent series of declarations concerning what the brave man is in comparison to the coward, embedded within it is a quatrain expressing chagrin and regret:

> Each more melodious note I hear
> Brings this reproach to me,
> That I alone afford the ear,
> Who would the music be.

The moon afforded Thoreau an example of cosmic ease and beauty that he longed to emulate. "The moon moves up her smooth and sheeny path / Without impediment." But that was not the case with him: "My cares never rest . . . my current never rounds into a lake." The moon has a serene indifference to all terrestrial suffering such as his own:

> She does not wane, but my fortune,

Which her rays do not bless,
My wayward path declineth soon,
But she shines not the less.

Even when the moon pales, she remains "alway in her proper
sphere / She's mistress of the night." By contrast, Thoreau felt uncertain,
out of place, unfulfilled. He sometimes tried to convince himself that the
wisest course was passivity in the face of the inevitable. "What first suggested that necessity was grim, and made fate so fatal," he asked himself in
his journal. "The strongest is always the least violent." Then, memorably:
"Necessity is a sort of Eastern cushion on which I recline."

But, too regularly agitated to be able to accept the condition of oriental ease, Thoreau plunged again and again into the fields and woods for
relief. These daily walks helped, for however random the experience they
furnished might be, they organized existence without greatly organizing it.
The bits and pieces of experience they offered did not require difficult assimilation to be appreciated. And, if one considers the literary forms on
which Thoreau relied, one can see that they either furnished the structure
that was missing or, as with the journal, sanctioned randomness and im-
provisation. Translation most obviously frees the writer from the burden
of original organization. Reviews such as "Paradise (To Be) Regained" and
assessments of careers like "Sir Walter Raleigh" and "Thomas Carlyle"
also provided stable, fixed entities on which Thoreau could elaborate. His
descriptions of walks as well as the narrative skeleton of the *Week* were
provided coherence by the movement across a landscape and by the passage of time, and *Walden,* of course, depended on a seasonal calendar for
its ordering form.

But, as Thoreau learned, his confusions were only contained, not resolved, by these contingent forms. "I am a parcel of vain strivings tied / By
a chance bond together." These, the opening lines of "Sic Vita," one of his
most imagistically effective poems, sums up Thoreau's condition as a
young man. Of no moment; expending effort without success; and existing, not in conformance to some grand conception, but randomly. The
poem itself was supposedly thrown in the window of Mrs. Lucy Jackson
Brown, but it is hardly a love lyric. Bronson Alcott, in fact, read it at Thoreau's funeral. Nor is it, as Canby suggests, a poem in which Thoreau indicates that he will mature—that "give him another year, and freedom, and
then his vain strivings will have strengthened his character, and have made
more virile the stock of talent in his mind." Quite the contrary. In the
poem there is no specified recipient of the bouquet, nor any gratified re-

sponse to its presentation. Rather, the speaking nosegay is placed in a bare cup where its tender buds mimic life, for they will not, they cannot, develop.

There *is* a resolution—the very oddest sort of rationalization. The speaker, it turns out, is to be regarded as a sacrifice, one that is necessary for the improvement of the plant. "Thus thinned," the parent stock will bear "more fruits and fairer flowers," "while I droop here." Now although the poem's opening line surely capture Thoreau's own sense of hopelessness and lack of purpose, this resolution is both specious and internally contradictory. Thoreau has specified the nosegay as composed of a mixture ture of violets and sorrel, seized "in haste" from the fields. So not only are the prophesied *fruits* inappropriate to the specific plants mentioned, but the spontaneous and hasty act of picking them can hardly be described as the deliberate thinning a gardener might perform. But Thoreau needed some positive explanation, some understanding of why, in an ostensibly harmonious world, he should feel himself no more than a motley collection of frustrated impulses, and so he generated this fable of productive sacrifice that supplied the poem with a formal but distinctly unsatisfactory conclusion.

Given the state of his frustration, Thoreau could not always uphold the strenuous position that insisted that the striving was all. Instead, like a village Hamlet, he sometimes longed for his sullied flesh to thaw and resolve itself into a dew. In 1839:

> Fain would I stretch me by the highway side,
> To thaw and trickle with the melting snow,
> That mingled soul and body with the tide,
> I too may through the pores of nature flow.

The relief of such a dissolution was, however, denied Thoreau. "But I alas nor trickle can nor fume." Therefore, once more as in "Sic Vita," he attempted a positive resolution. His role, he decided, was "to hearken while these ply the loom, / So shall my silence with their music chime." One cannot help but note how often Thoreau will attempt to make his negative qualities—his silence, his passivity, his distance, his frozenness—into virtues. Typically: "The most positive life that history notices has been a constant retiring out of life, a wiping one's hands of it, seeing how mean it is, and having nothing to do with it."

On the other hand, the desire to be literally absorbed into the all remained with him. One eccentric version of it was his evocation of the imagined pleasure of standing all day up to the chin in a swamp. A more common experience took place in 1839, when "drifting in a sultry day on the sluggish waters of the pond, I almost cease to live and begin to be. . . . I am never so prone to lose my identity. I am dissolved in the haze." That condition was clearly at once a union and an escape.

At the other extreme was Thoreau's celebration of crisp winter when each object had its firm definition. Such marble selfhood brought him reassurance. Melting was a rare phenomenon for him and generally one neither sought nor desired. In his hardened Roman state, Thoreau not only was armored against a wounding world but also evinced an indifference to suffering. He could look with fatalistic objectivity on a scene of disaster, transcending the pain of others and, by utilizing the same formula of paradox he employed with himself, could actually assert the attractiveness of such a scene. "When a freshet destroys the works of man, or a fire consumes them, or a Lisbon earthquake shakes them down, our sympathy with persons is swallowed up in a wider sympathy with the universe. A crash is apt to grate agreeably on our ears."

Nonetheless, at times such defenses failed, whereupon Thoreau was compelled to ask the question direct: "My friends, why should we live?" His gloomy perception was that "Life is an idle war a toilsome peace." If his metaphor for existence was military, his tone was pessimistic, not because he felt defeated but because he felt useless. "Shall we out-wear the year / In our pavilions on its dusty plain . . . ?" As the signal never comes "To strike our tents and take the road again," we are denied even the pleasure of purposeful movement. The poem's concluding stanza is utterly without hope, proposing as it does a wearisome and useless lifetime of illusory activity:

> Or else drag up the slope
> The heavy ordnance of nature's train?
> Useless but in the hope,
> Some far remote and heavenward hill to gain.

Although these sentiments are far from the whole of Thoreau, they do constitute a major component of his general mood—that there was neither purpose nor hope in a life that was marked by labor dedicated to a markedly dubious end. *Vain* then became an important operative term for him. "In vain I see the morning rise, / In vain observe the western blaze." These lines come from "The Poet's Delay," Thoreau's lament for his unresponsiveness to the presumably inspirational natural world. Nature may be boundlessly wealthy, but "I only still am poor within." Nature may celebrate fecundity, growth, and promise, "But still my spring does not begin."

Such laconic desolation was a recurrent feature of Thoreau's imagination. But, although he could describe his personal distress or embody his world in a bleak image, he rarely drew any explicit conclusions. Here is a complete poem:

> Between the traveller and the setting sun,
> Upon some drifting sand heap of the shore,
> A hound stands o'er the carcass of a man.

So, if not the bay horse and turtledove, Thoreau did at last find his hound. But he refused to interpret its significance. There was merely silence and stilled motion: sand, a hound, a human carcass, and beyond these the setting sun.

Here, then, is a background against which to read Thoreau's major writings. Highly personal, uncertainly ordered, and often perplexing compositions, they emerge out of such distress and confusion as these early pieces reveal. This study describes no sequential success story, but rather follows an intermittent struggle that is sometimes impressive, sometimes irritating, and often quite poignant in its urgency. Thoreau did manage some modest victories in time, as well as a quiet truce with himself and with the failings of those others who so regularly exasperated him. But self-conquest was a fantasy, and even that self-knowledge that Thoreau resisted so strenuously was a solvent of distinctly limited powers. Until his death Thoreau harbored demons of anxiety and resentment that he tirelessly tried to rationalize but that would not be stilled. Sometimes he rarefied his arguments to a point difficult to reconcile with his supposed commitment to the actualities of existence; at other moments, his prose grew opaque, evasive, and strangely insufficient. Pessimism, aggressive anger, and incoherence are all prominent features of Thoreau's writing, but because they fail to accommodate themselves to those positive versions of the man ranging from the gentle naturalist to the fiery independent, they have been largely overlooked. Still, they are symptoms of inner conflicts of a magnitude and endurance hardly acknowledged, and they mark his writing everywhere.

JOHN HILDEBIDLE

Suspectable Repetitions:
Cape Cod

C*ape Cod* has somehow acquired the reputation of being "Thoreau's sunniest, happiest book"—a reputation attested by the frequency with which copies of the book are to be found in souvenir shops today between Sandwich and Truro. Ironically, the work seems to have become the kind of historical guidebook which Thoreau himself carried along on his excursions to the Cape, in the form of "the eighth volume of the Collections of the Massachusetts Historical Society, printed in 1802." That Thoreau carried such a book indicates, in a very small way, both the strangeness and unfamiliarity of the place to him, and the degree to which he relies in his account on history of the most traditional kind as a means of understanding this alien land.

The peculiarity of the book's cheery reputation lies in the application of the term "sunny" to a work which begins with a long, and at times painfully detailed description of the immediate aftermath of the wreck of the brig *St. John,* and continues, often in the rain, to see shipwreck at almost every turn. The Cape as a whole, Thoreau imagines, is a potential wreck, preserved only by the most fragile means: "Thus Cape Cod is anchored to the heavens, as it were, by a myriad little cables of beachgrass, and, if they should fail, would become a total wreck, and ere long go to the bottom." Shipwrecks are not, to Thoreau, uniformly disastrous; the visual effect of the *St. John,* for instance, is ambiguous: "I saw that the beauty of the shore itself was wrecked for many a lonely walker there, un-

From *Thoreau: A Naturalist's Liberty.* © 1983 by the President and Fellows of Harvard College. Harvard University Press, 1983.

til he could perceive, at last, how its beauty was enhanced by wrecks like this, and it acquired thus a rarer and sublimer beauty still." The wrecks serve a very real economic purpose by helping to support the Cape Codders, most of whom work at least part of the time as wreckers or scavengers. Thoreau twice mentions the case of "Mr. Bell's nursery," wrecked on board the *Franklin* but thereby spread widely, as the seeds wash ashore. The case seems to Thoreau to be exemplary of a larger, ultimately regenerative, but chillingly (and literally) inhuman process:

> Vessels with seeds in their cargoes, destined for particular ports, where perhaps they were not needed, have been cast away on desolate islands, and though their crews perished, some of their seeds have been preserved. Out of many kinds a few would find a soil and a climate adapted to them,—become naturalized and perhaps drive out the native plants at last, and so fit the land for the habitation of man. It is an ill wind that blows nobody any good, and for the time lamentable shipwrecks may thus contribute a new vegetable to a continent's stock, and prove on the whole a lasting blessing to its inhabitants.

The reassurance to be found in such speculations rests on, at best, a chastened view of life. The sea, maker of shipwrecks, becomes in Thoreau's eyes an apocalyptic force; as such it is natural in the largest possible sense: "I sympathized rather with the winds and waves, as if to toss and mangle these poor human bodies was the order of the day. If this was the law of Nature, why waste any time in awe or pity? If the last day were come, we should not think so much about the separation of friends or the blighted prospects of individuals." The wreck of human hopes so evident as Thoreau watches the aftermath of the *St. John* disaster is, from this view, only a sign of the misdirection of those hopes. Is it not possible, he wonders, that "the mariner who makes the safest port in heaven, perchance, seems to his friends on earth to be shipwrecked, for they deem Boston Harbor the better place?" Thoreau, in the end, makes his stand clear; he knows the distance from heaven to Boston, and from heaven to Cape Cod as well: "I wished to see that seashore where man's works are wrecks; to put up at the true Atlantic House, where the ocean is land-lord as well as sea-lord, and comes ashore without a wharf for the landing; where the crumbling land is the only invalid, or at best is but dry land, and that is all you can say of it."

At an important moment in *Walden*, Thoreau observes the point at which "the pond asserts its title to a shore, and thus the *shore is shorn*."

Cape Cod is, in a sense, an extended consideration of precisely this kind of landscape, but on an immensely larger scale, and without the comforts to be found on the edge of the pond. Everywhere on the Cape Thoreau finds conflict and flux at the ocean's edge. Near Hull he sees "the sea nibbling voraciously at the continent" while at the same time making the "wrecks of isles . . . into new shores." "Everything," he notices, "seemed to be gently lapsing into futurity." But the lapse is not always, indeed not usually, so gentle or so well directed. The very edge of the beach takes him back to the primordial time which he glimpsed atop Ktaadn: "Before the land rose out of the ocean, and became dry land, chaos reigned; and between high and low water mark, where she is partially disrobed and rising, a sort of chaos reigns still, which only anomalous creatures can inhabit."

The shore is "a place of wonders," "a great country," "inexhaustible" in its fertility but also "unfruitful." The beach—that part of the Cape which Thoreau, by choice, makes the scene of almost all of his excursion— is "such a surface as the bottom of the sea made dry land," a world of "naked flesh" constantly being played with by the sea "as a cat plays with a mouse."

A similar confusion of the Empedoclean elements occurs in *Walden,* where the pond is sky-water and a landlord claiming his title to the shore. Thoreau makes the connection between the sea and smaller bodies of water explicit in *Cape Cod:* "The ocean is but a larger lake." But the possible reassurance to be gained by such an identity of waters is heavily qualified. Elsewhere the connection of sea and pond is assigned to a mistake of perspective, something to be gotten over: "We wished to associate with the ocean until it lost the pond-like look which it wears to a countryman. We still thought we could see the other side." At the same time that Thoreau calls the ocean a lake, he quickly returns to the main line of his argument: "Yet this same placid ocean, as civil now as a city's harbor, a place for ships and commerce, will ere long be lashed into a sudden fury."

He is of course no particular admirer of the civil or of commerce, nor is he likely to be afraid of curative fury. But the pages surrounding Thoreau's equation of the ocean and lake are full of the most violent images of the sea—the mythical Isle of Demons is there, as is a vision of a drowned continent "all livid and frothing at the nostrils, like the body of a drowned man" and of voracious bluefish "slicking" the water by their butchery of other fish, of a storm playing with vessels "like seaweed" and of the sea abusing "the rag of a man's body like the father of mad bulls." Such terrors are not only the mistaken views of Thoreau the inlander; he debunks the notion that "they who have been long conversant with the

ocean can foretell" and thus survive its violence—"probably no such ancient mariner exists."

The confusion of earth, air, and water in *Walden* is a sign of redemptive transformation, of mediation, of Eden. The chaos where earth, air,
and water meet on Cape Cod is, by contrast, a place of devastation, an
earthly hell. The sea may, momentarily, take on the calm aspect of a lake;
but its nature is anything but calm. At the top of Ktaadn Thoreau had seen
a nature with no relation to man; in the sea he finds a nature whose only
human relation is one of threat and outright destruction. It is terrible even
when calm:

> Though there were numerous vessels at this great distance in
> the horizon on every side, yet the vast spaces between them, like
> the spaces between the stars—far as they were distant from us,
> so were they from one another—nay, some were twice as far
> from each other as from us,—impressed us with a sense of the
> immensity of the ocean, the "unfruitful ocean," as it has been
> called, and we could see what proportion man and his works
> bear to the globe. As we looked off, and saw the water growing
> darker and darker and deeper and deeper the farther we
> looked, till it was awful to consider, and it appeared to have no
> relation to the friendly land, either as shore or bottom,—of
> what use is a bottom if it is out of sight, if it is two or three
> miles from the surface, and you are to be drowned so long be-
> fore you get to it, though it were made of the same stuff with
> your native soil?—over that ocean where, as the Veda says,
> "there is nothing to give support, nothing to rest upon, nothing
> to cling to," I felt that I was a land animal.

The faith that the naturalist-mystic brought to *Walden*—"let us settle ourselves . . . till we come to hard bottom and rocks in place, which we can
call *reality*, and *say*, This is and no mistake"—will not suffice at Truro.
Thoreau has attained what he set out after—"to get a better view than I
had yet had of the ocean"—only to find it an awful thing.

One clue as to why the vision is so awful can be found in Thoreau's
closing remarks. Like any good guide, he offers to the tourist some practical advice—where to go, where to stay, and, most significant of all, when
to visit:

> Most persons visit the seaside in warm weather. . . . But I sus-
> pect that the fall is the best season, for then the atmosphere is

more transparent, and it is a greater pleasure to look out over
the sea. The clear and bracing air, and the storms of autumn,
and winter even, are necessary in order that we may get the impression which the sea is calculated to make. In October, when
the weather is not intolerably cold, and the landscape wears its
autumnal tints, such as, methinks, only a Cape Cod landscape
ever wears, especially if you have a storm during your stay,—
that I am convinced is the best time to visit this shore.

Walden Pond was a perennial spring; the Cape is a landscape of fall, and,
applying one of Thoreau's favorite puns, of the Fall. The shore of the vast
ocean is the place where, even more clearly than in benighted Concord,
men suffer the curse of the Expulsion—cursed land bringing forth sea grass
as its own thorn and thistle, cursed sweating labor of the harshest kind,
ending only in sudden and inevitable death. The Cape Codders scrabbling
for a living from the remains of battered vessels are indeed the fallen; and
they are, Thoreau notices, terribly like all the rest of us: "Are we not all
wreckers contriving that some treasure may be washed up on our beach?"
But what is to be found in "the waste and wrecks of human art" thus
"vomited up" by the sea is more often a corpse or a piece of half-rotted
rope or a bottle of red ale than a treasure.

Cape Cod, to Thoreau, appears then as a polar opposite of Walden,
a damp grey littered inferno in contrast to the paradisal spot near Concord. History found little place in that paradise; but hell, as it turns out,
is for Thoreau the perfect place to show the applicability, however limited,
of the old authorities. Most frequently, history in *Cape Cod* is the record
of decay, and the means of seeing all the more clearly the continuing decline of human endeavor in this unregenerate land. He approaches, for example, the village of Sandwich by way of his volume of historical collections, only to find that the place is sadly disappointing: "Ours was but half
a Sandwich at most, and that must have fallen on the buttered side some
time." He discovers, as further evidence of the poor condition of the villagers, clear sign of that overdeveloped respect for the customs and ways of
the past which is the dark, entrapping side of a sense of history. The book
tells him that: "The inhabitants of Sandwich generally manifest a fond and
steady adherence to the manners, employments, and modes of living which
characterized their fathers." To which Thoreau adds the observation that
this "made me think that they were, after all, very much like all the rest
of the world." Much later, in Truro, Thoreau again consults his authorities
for evidence of the industry, supposedly once prosperous there, of raising

sheep. All Thoreau can find when he visits is one cow "tethered in the desert" and he comments that "the country looked so barren that I several times refrained from asking the inhabitants for a string or a piece of paper, for fear that I should rob them." Taken at face value, the "authoritative" records of the past show all the more clearly how barren the Cape is in Thoreau's present, and how much of the blame the inhabitants must bear for the decline.

It is a reversal of his usual method: the observable present is tested against the recorded past, and not vice versa. If the angle of vision is reversed, the question arises, as we shall see, of whether the authorities are reliable, since, measured against the hard reality of Cape Cod as Thoreau sees it, they are consistently wrong. The reasonable approach to the problem is a suspicious attitude; finding, in one case, a continuity of report from past and present, and one asserting the fertility even today of the Cape, Thoreau observes: "The recent accounts are in some instances *suspectable repetitions* of the old, and I have no doubt that their statements are as often founded on the exception as the rule, and that by far the greater number of acres are as barren as they appear to be" (my italics). That is the more usual, and more reliable, appeal—from account to observation. The recent statements are doubly suspect—because they are repetitious of old and questionable documents, and because they are at variance with the appearance of things now. Thoreau finds, on further investigation, that historical accounts generally are often also "suspectable repetitions," and as such must be used warily. The one historical fact that seems to hold true continuously on Cape Cod is the sad and meaningful prevalence of shipwreck. The Cape is indeed, and has always been, that shore where man's works and hopes are wrecked.

Armed, however ineffectually, with his guidebook and prepared for his encounter with the grim facts of Cape Cod life by his observation of the wreckage where the *St. John* had foundered, Thoreau sets off on his trip to the sea. He presents the trip as a continuation of his earlier ventures, which had led to *Walden:* "I have been accustomed to make excursions to the ponds within ten miles of Concord, but latterly I extended my excursions to the seashore." But by traveling so far from Concord, he encounters the problem of perspective.

In *Walden,* we remember, he had insisted that the fundamental act was settling, not traveling. He had dismissed the second-hand accounts of travelers and had missed no opportunity to point out the futility of those who travel in search of wealth or peace. One sign of his superiority to John Field is that Thoreau "had set there [where Field now lives] many times of old before the ship was built that floated his family to America." The issue seems clearly drawn; it is the native, the deliberately still and settled man who can best front the essential facts.

In *Cape Cod* Thoreau is a stranger. He acknowledges in the very first sentence that the ocean, to one "who lives even a few miles inland," is "another world." His effort to overcome his own ignorance of the sea is represented not by settling on its shore but by wandering on the beach, moving almost continuously. Now it is the stranger to whom he gives the advantage: "A stranger may easily detect what is strange to the oldest inhabitant, for the strange is his province." Repeatedly he reminds his readers that he is an "inlander," a landsman, a "countryman." The freshness of observation which a traveler may bring has its clear advantages—the natives, dulled by familiarity, miss entirely the "inspiriting sound" of the sea roar. The inlander is frequently subject to mistakes of vision—"Indeed, to an inlander, the Cape landscape is a constant mirage"—but that is, to Thoreau, no conclusive drawback.

In fact, the confusion may be productive of fable and myth. It is the landsman's confusion which, in part, allows at the seashore "the animal and vegetable kingdoms" to be "strangely mingled." Even the more foolish errors which a traveler makes have their beneficial effects. Thoreau visits the Shank-Painter Swamp only because "as a landsman naturally would" he misunderstands the name and expects something colorful. Instead, he finds a wealth of natural history on the way—spiders, beach grass, tortoises, toads, and strawberries. And in the end the trip is transcendentally rewarding as well. The landscape he sees en route to the swamp is "the dreariest scenery imaginable," but then he is not interested in mere scenery. In the desert there he finds more evidence of the peculiar nature of the Cape, the dead remains of what had been a flourishing forest, signs of "inundations" and evidence of the continuing strife of the shore, with the operative force being an especially concise union of the elements—"a tide of sand impelled by waves and wind." The trip culminates in Thoreau's realization of the Cape's fragile moorings, which I have already quoted: "This Cape Cod is anchored to the heavens, as it were, by a myriad little cables of beach grass."

There are more mundane advantages. Only because he is a stranger, and thus unlikely to return and make use of the information, Thoreau is shown "the best locality for strawberries" and, ironically, is given some information about the location of the only substantial rock near Eastham, which, by its rarity, had acquired a peculiar value to the natives, "equal to a transfer of California 'rocks,' almost." The two instances provide a useful key to the mixed nature of the natives. Their knowledge of strawberries is undoubtedly to be admired; we remember Thoreau's own fondness for berries on Fair-Haven Hill, and his insistence that only the man who picks and eats them knows fruit truly. But Thoreau the traveler is particularly equipped to see the foolishness of the Cape Codders' misplaced interest in rocks, since he has visited such rocky places as Cohasset and Marblehead. It is this breadth of comparative knowledge which constitutes the stranger's advantage over the native (unless, like Thoreau, the native is also a traveler). Any one fact, as we are told in *Walden* and as such incidents in *Cape Cod* as the discovery of the ale bottle re-emphasize, can yield a sense of the whole if transcendentally viewed. Or so, at least, can the essential facts. But how is one to know the essential? We remember that the task of accumulating, sorting, and assessing is fundamental to the kind of historiography Thoreau undertakes in his chapter on Provincetown. Natural history (in its written form), travelogue, and history are to the reader what travel is to the first-hand observer: a way of assembling the range of knowledge necessary to counterweigh the possible misdirection of a more narrow and deliberate vision; a way of knowing the uniqueness of Walden to be true and the uniqueness of Eastham rock to be false.

The natives whom Thoreau encounters on Cape Cod (and of course the majority of those settled in and around Concord) are brave enough (as was John Field), but not especially percipient. Thoreau's well-known dialogue with the Wellfleet oysterman is a small exemplary summary of the generality of his meetings with the natives. The oysterman is a curious mixture of ignorance and knowledge. He knows about the Concord Fight but not precisely where Concord is and knows his Bible but speaks well of it only out of "prudence," not faith. His trade, while providing him a "competency," is yet another declining Cape industry—the native oysters have died out and the business continues now only by importing stock from the south. Even about oysters he has less than complete knowledge. He insists that oysters can move only "just as much as my shoe," which Thoreau the naturalist knows is not necessarily the case. The oysterman knows the names of ponds—surely an important skill to Thoreau—and of vegetables but has some trouble recalling his wife's name and his days as a pilot have passed because "now they had changed the names so he might be bothered." The oysterman's first-hand knowledge of history serves to Thoreau the useful purpose of corroborating written records, and, being a man of the sea, the oysterman is especially well informed about shipwrecks.

Between Thoreau the inland traveler and the native shore-living oysterman, things end more or less in a standoff. The traveler's freshness of experience (the oysterman thinks it is simple ignorance) allows him to taste the "sweet and savory" sea clam and to handle the sun-squall—an opportunity Thoreau would not have wanted to miss, if only for its potential as a mystical pun. The oysterman explains that the clam is partly poisonous and the sun-squall noxious to handle, which in turn allows Thoreau to feel noticeably superior (and unusually tactful); as for the clam, "I did not tell him that I had eaten a large one entire that afternoon, but began to think that I was tougher than a cat." The pride passes away—"In the course of the evening I began to feel the potency of the clam which I had eaten. . . . I was made quite sick by it for a short time while [the oysterman] laughed at my expense." His only consolation is to find in *Mourt's Relation* an account of the same error—and the same illness—among the Pilgrims. So much, at any rate, for the absolute virtue of the unmediated experience of Nature; there is at least some advice "from my seniors" which, pace *Walden,* Thoreau might profitably have listened to. On the other hand, the wariness based on custom, which is characteristic of the oysterman, is no more absolutely reliable; Thoreau suffers not an itch from the "poisonous" sun-squall.

What Thoreau settles upon, then, is not an unequivocal preference for either strangers or natives, but a kind of synthesis which approximates "neutral ground," a way of seeing that is neither parochial (in the negative sense) nor superficial. This angle of vision is a beneficial effect of Thoreau's visit to the awful seaside:

> The seashore is a sort of neutral ground, a most advantageous point from which to contemplate this world. It is even a trivial place. The waves forever rolling to the land are too far-travelled and untamable to be familiar. . . . It is a wild, rank place, and there is no flattery in it. Strewn with crabs, horseshoes, and razor clams, and whatever the sea casts up,—a vast *morgue,* where famished dogs may range in packs, and crows come daily to glean the pittance which the tide leaves them. The carcasses of men and beasts together lie stately up upon its shelf, rotting and bleaching in the sun and waves, and each tide turns them in their beds, and tucks fresh sand under them. There is naked nature,—inhumanly sincere, wasting no thought on man, nibbling at the cliffy shore where gulls wheel amid the spray.

The value Thoreau finds is not objectivity; in a journal entry of May 6, 1854, Thoreau insists that "there is no such thing as a pure *objective* observation." He goes on to raise again the issue of travel: "It matters not where or how far you travel,—the farther commonly the worse,—but how much alive you are." Or, we might say, it matters not where you travel but how, as it matters not where but how you settle. The peculiar experience of Cape Cod is that it allows Thoreau to be especially alive to and in a landscape that is a morgue, a collection of momentos of death and of the vanity of earthly hope.

But even in that landscape Thoreau finds his moments of insight. One of the most important occurs in the chapter devoted to "The Beach." Thoreau seeks out a "charity house," a shelter set up for the care of shipwrecked sailors. Putting his eye to "a knot-hole in the door" he sees more than a derelict building:

> After long looking without seeing, into the dark,—not knowing how many shipwrecked men's bones we might see at last, looking with the eye of faith, knowing that, though to him that knocketh it may not always be opened, yet to him that looketh long enough through a knot-hole the inside shall be visible,— for we had had some practice at looking inward,—by steadily keeping our other ball covered from the light meanwhile, putting the outward world behind us, ocean and land, and the beach,—till the pupil became enlarged and collected the rays of light that were wandering in that dark (for the pupil shall be enlarged by looking; there never was so dark a night but a faithful and patient eye, however small, might at last prevail over it)—after all this, I say, things began to take shape in our vision,—if we may use this expression where there was nothing but emptiness,—and we obtained the long-wished-for insight.

It is Thoreau's most clever answer to his own question—will you be a student merely or a seer? Be a pupil and you are at the same moment both student and see-er. It is the moment he went to the Cape for, or at least a moment he went to the Cape to rediscover, another chance to "link my facts to my fable." Notice how easily the scientific fact of the enlargement of the pupil of the eye becomes a symbolic pun. Thoreau is once again writing a new scripture, in part by turning the old Scripture inside out; he revises the familiar words of Matthew 7:7 in a subordinate clause. He identifies this vision—which, like a good mystic, he is not sure he has the power to express—with the sense of apocalyptic threat he finds elsewhere on the edge of the sea; he is "at last, looking with the eye of faith." He shows that he has learned the chastening lesson of this purgatory, by putting the outward world behind him. His final words in *Cape Cod* are an extension of this—"A man may stand there and put all America behind him."

It appears at first, however, that all this complexity of syntax and allusion amounts to a Transcendental shaggy-dog story; for what Thoreau sees, after identifying himself with the "blind bard" Milton, is a chimney, "some stones and some loose wads of wool on the floor, and an empty fireplace at the further end"—hardly worth putting aside the world for. But this is only the visible, in the mundane sense; he had rebuked, in his journal, those who "take cognizance of outward things merely." The real vision, the "long-wished-for insight" constitutes yet another proof of the bitter lessons of the whole excursion: "Turning our backs on the outward world, we thus looked through the knot-hole into the Humane house, into the very bowels of mercy; and for bread we found a stone. . . . This, then, is what charity hides! Virtues antique and far away, with ever a rusty nail over the latch; and very difficult to keep in repair, withal, it is so uncertain whether any will ever gain the beach near you." As Thoreau remarks at the end of the chapter, a few sentences later, "I did not intend this for a sentimental journey," and indeed it is not. But if this is where he ends, where did he begin? His conclusion is to put behind him all outward things; but he finds the site of this inward vision by a long wandering in the out-of-doors.

More literally, the chapter which ends at the charity house consists primarily, up until its final pages, of natural history and antiquarianism. Thoreau spends some time observing wreckers, naturalizing man, as he had done in "The Village." He discusses, with appropriate citations, the uses and nature of driftwood; he observes and describes the topography of the beach. He finds the time to record "a remarkable method of catching gulls, derived from the Indians" and to read, apparently in " 'Description of the Eastern Coast of the County of Barnstable,' printed in 1802," about the habits and names of gulls. In the end, he is directed to the charity house into which he looks so productively by the same "authority" that explains the function of the houses and gives him detailed instruction about where they are to be found.

We have here, again, a gathering of the ways in which the world's methods and the world's authorities may be used by the man seeking a kind of "insight and far-sight" which is normally beyond the reach of scientist or historian, and which may depend upon turning one's back on the world. By going over the ground with the eye of the naturalist and with the range of information to be gained from historical accounts, Thoreau finds the place where insight occurs.

Blessed men, Thoreau loves to remind us, have no need of history. But on Cape Cod Thoreau can find his blessedness only in the negative, in his estrangement from the purgatorial world of sand, wind, ocean, beach grass, and wreckage. There, history is not only relevant, it is inescapable. Thoreau carries it with him, in the form of his historical guidebook and his knowledge of the early chroniclers of the New World: Thomas Morton, Edward Winslow, John Smith, Beverly, William Wood. The records of the past are there in any case, in the Truro graveyard or in the relics, human and otherwise, on the beaches. And there is the constant sea, with which "we do not associate the idea of antiquity" since it changes not at all over time, but whose ominous timelessness makes the records of human time all the more noticeable, and all the more pitiable.

In this time-bound, relic-strewn, fallen world, Thoreau finds the occasion to undertake his most extended historical investigations: the ecclesiastical history of Eastham, and the attempt to find in all written records the true discoverer of Cape Cod. The two are exemplary, indeed monitory histories. And they are set in a context of a more general consideration of the role and value of history. We remember Thoreau's comments about "suspectable repetitions." But Thoreau's affection for old accounts—"I love to quote so good authority"—is apparent. Indeed, repetition is, in its way, a virtue, as is the eye for detail he finds in the old books: "The old accounts are the richest in topography, which was what we wanted most; and, indeed, in most things else, for I find that the readable parts of the modern accounts of these towns consist, in a great measure, of quotations, acknowledged and unacknowledged, from the older ones, without any other information of equal interest." By reading the old accounts for their topography, Thoreau again uses them, not for their own, but for his purposes. History, properly read, need not be read on the authors' terms.

No account is truly satisfactory. As in *The Maine Woods* the particular evidence of this is to be found in maps, but Thoreau generalizes the point: "[Cape Cod] was not as on the map, or seen from the stage coach; but there I found it all out of doors, huge and real, Cape Cod! as it cannot be represented on a map, color it as you will; the thing itself, than which there is nothing more like it, no truer picture or account." Thoreau indulges himself at one point by recording a more blunt rejection of accounts (" 'Dam book-peddlars,—all the time talking about books. Better do something. Damn 'em. I'll shoot 'em.' ") but those are only the mutterings of the oysterman's "fool." In a more serious way, Thoreau raises again the point that time, pursued back far enough, defeats itself. Quoting a Swiss colleague of Agassiz, Édouard Desor, he argues that " 'in going back through the geological ages, we come to an epoch when, according to all appearances, the dry land did not exist, and when the surface of our globe was entirely covered with water,' " which is, as he has asserted elsewhere, the most timeless of elements.

The decline from myth to history to the sketchy records of modern life is a sign of the more general decline from ancient and heroic times. Speaking of the difficult voyage of a Cape Cod sea captain, Thoreau claims that: "In ancient times the adventures of these two or three men and boys would have been made the basis of a myth, but now such tales are crowded into a line of shorthand signs, like an algebraic formula in the shipping news." Compared to the newspapers, history is better. But its limitations are sharply delineated: useful not for its own ends, below myth in ultimate value, and subject to the test of current observation, always to be known as questionable and secondhand.

Why then use it at all? Having told the tale of the Wellfleet oysterman, Thoreau asks, "*Quid loquar?* Why repeat what he told us?" His answer is to quote Virgil's *Eclogue VI*, where the poet asks the same question concerning the songs of Silenus. The answer is, in the immediate sense, no answer at all; Thoreau replies to his own question by quoting Virgil's. The passage mentions the story of Scylla, who tore apart sailors in the depths of the sea—a monster still likely inhabiting the ocean off Cape Cod. The Virgilian parallel at least implies that the oysterman's history (he has been telling about his memories of George Washington) is of value as myth and as literature, if not as fact.

And history is a tonic against idleness. Thoreau introduces his survey of the history of Eastham by suggesting it will pass the time: "As it will take us an hour to get over this plain, and there is no variety in the prospect, peculiar as it is, I will read a little in the history of Eastham the while." Although it soon appears this is more than a pastime, we have been warned not to expect anything too lively. Thoreau has, on the previous page, provided a short, sour, but accurate precis of such histories: a matter of pastors, old prayers, and ecclesiastical councils.

Thoreau begins, however, with an issue of more import than ecclesiastical councils, and one of wider application than Eastham. The town, he records, was acquired in small part by purchase, in larger part simply by claiming that "Not Any" other being owned the lands taken by settlers: "Perhaps this was the first instance of that quiet way of 'speaking for' a place not yet occupied, or at least not improved as much as it may be, which their descendants have practiced, and are still practicing so extensively." Finding, in the case of Eastham, an Indian, Lieutenant Anthony, who years later appeared, claimed, and received payment for lands north of Eastham, Thoreau wonders if a similar event may take place "at the door of the White House some day"—perhaps as repayment for the dispossession of the Cherokee. But it is not only a matter of mistreatment of the natives, or a reminder that the natives he encounters on the Cape are in fact not so native as they seem. There is a larger point, a contributory explanation of why this place is the home of the damned: "I know that if you hold a thing unjustly, there will surely be the devil to pay at last."

Having established the shoddy foundation of the town, Thoreau mounts an anecdotal survey of the early religious history of Eastham. As one might expect, he misses few opportunities to see the shallowness and misdirection of the religious practices he observes. The overall intent of the survey is, first of all, to identify the self-deluding and even hysterical roots of Eastham's ecclesiastical establishment. Thoreau does this good-humoredly and at a distance; he makes few references to contemporary practices of the more widely accepted sort, and thus he avoids directly offending his readers. He does tell about camp meetings which are, unmistakeably but quietly, identified as conventions of lunatics: "They select a time for their meetings when the moon is full." Few of the readers of *Putnam's Weekly* were likely to take offense at the ridicule of religious extremism; Thoreau will not, however, allow his readers wholly to escape the brunt of his charge simply by separating themselves, as most would do willingly, from the more extravagant and déclassé religious enthusiasms. Acknowledging his own inability to follow the complications of doctrine in one case he recounts, Thoreau falls back on a vague but pointed summary: "And many the like distinctions they made, such as some of my readers, probably, are more familiar with than I am." Eastham is, after all, one example of the Puritan roots of the general moral polity of New England in Thoreau's time; if the proud parishoners of early Cape Cod are misguided, are not their descendants equally so?

Thoreau softens the case by admitting that Cape Cod is a unique place: "We conjectured that the reason for the perhaps unusual, if not unhealthful development of the religious sentiment here, was the fact that a large portion of the population are women whose husbands and sons are either abroad on the sea, or else drowned, and there is nobody but they and the ministers left behind." The effects are hysterical and dehumanizing. Thoreau finds one "singularly masculine woman" who escapes madness only at the price of any sort of human feeling; she is "hard enough for any enormity." These are not, we must suppose, peculiar accidents— they are only "*perhaps* unusual"—but rather the direct result of the misdirection of spirit Thoreau finds in Puritan religion. It is yet another explanation of why the Cape is a place of spiritual death, producing, by way of art, no more than commendatory occasional verses on the fall of Governor Prence's pear tree, which Thoreau can bear to quote only in part. By recounting the very events which the settlers took enough pride in to record, Thoreau manages to show how little they lived "an Achillean life." He uses the history of the place against itself: by your own chronicles shall ye be judged.

The case of Reverend Samuel Osborn shows this. Osborn, accused of having "embraced the religion of Arminius," is tried and found inadequate by "an ecclesiastical council consisting of ministers" which—a lovely pun—"sat upon him, and . . . naturally enough, spoiled his usefulness." Osborn is dismissed and moves to Boston to keep a school. But, alone among the clergy Thoreau mentions, Osborn was indeed useful, and in the practical way of which Thoreau is completely approving. He "taught his people the use of peat, and the art of drying and preparing it, which, as they had scarcely any other fuel, was a great blessing to them." In addition he was an agriculturalist. Such usefulness is no defense against a sitting council. Thoreau observes, knowingly using the language of a doctrine which is fundamental (and fundamentally in *error*) according to the fathers of Protestantism, that Osborn "was fully justified, methinks, by his works in the peat meadow." Had there been more hewing of peat and hoeing of beans, and less preaching of the sort which Thoreau quotes at length, both the crops and the spirit of the Cape might be less barren.

Thoreau, at the last, seems to turn aside his wrath, in a passage which is a fine example of damnation disguised as courtesy: "Let no one think that I do not love the old ministers. They were, probably, the best men of their generation, and they deserve that their biographies should fill the pages of the town histories." This, of men who frighten "comparatively innocent" young men "nearly out of [their] wits," and who, apparently, cannot tell Latin from Nipmuck: if such are the best, what of the commonality?

In "Provincetown" the Pilgrims are examined more extensively, and somewhat less antagonistically, as possible exemplars of the properly deliberate life. Here Thoreau indulges in a sort of criticism of the New England foundation which we have in the twentieth century come to accept as stereotypically correct. He makes his point, as later critics have done, by using the settlers' own historical account against them. He does not, we notice, question the accuracy of these accounts, perhaps because, as in the case of Millennium Grove meeting ground and the murderous Nauset woman, he finds ample corroboration within the sight of his own eyes.

What he does is to define, in the words of the damned, the elements of the damnation he sees, and to show how, properly read, history may have a salutary effect utterly opposed to the intentions of its writers.

The pages which Thoreau devotes in his "Provincetown" chapter to the question of who first and best explored Cape Cod offer a more complex example of Thoreau as historian. Here he addresses directly the question of the comparative validity of sources. His basic tests, not surprisingly, are language (especially the language of naming) and geographic detail. His effort is not so single-mindedly condemnatory as it was in his survey of Eastham. Now he tries to find not only examples of delusion and failure, but exemplary lives in the positive sense. The moment of discovery is not, to him, a time of purely historical interest; could he find in the record of the past a detailed account of true discovery, he might better be able to recognize and to describe his own attempt always to live in an attitude of discovery. Failing that, he can see in the record of repeated discovery and rediscovery a type of the kind of self-renewing Transcendental holiness which he hopes to make the fundamental element of his life: "If America was found and lost again, as most of us believe [and as his documents seem to prove], then why not twice? especially as there were likely to be so few records of an earlier discovery. Consider what stuff history is made of,—that for the most part it is merely a story agreed upon by posterity. . . . I believe that, if I were to live the life of mankind over again myself (which I would not be hired to do), with the Universal History in my hands, I should not be able to tell what was what."

As with science, Thoreau is always aware of the potential hazards of his mode of inquiry; the acquisition of more knowledge is less preferable than the acquisition of better knowledge. More information might only lead to the kind of entrapment in detail which Thoreau lamented in his journal. With that in mind, he shifts his ground, working deep rather than broad, and considers at length the Pilgrims, "discoverers" at least in the common legend. Thoreau can, in studying them, consider exactly what the nature of discovery and its potential failures are. It is very much to his taste to find an example of failure; if earlier discoverers have, in some recognizable way, missed their chance, it leaves the field open to Thoreau himself, to be not merely a rediscoverer but a true discoverer. For a man convinced of the value of individuality and originality, the distinction is by no means unimportant.

It is a question of naming which begins Thoreau's venture backward. He notices how "on successive maps, Cape Cod appears sprinkled over with French, Dutch, and English names, as it made part of New France,

New Holland, and New England." That leads, in its turn, to the larger question of exploration, and to the first of Thoreau's historiographic points: "It is remarkable that there is not in English any adequate or correct account of the French exploration of what is now the coast of New England, between 1604 and 1608." Such an account does exist in French, and constitutes "the most interesting chapter of what we may call the ante-Pilgrim history of New England." Thoreau goes on to show both the general ignorance, on the part of English and American historians, of this account in its full form, and the frequent unacknowledged use—indeed, copying—of portions of the French account by these same English and American authorities. He spends some time asserting the priority and the extent of the French experience in New England. In passing he raises again the issue of "just title" and points out how, by comparison with the French, the English settlers show a sad inability to derive adequate information even from those things they should have known first hand. Here is one major theme of Thoreau's historical excursion: the measurement of the Pilgrim experience against that of the French. It is the French, and especially Champlain, who seem, at first, to win the contest.

But at least on the point of priority, even the French are inadequate, as Thoreau shows by citing the history, before Champlain, of visits to "this country of 'Norumbega,' " including an extended description of the moment when "Cape Cod is commonly said to have been discovered in 1602" by Bartholomew Gosnold. The problem with this legendary discovery, as Thoreau demonstrates, is its vagueness, especially when tested against the standard of detail and accuracy represented by Champlain's *Voyages*. The story as Thoreau tells it is full of errors of judgment (Gosnold at first mistakes the "savages" for "Christians distressed"), and there is plenty of evidence that Gosnold was not the first to visit these shores. One of the savages he meets comes dressed, roughly, as an Englishman. There are also repeated mistakes of language (the aborigines are, in the words of the chronicler, able "to understand much more than we . . . for want of language, could comprehend,") and failures of naming. Most of Gosnold's names for the features he "discovered" do not remain in use.

Thus weak on the face of it, the case of Gosnold proves susceptible to attack on another front: consulting "old Icelandic manuscripts" Thoreau raises the possibility of visits by the "hardy race" of Northmen, as well as "the claims of several other worthy persons." The Northmen are particularly of interest to him, since they allow Thoreau to name himself as the true discoverer. The possible first visitors he names—Thor-finn, Thor-wald—share with Thoreau the same initial syllable. One of them "is said

to have had a son born in New England." Explicitly, that son was the an-
cestor of "Thorwaldson the sculptor." But implicitly it is Thoreau himself.
Some pages before, discussing a mirage he sees in Truro, Thoreau made
the connection directly: "But whether Thor-finn saw the mirage here or
not, Thor-eau, one of the same family, did; and perchance it was because
Leif the Lucky had, in a previous voyage, taken Thor-er and his people off
the rock in the middle of the sea, that Thor-eau was born to see it."

The overall effect of Thoreau's researches is twofold. First, it emphasizes the recurrence of discovery; second, it makes it clear that it was Thoreau himself who was "born to see it" truly for the first time. The point is
not so much, after all, the priority as the *quality* of discovery; and to investigate that Thoreau devotes himself to the most familiar case, that of the
Pilgrims who landed in Provincetown Harbor "on the 11th of November,
1620, old style." Using their own chronicle, the misnamed *Mourt's Relation,* he considers their strengths and weaknesses as discoverers, and as
models for his own exploratory excursion. It is the clearest example of
Thoreau using the method of the naturalist to assess the validity of a historical authority. Thoreau tests each element of the account in *Mourt's Relation* against the observations he himself makes. The Pilgrims are correct
about the shallowness of the harbor, but wrong in most other ways. At
least Thoreau can find no corroboration for what the chronicle says about
fowl, wood, soil, and vegetation.

It is a troublesome point. The fault could be one of inaccuracy of the
chronicle, or yet another sign of the progressive decline of the Cape since
the arrival of the profaning hand of man: "All accounts agree in affirming
that this part of the Cape was comparatively well wooded a century ago.
But notwithstanding the great changes which have taken place in these respects, I cannot but think that we must make some allowance for the
greenness of the Pilgrims in these matters, which caused them to see
green. . . . Their account may be true particularly, but it is generally false."
This is, if you will, the obverse of the necessary and virtuous subjectivity
of observation which Thoreau asserts in his journal entry of May 6, 1854.
And it serves to complicate further the balance between strangers and natives; here are strangers who bring not insight but preconception to their
observation.

In the end, the Pilgrims will not serve as adequate models of discovery—"they possessed but few of the qualities of the modern pioneer." This
is due in large part to their refusal to act as individuals—"they were a family and a church, and were more anxious to keep together, though it were
on the sand, than to explore and colonize a New World." The connection

to those who sit in Concord reading newspapers or the riders on the Iron Horse who barely find the time to glance at Walden Pond is clear. Again Thoreau invokes the example of Champlain; he, in the same circumstances, "would have sought an interview with the savages, and examined the country as far as the Connecticut, and made a map of it, before Billington had climed his tree." It is Champlain who leaves behind him "a minute and faithful account." While the English "fable"—in this case, not a useful occupation—Champlain acts, bringing to the task the virtues of the naturalist, and of Thoreau at Walden, "measuring and sounding." Champlain, too, is imperfect; he is French, for one thing, and decidedly unfriendly to the Indians. But he shows what a man of action and of observation might do.

This search for exemplary predecessors is a further and important use to which Thoreau puts history. It is a task of peculiar significance, and peculiar difficulty, to the American saint (a genus of which Thoreau and Whitman are representative). The very hope of finding full-scale examples in the past is, in its way, a denial of one's own sainthood, since holiness in the New World style is inherently unique and individual. The true American saint can have no predecessor, no model after which to pattern his life. Necessarily, his only hero is the self. It is for this reason that the exemplars he finds are, most commonly, obscure and failures. Their obscurity insures that they do not represent the weight of custom which the American saint hopes to avoid; were they less eccentric, posterity would have agreed to remember them as a part of received history. Their failure serves the purposes of allowing the saint to retain his originality while deriving the reassurance that the task is worthy. So too does the saint's choice of exemplary figures whose explicit action is unlike his own; Columbus' voyage is vastly different from Thoreau's.

But the search for usable predecessors goes on. History serves the purpose, then, of proving that the discovery of "the only true America" is an old and esteemed goal, and that it has never quite been done. So it remains a prospect worth the most intense effort. With that knowledge one may face with some serenity even the ominous and inhumanely sincere ocean, with all America behind him, knowing that he faces yet another wilderness with another, truer America yet to be found.

MICHAEL T. GILMORE

Walden *and the "Curse of Trade"*

Among the many paradoxes of *Walden* perhaps none is more ironic than the fact that this modernist text—modernist in its celebration of private consciousness, its aestheticizing of experience, its demands upon the reader—starts out as a denunciation of modernity. It is inspired by the agrarian ideals of the past, yet in making a metaphor of those ideals it fails as a rejoinder to the nineteenth century and creates as many problems as it lays to rest. Personal and historical disappointment determines the shape of Thoreau's masterpiece. In important ways it is a defeated text. Though Thoreau begins with the conviction that literature can change the world, the aesthetic strategies he adopts to accomplish political objectives involve him in a series of withdrawals from history; in each case the ahistorical maneuver disables the political and is compromised by the very historical moment it seeks to repudiate.

This is not to deny *Walden*'s greatness, but rather to emphasize the cost of Thoreau's achievement and to begin to specify its limits. No reader of the book can fail to notice the exultant tone of the "Conclusion"; the impression it leaves is of an author who has made good on his promise not to write "an ode to dejection." But one might say, in another paradox, that *Walden*'s triumphant success is precisely what constitutes its defeat. For underlying that triumph is a forsaking of civic aspirations for an exclusive concern with "the art of living well" (in Emerson's phrase about his former disciple). And to say this is to suggest that *Walden* is a book at

From *American Romanticism and the Marketplace.* © 1985 by the University of Chicago. University of Chicago Press, 1985.

odds with its own beliefs; it is to point out Thoreau's complicity in the ideological universe he abhors.

II

At the heart of Thoreau's dissent from modernity is a profound hostility to the process of exchange, to what he calls the "curse of trade." He pictures a contemporary Concord where everyone is implicated in the market, and he mounts a critique of that society as antithetical to independence, to identity, and to life itself. His antimarket attitude, though it has similarities to pastoralism, is more properly understood as a nineteenth-century revision of the agrarian or civic humanist tradition. Civic humanists regarded the economic autonomy of the individual as the basis for his membership in the polis. The self-sufficient owner of the soil, in their view, was the ideal citizen because he relied on his own property and exertions for his livelihood and was virtually immune to compromising pressures. Commercial enterprise, in contrast, endangered liberty because it fostered dependence on others and, by legitimating the pursuit of private interest, undermined devotion to the common good. Jeffersonian agrarianism, the American development of this tradition, retained its antimarket bias and its stress on freedom from the wills of others. In Jefferson's own formulation from the *Notes on the State of Virginia,* commerce is productive of subservience, and the independent husbandman uniquely capable of civic virtue.

Thoreau, writing some sixty years after Jefferson, shows a similar antipathy to exchange but entertains no illusions about either the present-day husbandman or the benefits conferred by real property. Several pages into *Walden* appears his well-known indictment of the various forms of ingratiation and venality practiced by his neighbors in order to make money—an indictment that applies to the farmer as much as to the tradesman.

> It is very evident what mean and sneaking lives many of you live, . . . always promising to pay, promising to pay, tomorrow, and dying to-day, insolvent; seeking to curry favor to get custom, by how many modes, only not state-prison offences; lying, flattering, voting [cf. Thoreau's attack on democracy of "Civil Disobedience"], contracting yourselves into a nutshell of civility, or dilating into an atmosphere of thin and vaporous generosity, that you may persuade your neighbor to let you make his shoes, or his hat, or his coat, or import his groceries for him.

Thoreau's position in this passage is directly opposed to the laissez-faire ideology gaining in popularity among his contemporaries. He sees the marketplace not as a discipline in self-reliance, an arena where the man of enterprise can prove his worth, but rather as a site of humiliation where the seller has to court and conciliate potential buyers to gain their custom. The interactions of exchange, in his view, breed not independence but servility. Nor, insists Thoreau, does nineteenth-century agriculture offer an exemption from the abasements and dependencies of the exchange process. The land has become an investment like any other and the farmer a willing participant in the marketplace. The husbandmen of Concord, immortalized by Emerson for their stand "by the rude bridge that arched the flood," are now "serfs of the soil" who spend their lives "buying and selling" and have forgotten the meaning of self-reliance. Thoreau envisions them, in a celebrated image, "creeping down the road of life," each pushing before him "a barn seventy-five feet by forty . . . and one hundred acres of land, tillage, mowing, pasture, and wood-lot!"

For Thoreau, commercial agriculture has an impact on the physical world which is just as devastating as its effect on the farmer. In the chapter "The Ponds" he describes an agricultural entrepreneur named Flint for whom nature exists solely as commodity. Indeed, on Flint's farm the use value of natural objects has been consumed by their exchange value; their abstract character as potential money has completely obliterated their "sensuous" reality (to use a favorite adjective of Marx's in this connection) as fruits and vegetables. The result is an impoverishment of the thing, an alteration of its very nature. "I respect not his labors," Thoreau writes of Flint,

> his farm where every thing has its price; who would carry the landscape, who would carry his God, to market, if he could get any thing for him; . . . on whose farm nothing grows free, whose fields bear no crops, whose meadows no flowers, whose trees no fruits, but dollars; who loves not the beauty of his fruits, whose fruits are not ripe till they are turned to dollars.

A companion chapter, "The Pond in Winter," shows this destruction of nature actually coming to pass through the speculations of "a gentleman farmer" who carries the landscape off to market. Wanting "to cover each one of his dollars with another," the farmer has hired a crew of laborers to strip Walden of its ice. Thoreau treats the entire opeartion as though the ice-cutters were "busy husbandmen" engaged in skimming the land: "They went to work at once, ploughing, harrowing, rolling, furrowing . . . [and] suddenly began to hook up the virgin mould itself, with a peculiar jerk, clear down to the sand, or rather the water, . . . all the *terra firma* there was, and haul it away on sleds."

As Thoreau's denunciation of Flint makes clear, his quarrel with the marketplace is in large measure ontological. He sees the exchange process as emptying the world of its concrete reality and not only converting objects into dollars but causing their "it-ness" or being to disappear. A particularly powerful statement of this idea occurs at the beginning of "The Ponds," in the passage where Thoreau assails the marketing of huckleberries. He argues that nature's fruits "do not yield their true flavor" either to the man who raises them commercially or to the urban purchasers. The huckleberry cannot be tasted or even said to exist outside its native habitat: invariably it undergoes a fatal transformation en route from the countryside to the metropolis. What reaches Boston is not the fragrant berry itself but the "mere provender" that the fruit has become in being transported to the customer. Its bloom has been "rubbed off in the market cart" and its "ambrosial and essential part" extinguished by its conversion into an article of trade.

Thoreau believes that along with the degradation of the physical object in exchange there occurs a shriveling of the individual. Men in the marketplace, according to *Walden,* do not relate as persons but as something less than human; they commit violence against their own natures in their incessant anxiety to induce others to buy their products or their labor. "The finest qualities of our nature," Thoreau says in a passage paralleling his discussion of the huckleberry, "like the bloom on fruits, can be preserved only by the most delicate handling. Yet we do not treat ourselves or one another thus tenderly." The laborer's self, his authentic being, has as little chance to survive the exchange process as a genuine huckleberry. To satisfy his employer, he has to suppress his individuality and become a mechanical thing: "Actually, the laboring man has not leisure for a true integrity day by day; he cannot afford to sustain the manliest relations to men; his labor would be depreciated in the market. He has no time to be anything but a machine." The final disappearance of the person, the most extreme form of absence, would be death, and Thoreau does in fact equate exchange with the deprivation of life. "The cost of a thing," he writes, "is the amount of what I will call life which is required to be exchanged for it, immediately or in the long run." Exchange brings about the ultimate alienation of man from himself; to engage in buying and selling is not merely to debase the self but to extinguish it, to hurry into death.

Thoreau's analysis of commodification has certain affinities with the

Marxist critique of capitalism. His comments on the erosion of human presence in exchange evoke the notion of reification, a concept developed in the twentieth century by Georg Lukács. Reification refers to the phenomenon whereby a social relation between men assumes the character of a relation between things. Because they interact through the commodities they exchange, including the commodity of labor, individuals in the capitalist market confront each other not as human beings, but as objectified, nonhuman entities. They lose sight altogether of the subjective element in their activity. An important corollary to this loss of the person is a confusion of history with nature. By mystifying or obscuring man's involvement in the production of his social reality, reification leads him to apprehend that reality as a "second nature." He perceives the social realm as an immutable and universal order over which he exerts no control. The result is greatly to diminish the possibility of human freedom.

Thoreau reaches a similar conclusion about the decline of liberty under capitalism: he portrays his townsmen as slave drivers of themselves. The weakness of his position, a weakness to which we shall return, is that he launches his attack against history rather than in its name, with the result that he mystifies the temporality of his own experience, presenting it as natural or removed from social time. He is outspoken in debunking such "naturalization" when it functions as a way of legitimating social codes. In his disquisition on clothing, for example, he points out how the fetishism of fashion invests the merely whimsical with the prestige of inevitability. "When I ask for a garment of a particular form," he explains, "my tailoress tells me gravely, 'They do not make them so now,' not emphasizing the 'They' at all, as if she quoted an authority as impersonal as the Fates. . . . We worship not the Graces, nor the Parcae, but Fashion."

Thoreau constantly challenges the false identification of what "they" say or do with the course of nature. He maintains that social reality, to which men submit as though to "a seeming fate," is in fact made by men and subject to the revision. His neighbors, whose resignation only masks their desperation, do not adopt the customary modes of living out of preference but "honestly think there is no choice left." Although they deny the possibility of change and say, "This is the only way," Thoreau insists that they are mistaken, that "there are as many ways" to live as "can be drawn radii from one centre." His lack of deference toward his elders stems from the same impatience with a reified social reality. Old people, he finds, regard their own experience as exemplary and refuse even to contemplate alternatives to the existing order of things. But "what old people say you cannot do you try and find that you can." What they fail to realize, what

Thoreau feels all his neighbors are unable to see, is that "their daily life of routine and habit . . . is built on purely illusory foundations." They "think that *is* which *appears* to be."

III

To negate the "curse of trade" during his stay in the woods, Thoreau supports himself by farming. This is the occupation followed by the majority of his neighbors, but his own experiment in husbandry differs significantly from the commercial agriculture prevalent in Concord. By building his own house and growing his own food, by concentrating on the necessaries of life and renouncing luxuries, he minimizes his dependency on others and removes himself as far as possible from the market economy. In keeping with his precept, "Enjoy the land, but own it not," he squats on soil belonging to someone else (Emerson, as it happens) and endeavors to "avoid all trade and barter." "More independent than any farmer in Concord," he claims to have learned from his experience that something approaching self-sufficiency is still practicable in mid-nineteenth-century America, if only "one would live simply and eat only the crop which he raised, and raise no more than he ate, and not exchange it for an insufficient quantity of more luxurious and expensive things."

Something *approaching* self-sufficiency: Thoreau makes no attempt to disguise the fact that he is unable to emancipate himself completely from exchange relations. He freely "publishes his guilt," as he puts it, that his venture at subsistence farming is not strictly speaking an economic success. He raises a cash crop of beans and uses the proceeds to give variety to his diet, and he is forced to supplement his income from farming by hiring himself out as a day laborer, the employment he finds "the most independent of any, especially as it required only thirty to forty days in a year to support one." He recognizes, in other words, the obsolescence of his program as a *literal* antidote to the ills of market civilization.

What Thoreau does affirm, and affirm consistently, is the possibility even in the nineteenth century of a way of life characterized by self-reliance and minimal involvement in exchange. Following the civic humanist tradition, he identifies this ideal with husbandry, and husbandry in turn supplies him with a metaphoric solution to the problems of the marketplace. Agriculture, he states, "was once a sacred art; but it is pursued with irreverent haste and heedlessness by us, our object being to have large farms and large crops merely." Thoreau makes a point of actually farming in the traditional way, going down to the woods and living by himself, because he refuses to sacrifice the use value of husbandry to its symbolic value in the manner of Flint. He wants to earn his metaphor by dwelling "near enough to Nature and Truth to borrow a trope from them."

Thoreau has an acute sense of the relationship between commodity and symbolism—or rather of the commodified thinking concealed in symbolization. The commodity, like the symbol, is both what it is and the token of something else (i.e., money); on Flint's farm, the something else has totally displaced the concrete reality. To use farming as a trope for self-sufficiency without literally farming would be to perform in thought the same violation Flint commits on his land. Thoreau finds this commodified habit of mind to be the common practice of his contemporaries. "Our lives," he complains, "pass at such remoteness from its symbols, and its metaphors and tropes are so far fetched." At Walden he redeems his own life from such distancing and loss of the real; he farms the land, as he says in "The Bean-Field," "for the sake of tropes and expression, to serve a parable-maker one day."

Thoreau suggests that the values formerly associated with farming are available to all men, in all pursuits. "Labor of the hands," as he describes his hoeing, ". . . has a constant and imperishable moral, and to the scholar it yields a classic result." The moral yielded by *Walden* is that virtually any kind of workman can be a figurative farmer and any kind of work independent "labor of the hands." The centrality of this phrase to Thoreau's undertaking is suggested by its position at the very outset of the book; it appears in the opening sentence: "When I wrote the following pages, or rather the bulk of them, I lived alone, in the woods, a mile from any neighbor, in a house which I had built myself, on the shore of Walden Pond, in Concord, Massachusetts, and earned my living by the labor of my hands only." Labor of the hands is clearly meant to encompass intellectual as well as manual work. As Thoreau says in explaining what he lived for, "My head is hands and feet. I feel all my best faculties concentrated in it."

A difficulty that arises immediately with Thoreau's metaphoric solution to exchange is that it has the effect of privatizing a civic virtue. Farming as a way of life enjoyed the high standing it did in civic humanist thought because it was a training for participation in the public or political sphere. In *Walden*, as a figure for self-reliant labor, it has become a private virtue—a virtue without civic consequences. And there is no doubt that Thoreau hoped his text would result in some form of political awakening. Indeed, one of his principal objectives in writing *Walden* is to restore his countrymen to the freedom which they have lost under the market system.

He moves to the woods on "Independence Day, or the fourth of July, 1845" because he considers this a civic enterprise, requiring a reformation or new foundation of American liberty. A close connection can be seen here between the project of *Walden* and Thoreau's appeal at the end of "Civil Disobedience" for a founder or reformer whose eloquence will revive the polity. In the essay, which he wrote while working on the early drafts of the book, he criticizes the country's lawmakers for their failure to "speak with authority" about the government. Implicitly he projects a role for himself as a model legislator, one whose effectiveness will lie in his ability to inspire others through his words:

> No man with a genius for legislation has appeared in America. They are rare in the history of the world. There are orators, politicians, and eloquent men, by the thousand; but the speaker has not yet opened his mouth to speak, who is capable of settling the much-vexed questions of the day. We love eloquence for its own sake, and not for any truth which it may utter, or any heroism it may inspire.

In *Walden* Thoreau assumes the duties of this reformer-legislator as a writer rather than a speaker because of the greater range and authority of literature. The orator, he says in the chapter "Reading," addresses the mob on the transitory issues of the moment, but the author "speaks to the heart and intellect of mankind, to all in any age who can *understand* him." Great writers, he adds, "are a natural and irresistible aristocracy in every society, and, more than kings or emperors, exert an influence on mankind." Twentieth-century readers, with their very different ideas about the functions of texts and the role of the writer, may find it difficult to take these statements seriously. But it is a mistake to treat *Walden* as though it were imbued with the modernist sentiment (to paraphrase W. H. Auden) that literature makes nothing happen. This kind of accommodation with "reality"—of reified consciousness—is precisely what Thoreau is arguing against in the book. Nor for the time and place is there anything especially unusual about his civic ambitions; on the contrary, they are perfectly consistent with the New England ideal of the literary vocation.

Lewis P. Simpson has shown that a conception of the writer as a spiritual and intellectual authority was particularly strong around Boston and Concord during the early decades of the nineteenth century. Simpson uses the term "clerisy," a borrowing from Coleridge, to designate the literary community that emerged at this time and sought to claim for men of letters the influence formerly exercised by the ministry. The wise and learned, it was felt, had a special obligation to educate the nation; through the practice of literature, they were to provide moral guidance and enlightenment. While Thoreau was hardly a conventional member of the New England elite, he shared his culture's emphasis on the usefulness of the literary calling. He conceives *Walden* as a reforming text meant to produce results in the world, and hopes to be remembered, like the heroic writers whom he so admires, as a "messenger from heaven, [a] bearer of divine gifts to man."

But in this respect *Walden* is a notably different text from "Civil Disobedience": though both works begin, as it were, in the social world, *Walden* retreats into the self while "Civil Disobedience" calls for resistance to the government. This change can be seen in the book's very structure, its transition from "Economy" to "Conclusion," from Concord and Thoreau's neighbors to the inwardness of self-discovery. A mood of withdrawal totally dominates the final pages, as Thoreau urges his readers to turn their backs on society and look inside themselves. "Be a Columbus to whole new continents and worlds within you," he exhorts, "opening new channels, not of trade, but of thought. . . . [E]xplore the private sea, the Atlantic and Pacific Ocean of [your] being alone." The ending contains some of the book's best-known aphorisms, most of which revolve around the sentiment that "every one [should] mind his own business, and endeavor to be what he was made." The image left is of a solitary individual pursuing his own development, cultivating his own consciousness, in utter indifference to the common good. Such an image is not only radically at odds and the tone of *Walden*'s beginning; it also amounts to a distorted—and reified—reflection of the laissez-faire individualist pursuing his private economic interest at the expense of the public welfare.

Thoreau's unwitting kinship with social behavior he deplores can also be seen in his effort to create a myth of his experience. As the narrative progresses, he seems to grow intent upon suppressing all traces of autobiography and treating his two years at the pond as a timeless and universal experience. The patterning of the book after the cycle of the seasons contributes to this sense of the mythological, as does perhaps even more strongly the almost purely metaphorical character of the "Conclusion." In contrast to the specificity of the opening chapter, which takes place in Concord, Massachusetts, in the year 1845, the ending is situated in no time and no physical location. Thoreau declares open war on history: after ridiculing the "transient and fleeting" doings of his contemporaries, he vows "not to live in this restless, nervous, bustling, trivial Nineteenth Century, but stand or sit thoughtfully while it goes by." The text's denial of history, its flight from Jacksonian America, paradoxically resembles the commodified mode of thought which Thoreau charges against his countrymen and which permits a Flint to perceive his fruits and vegetables as dollars. In an analogous way, Thoreau allows the mythic value of his Walden experiment to displace the actual circumstances of its occurrence. Moreover, his determination to empty his adventure of historical content replicates a basic feature of reified consciousness. As he himself has pointed out repeatedly, market society engenders a conflation of history with nature. By presenting its limited, time-bound conventions as eternal, the existing order in effect places itself outside time and beyond the possibility of change. Although Thoreau rigorously condemns his society's "naturalizing" of itself in this fashion, he can be charged with performing a version of the same process on his own life by erasing history from *Walden* and mythologizing his experiment at the pond.

IV

The privatizing and antihistorical tendencies which blunt *Walden*'s critical edge reappear in Thoreau's attempt to devise a conception of reading and writing as unalienated labor. He is obliged to seek such a formulation because as a maker of texts, a would-be reformer in literature, he encounters the same problem that his neighbors experience in their daily transactions as farmers, merchants, and workmen: he has to confront the specter of the marketplace. In this area too Thoreau's rebuttal to exchange embroils him in difficulties he is unable to overcome. Indeed, the two goals he sets himself as an author, to initiate civic reformation while resisting the exchange process, turn out to be so incompatible by the mid-nineteenth century as to render their attainment mutually exclusive.

Trade, Thoreau keeps insisting, "curses every thing it handles; and though you trade in messages from heaven, the whole curse of trade attaches to the business." Anything that is done for money, including the effort to instruct mankind, to be a "messenger from heaven" as Thoreau desires, is compromised by that very fact. Of his brief experience as a schoolteacher, he observes: "As I did not teach for the good of my fellowmen, but simply for a livelihood, this was a failure." In *Walden* he regularly refers to his readers as students—"Perhaps these pages are more particularly addressed to poor students," he says as early as the second paragraph—and he clearly sees the threat of failure hanging over his writing unless he can circumvent exchange in his dealings with his audience.

Thoreau regards life and presence, two qualities nullified by the capitalist market, as fundamental to his efficacy as an author-legislator. In censuring philanthropists, he says that their error is to distribute money rather than spending themselves. "Be sure to give the poor [i.e., poor students] the aid they most need, though it be your example which leaves them far behind." When he introduces himself on the first page as *Walden*'s narrator, he emphasizes his own determination to retain the "I" or the self in his writing, to speak in the first person, and he adds that he requires of every writer "a simple and sincere account of his own life, and not merely what he has heard of other men's lives." This conception of literature as synonymous with life and the person recurs throughout the book, for example, when Thoreau states of the written word that it "is the work of art nearest to life itself. It may be translated into every language, and not only be read but actually breathed from all human lips." But if words have to be alive to "inspire" the reader, there are two senses in which exchange turns them into dead letters and kills the text. Since the cost of a thing is the amount of life expended for it, the book as commodity becomes an instrument of death like any item sold on the market. It also suffers an internal demise, commodification destroying literature's "bloom" just as surely as it blights the fruits and flowers on Flint's farm.

The literary work as article of exchange and the author as tradesman was the accepted state of affairs when Thoreau wrote *Walden*. As Tocqueville noted after his visit to America, the aristocratic domain of letters had become in democratic-capitalist society "the trade of literature." Thoreau, who claims to want "the flower and fruit of a man, that some fragrance be wafted from him to me, and some ripeness flavor our intercourse," views the situation of literary culture with dismay. The books read and written by his countrymen, he feels, are not literature at all but commodities with the impoverished nature of commodities. Singularly lacking in either fragrance or flavor, they are fit only to be consumed by "those who, like cormorants and ostriches, can digest" any sort of foodstuff. To Thoreau, they are simply one more piece of merchandise in the unending stream of commerce which connects "the desperate city" to "the desperate country"; and like the huckleberries transported to the Boston market from the country's hills, they lose their most essential qualities in transit. "Up comes the cotton, down goes the woven cloth; up comes the silk, down goes the woolen; up comes the books, but down goes the wit that writes them." Popular writers are "the machines to provide this provender," Thoreau contends, evoking his characterizations of both the huckleberry and the laboring man, and his neighbors are "the machines to read it." He proceeds to deliver a lengthy diatribe against fashionable literature

and the public that devours it "with unwearied gizzard," concluding with
the statement that "this sort of gingerbread is baked daily and more sedulously than pure wheat or rye-and-Indian in almost every oven, and finds
a surer market."

In addition to changing the text into a commodity and taking away
its life and essence, the marketplace endangers Thoreau's literary-civic enterprise because it encourages the reader in his addiction to mediation. Mediation, the substitution or replacement of one thing or person by another,
is the heart and soul of the exchange process. In "Civil Disobedience"
Thoreau disapproves of money, the medium of exchange, on precisely the
grounds that it "comes between a man and his objects, and obtains them
for him," thereby reducing his capacity for self-reliance. In *Walden* he
states repeatedly that he wants the reader to obtain his objects by his own
exertions (see his definition of a *"necessary of life"*). To allow the reader
to accept Thoreau's experience as a substitute for his own would be the
literary equivalent of the use of money. "I would not have any one adopt
my mode of living on any account," he declares; rather, "I would have
each one be very careful to find out and pursue his *own way*." Reading or
studying something should never become a substitute for doing it, according to Thoreau, who expresses disdain for the "common course" of instruction whereby the student (or reader) is required "to study chemistry,
and not learn how his bread is made, or mechanics, and not learn how it
is earned." " 'But,' " he continues, anticipating a probable critic,

> "you do not mean that the students go to work with their
> hands instead of their heads?" I do not mean that exactly, but
> I mean something which he might think a good deal like that;
> I mean that they should not *play* life, or *study* it merely, while
> the community supports them at this expensive game, but ear-
> nestly *live* it from beginning to end. How could youths better
> learn to live than by at once trying the experiment of living?

As Thoreau also points out, those who make a habit of depending on
others through exchange and the division of labor court the risk of not
being able to use their heads at all. "No doubt another *may* also think for
me; but it is not therefore desirable that he should do so to the exclusion
of my thinking for myself."

The reader who lets another do his thinking or his acting for him is a
reader whose consciousness has been reified. He reacts to the words on the
printed page with the same passivity and sense of noninvolvement as he
feels in bowing to social reality. Most readers, in Thoreau's view, are in
exactly this position; they limit themselves to books meant for deficient in-

tellects and children and so "dissipate their faculties in what is called easy reading." To read in this feeble way, without exerting one's mind or relying on oneself, is merely to be confirmed in one's present condition. "Easy reading," like the writing which elicits it, obviously cannot promote the spirit of independence Thoreau seeks to nurture as the author of *Walden*.

Thoreau's task as a writer-reformer accordingly requires him to make a book which is not a commodity. To spare *Walden* the fate of the huckleberry, he has to ensure that like the pond it contains "no muck" and is "too pure to have a market value." He also has to find some way for the reader to eliminate mediation and achieve independence in his own right. And here again Thoreau has recourse to the civic humanist ideal of husbandry for his solution. He links authorship and agriculture and portrays both the artist and his audience as figurative husbandmen, extricating *Walden* from the marketplace by means of metaphor.

In "The Bean-Field" Thoreau draws a sustained comparison between composing a text and planting a crop. He likens himself at his hoe to "a plastic artist in the dewy and crumbling sand," and he speaks of "making the yellow soil express its summer thought in bean leaves and blossoms rather than in wormwood and piper and millet grass, making the earth say beans instead of grass." The writer as metaphorical farmer remains outside the exchange process and never deals in commodities because he never sells his crop for money. His text, which never reaches the Boston market, preserves its effectiveness as a living expression of his individuality.

Thoreau also depicts the reader as a laborer "of the hands" and contrasts the toil of reading *Walden* with the "easy reading" suitable to popular literature. He claims that the diligent student who sits alone with his books throughout the day and late into the night is "at work in *his* field, and chopping in *his* woods, as the farmer is in his." Such strenuous intellectual exertion is the price of comprehending *Walden*, which requires a "heroic reader" to emulate its heroic author. "The heroic books, even if printed in the character of our mother tongue, will always be in a language dead to degenerate times; and we must *laboriously* seek the meaning of each word and line, conjecturing a larger sense than common use permits out of what wisdom and valor and generosity we have" (italics added). The reader as symbolic farmer, tasked more by *Walden*'s intricacies than by "any exercise which the custom of the day esteem," triumphs over mediation by having the same "laborious" experience at his desk that Thoreau has at the pond. Reading *Walden* becomes figuratively identical with being at Walden, a discipline in the mental self-reliance which enables one, or so Thoreau believes, to penetrate the "veil of reification."

The qualification is in order because in metaphorizing reading and writing as activities outside history and the marketplace Thoreau disregards the realities of the text's evolution and his relation to the public. History forcibly enters *Walden* in the changes and additions made between the first draft and the published version, changes stretching over a period of nearly ten years. J. Lyndon Shanley, who has done the most thorough study of the original draft, finds that Thoreau enlarged the second half of the manuscript far more than the first, adding "more to the account of his life in the woods than to his criticism of contemporary ways," and that his major revisions were intended to emphasize the cycle of the seasons. The development *within* the text, in other words, corresponds to a development *outside* the text, a shift in attitude suggesting a deepening estrangement from the social realm. Thoreau seems to have suffered a crisis of confidence in the likelihood of civic reform and the idea of his writing as a means of instigating it. Besides the addition of the "Conclusion," none of which appeared in the first draft, one change in particular is unequivocal in suggesting his disenchantment with the role of educator-legislator. In both versions he speaks of planting in his readers the seeds of sincerity, truth, and simplicity, to "see if they will not grow in this soil." But missing from the original manuscript is the sentence which comes next in the book: "Alas! I said this to myself; but now another summer is gone, and another, and another, and I am obliged to say to you, Reader, that the seeds which I planted, if indeed they *were* the seeds of those virtues, were wormeaten or had lost their vitality, and so did not come up."

Between 1846, when he began *Walden,* and 1854, when he completed it, Thoreau had good reason to lose confidence in the viability of his civic aspirations. "Civil Disobedience" (1849) and *A Week on the Concord and Merrimack Rivers* (1849) had been published in that time; the first elicited no reaction whatsoever from the public, and the second has been described as "one of the most complete failures in literary history." In the final version of *Walden* Thoreau himself alludes to the discouraging reception of his earlier work. He tells the story of an Indian who came to Concord to sell baskets but learned to his chagrin that the inhabitants did not want to buy any. The Indian wrongly supposed that he had done his part by making the baskets, "and then it would be the white man's to buy them. He had not discovered," comments Thoreau,

> that it was necessary for him to make it worth the other's while to buy them, or at least make him think that it was so, or to make something else which it would be worth his while to buy. I too had woven a kind of basket of delicate texture, but I had

not made it worth any one's while to buy them. Yet not the less, in may case, did I think it worth my while to weave them, and instead of studying how to make it worth men's while to buy my baskets, I studied rather how to avoid the necessity of selling them.

The "kind of basket" woven by Thoreau prior to *Walden* was of course *A Week*, a book which sold so poorly, as he reveals in a journal entry for 1853, that he was obliged to take possession of "706 copies out of an edition of 1000." He confides to the journal, and the bravado does not hide his own feelings of hurt and vexation, "I believe that this result is more inspiring and better for me than if a thousand had bought my wares. It affects my privacy less and leaves me freer."

Under the market system, there is no way for an author to exert influence to a significant degree without attracting a popular audience. If a book never reaches Boston, it is not likely to have much impact there. The influential writers praised by Thoreau enjoyed an "advantage" that was unavailable to him in the United States in the middle of the nineteenth century: the advantage of patronage by kings, noblemen, and warriors. Thoreau is caught in a contradiction of his own and history's devising: while he craves the authority of a founder, he refuses to view his text as a commodity and to accept "the necessity of selling" it. The failures of "Civil Disobedience" and *A Week* strengthen his antimarket resolution, but at the same time they force him to retreat from his ambition to reform the polity. Since he cannot shape popular opinion without large sales, he effectively abandons his civic project by striving to make *Walden* a difficult text at which the reader has to labor—hence a text which is inaccessible to the great majority of the public. "It is a ridiculous demand which England and America make," he writes in the "Conclusion," "that you shall speak so that they can understand you." And he goes on to voice defiant satisfaction that his own pages "admit of more than one interpretation," approximating the obscurity of the Walden ice. At this point Thoreau's celebration of figurative husbandry has become indistinguishable from the modernist credo of textual complexity, even incomprehensibility. The first draft of *Walden* was "Addressed to my Townsmen," but the last, colored by disappointment, seeks to exclude the many and narrow its appeal to a "fit audience, though few."

Thoreau worked five years longer on *Walden* than he had originally intended. Expecting a success with his first book, he hoped to bring out the second as early as 1849; copies of *A Week* included the announcement that *Walden* would be published shortly. But when it became evident that *A Week* was not selling, his publishers refused to issue *Walden,* and Thoreau spent five additional years revising and refining it. Since neither *A Week* nor the first draft of *Walden* is a masterpiece, this brief account of Thoreau's publishing difficulties suggests some final ironies of history. Insofar as *Walden* does "transcend" the Age of Jackson, does rise above its historical moment as a consequence of its excellence as an artwork, it does so precisely because of the particular nineteenth-century circumstances under which it reached print. Its transcendence of history is rooted in the conditions of its production—its *belated* production—as a commodity to be marketed by publishers. And still more: there is the additional irony that *Walden* is its own most effective reply to Thoreau's denigrations of commercial enterprise. One need not even point out that the values of brotherhood and love, values conspicuously absent from *Walden,* are inextricably bound up with the principle of "exchange." On strictly aesthetic grounds, the text disputes the contention that "trade curses every thing it handles." Far from impairing the quality of *Walden,* commercial considerations conspired to make it a better work. *Walden* is the one undeniably great book Thoreau ever wrote, thanks in part to the operations of the marketplace.

ROBERT WEISBUCH

Thoreau's Dawn
and the Lake School's Night

A perfect earliness would be free of influence, and its literary statement would eschew allusion and all debate with other texts. The earliest author would be in immediate relation to Nature, in which, as Bergson tells us, no negative exists. One foot planted on the first grounds, the other on the ephemeral Ground of Spirit from which Nature spontaneously arises, the colossus of dawn would acknowledge nothing alien with which to bicker.

Such an uninfluenced earliness is Thoreau's goal, and he begins *Walden* by a bombardment of earliness images. He will write in the first person for "it is, after all, always the first person that is speaking." That is, he will speak truly, not just *in* but *as* the first person. He will hear no other voices, least those of elders, for age "has not profited so much as it has lost." He will write for "poor students" who must rely on their own experience for "If I have any experience which I think valuable, I am sure to reflect that this my Mentors said nothing about." Not to "*play* life, or *study* it merely," youth must "earnestly *live* it from beginning to end," where study would afford no authentic beginning from which to set out. The first person's only mentor, the one respected elder, is that "elderly dame," Nature, who "can tell me the original of every fable, and on what fact every one is founded, for the incidents occurred when she was young."

To be at the source of myth, "at the fountain head of day" with the "old settler and original proprietor" of Walden, "who tells me stories of

From *Atlantic Double-Cross: American Literature and British Influence in the Age of Emerson.* © 1986 by the University of Chicago. University of Chicago Press, 1986.

old time and of new eternity": this is the only influence Thoreau will accept. Thoreau locates a Walden spun out of the self's morning, "when I
am awake and there is dawn in me," a place "to front only the essential
facts of life," And like the actual frontiersman/backwoodsman, he moves
forward to move backward, though in his act of cultural undoing he
moves not at all. With no great interest in the actual West or the factual
frontier, Thoreau temporizes the spatial promise. For him, as Edwin Fussell writes, "it was far more agreeable to step backward in time, while remaining in the same place." He wishes to be prelapsarian at a Walden "already in existence" perhaps "on the spring morning when Adam and Eve
were driven out of Eden." It is time before time and scope beyond all
space.

It is an impossibility. "I am not aware that any man has ever built on
the spot which I occupy," Thoreau boasts. "Deliver me from a city built
on the site of a more ancient city, whose materials are ruins, whose gardens cemeteries." Yet earlier he had confessed that his hoeing "disturbed
the ashes of unchronicled nations." This is an act of recovery, but it shows
that the New World is old even if the nation is young; and America in any
case is busy refusing what youth it truly possesses. Nature's scope is ignored in favor of a going-indoors. "The nation itself, with all its so-called
internal improvements, which, by the way, are all external and superficial"
is "an unwieldy and over-grown establishment, cluttered with furniture."
Even those unencumbered by an admiration for false improvements must
front history and their postheroic moment. Elsewhere, travelling to Concord, New Hampshire, Thoreau confesses, "we found that the frontiers
were not this way any longer. This generation has come into the world
fatally late for some enterprises."

The very vocation of writer prevents primacy. Thoreau's first and final
dawn is by definition pre- and postlinguistic as it is before and beyond
usual consciousness. As Eric Sundquist argues, its only expression would
be an *ur*-language from "an Eden at the outset of the history of rhetoric,
. . . like the speech of a lost God." And in *The Maine Woods,* Thoreau
admits sadly, "The poet's, commonly, is not a logger's path, but a woodman's. The logger and the pioneer have preceded him like John the Baptist:
eaten the wild honey, it may be, but the locusts also." For his ease, the
poet sacrifices priority and the wild.

Thoreau may wish "not to live in this restless, nervous, bustling, trivial Nineteenth Century, but stand or sit thoughtfully while it goes by"; he
cannot. Bedeviled by an enforced lateness, Thoreau's rage at any chosen
lateness invades his dawn wonder. "This hostility affects him," Charles

Feidelson, Jr., writes. "His writing, explicitly or by implication, is always polemic and never, as he doubtless would wish, blandly indifferent to the assumptions of the enemy." Thoreau knows that earliness can become American blather, knows, as Stanley Cavell puts it, "that we are not free, not whole, and not new, and we know this, and are on a downward path because of it." But that means only "that the present is a task and a discovery, not a period of America's privileged history."

Earliness will be an act of will enabled by an acknowledgment of age, one's personal lateness and not alone the nation's or the nineteenth century's: "I long ago lost a hound, a bay horse, and a turtle-dove, and am still on their trail." But Thoreau's hoeing can renew the lost earliness. If writing is itself notice of a separation from the booming Eternal Now (and it is: "The volatile truth of our words should continually betray the inadequacy of the residual statement"), Thoreau will take measures against a too-careful appearance of order to stress extra-vagance rather than unity. Finally, as a self-reward, he will melt his structure of words into the seasonal cycle, and then he will surpass nature to create eternal spring. If his very words come out of a language with a history, he will shed their habitual meanings and drive them etymologically back to their origins, not *OED* origins but "a larger sense than common use permits out of what wisdom and valor and generosity we have." If Thoreau is drawn to acknowledge the century's issues and disciplines, these too will be treated to his extra-vagant etymology, as when economy becomes "the cost of a thing" and cost "the amount of what I will call life which is required to be exchanged for it, immediately or in the long run." If he is not as poor a student as he would wish, then he will quote approvingly only from the earliest books from classical and oriental places, eastward, where the sun rises; and his quotings will be signs of confluence, not influence, for "I gaze upon as fresh a glory" as the Egyptian or Hindu philosopher, "since it was I in him that was then so bold" as to raise "a corner of the veil from the statue of the divinity" just as "it is he in me that now reviews the vision." And if Thoreau must debate and if argument confesses intrusion, if the voice of wonder, epic celebration, and biblical prophecy must sometimes give way to the satirist's thrust, then that voice will be toned as the rustic churl's. Northrop Frye tells us that such a character, whose name connotes the agriculturally early, refuses "the mood of festivity" in comic narratives. Usually we do not like him. But, Frye notes, "The more ironic the comedy, the more absurd the society, and an absurd society may be condemned by, or at least contrasted with, a character that we may call the plain dealer, an outspoken advocate of a kind of moral norm who has the sympathy of the audience." Just so, Thoreau cries, "Simplicity, simplicity, simplicity!" at his "restless, nervous, bustling, trivial Nineteenth Century." In all, if he cannot be prelinguistic and totemic really, he can be so figuratively and drive back time a little bit at least by calling his writing notchings on a stick. Having accepted the latecoming status of woodman in that passage in *The Maine Woods*, Thoreau suddenly makes a choice of what had seemed an inevitability: "not only for strength, but for beauty, the poet must, from time to time," (and there is a pun here on the imaginative capacity for travel in time) "travel the logger's path and the Indian's trail, to drink at some new and more bracing fountain of the Muses, far in the recesses of the wilderness."

Most largely, as many commentators have noticed, Thoreau secedes from an America that, in its lateness, has lost itself. But he secedes by reenacting the American separation from England. He takes up his "abode in the woods," he reports, "by accident, . . . on Independence Day, or the fourth of July, 1845," a by-accident suggesting not meaninglessness but unplanned and thereby significant coincidence, as the double naming of the day implies. That is, Thoreau refuses the official nation for the American *patria*. Speaking of tea, coffee, and milk, the availability of which his visitor John Field considered a chief American advantage, Thoreau replies, "But the only true America is that country where you are at liberty to pursue such a mode of life as may enable you to do without these." The accusations he must rebut—that he is neglecting his social responsibilities, that he will become a heathen, that his venture is wildly impractical—recall the seventeenth-century British animadversions against the colonists; and his planting activities recapitulate the Puritan settlement.

I would add to this commonplace a simple emphasis on what Thoreau is seceding from it: it is England, or an America gone specifically English. England as a term in *Walden* stands simply and consistently for that which is too premeditated and overcultivated (like English hay) and for that which is too circumscribed (like the hunting grounds of English noblemen or the official English holidays implying the scheduled limiting of joys that should be daily). England stands for that which is decadent ("The government of the world I live in was not framed, like that of Britain, in after-dinner conversations over the wine") or exploitative ("England, which is the great workhouse of the world"). England has nothing to tell us: "as for England, almost the last significant scrap of news from that quarter" (notice the employment of Sydney Smith's word from the phrase "In the four quarters of the globe, who reads an American book?") "was the revolution of 1649." But America's own revolution has done nothing to halt the infiltration of British lateness. Our workers live in conditions "every day more like that of the English," and Irish John Field stands for an America still deeply colonial in "thinking to live by some derivative old country mode in this primitive new country."

Thoreau makes portable the idea of America to take it away from that Englamerica, the existent America that is a traitor to its own earliness. Part of that removal is explicitly literary, Thoreau's attempt to separate from English romanticism. And in that rebellion, the idea of the Wild, which elsewhere Thoreau figures with the fruitful nervousness of a civilized thinker, becomes an unambiguous value.

II

On the title page of the first edition appears, in bold capitals, this sentence. I DO NOT PROPOSE TO WRITE AN ODE TO DEJECTION, BUT TO BRAG AS LUSTILY AS CHANTICLEER IN THE MORNING, STANDING ON HIS ROOST, IF ONLY TO WAKE MY NEIGHBORS UP. Coleridge is Thoreau's chosen opposite, specifically the night waking poet of "Dejection: An Ode." He is the insomniac in rooms who looks out on an ill-omened moon through too literary eyes that have lost the creative power to unite nature and mind in an act of godly joy. And he is everyway rejected as a model by an American who situates himself outdoors not only at dawn but at the dawn of his opponent's home literature. Chanticleer is a type-name for a rooster, but it is Chaucer who is implied by the name in this literary sentence; and, like Thoreau, Chaucer was another poet of national earliness who had to battle foreign influence. Coleridge's fatigued self-pity marks a long English decline from Chaucer's morning cheer. It is Thoreau's New England neighbors who are to be awakened, but clearly neighbor England, in its originary spirit, is to be saved from its own lateness as well.

Why Coleridge as the negative English representative? I have implied one reason. The most self-disappointed of romantic personae, one who, even when he proclaims an imaginative faith at ode's end, sees himself barred from active participation in that faith, would be a large and likely target. Who better than the author of "Dejection" could be accused of exporting to America an attitude that would cause "lives of quiet desperation"? The man who complains that the "dull sobbing draft" of melancholic weather upon his Aeolian lute makes him wish that romantic emblem of sounding spirit "mute" announces a death wish. Thoreau wishes to be awake and all natural while Coleridge accuses himself of choosing "by abstruse research to steal / From my own nature all the natural man." Coleridge chronicles a lateness-decline within the course of his own life, aside from English literary history. He is set off against a man who self-approvingly chooses to imitate both an unthinking natural animal and a god in order to initiate a world.

But of course there is more to Thoreau's choice of Coleridge for a specific rejection. This is not so plainly a case of kicking a good man when he is down. Indeed Thoreau does trivialize the ode. The night of self-pity is spectacularly transformed, first when Coleridge refuses his own melodramatic comparison to Lear to see himself as merely "a little child / Upon a lonesome wild, / Not far from home, but she hath lost her way"; and then in an act of outgoing generosity as he wishes for the "Dear Lady" that inner joy of which he has become incapable. Hard honesty and a love for the other which survives despair may mark more of a recovery than the poet knows or owns. Indeed, Coleridge's speaker finally enacts Thoreau's own dictum, "We may waive just so much care of ourselves as we honestly bestow elsewhere," another of the poem's implications that Thoreau's allusion discounts.

Thoreau strikes at Coleridge not because Coleridge is a good man down but because Coleridge is a giant keeping him under, an influential poet and thinker whom Thoreau so resembles in many points that differences need to be dramatized for Thoreau to make his own home in an American woods.

Most largely, as Lawrence Buell notes, Coleridge is credited with the importation to America of European pantheisms that emphasize "a metaphysical correspondence between nature and spirit," and it is precisely this sense that Emerson named Thoreau's best gift, the drawing of "universal law from the single fact." Further, Coleridge everywhere stresses that "priority of relation over substance," which Charles Feidelson, Jr., sees as vital to Thoreau's art of perception. Neither Coleridge nor Thoreau consistently believes in a plain projectivism whereby the self utterly produces the out-there, but both can be drawn to such a view. The Coleridge who writes in "Dejection"

> O Lady! we receive but what we give,
> And in our life alone does Nature live:
> Ours is her wedding garment, ours her shroud!
> . . . .
> Ah! from the soul itself must issue forth

> A light, a glory, a fair luminous cloud
> Enveloping the earth—

is perfectly met by the Thoreau who argues that architectural beauty "has gradually grown from within outward, out of the necessities and character of the indweller, who is the only builder—out of some unconscious truthfulness, and nobleness, without ever a thought for the appearance." And Thoreau again, perhaps via Emerson, sounds the Coleridgean idea when he devalues the making of beautiful objects by calling it "far more glorious to carve and paint the very atmosphere through which we look, which morally we can do."

Finally, Coleridge and Thoreau share, in James McIntosh's words, a "sense of nature as one, as alive, and as the aggregate of things," a sense generally romantic. But it is named most succinctly by Coleridge in "The Eolian Harp," where he glorifies "the one Life within us and abroad, / Which meets all motion and becomes its soul," and Thoreau takes up Coleridge's image when he writes of distant sound as creating "a vibration of the universal lyre."

Yet McIntosh goes on to insist that "Thoreau and his European counterparts are romantics, not Orphists or Parsees or Buddhists, partly because they share a more or less open awareness of their separation from nature, however much they may desire to be at home in it." Here the two writers begin to differ. McIntosh's generalization is importantly valid, but consider that no other romantic poet stresses depressive isolation so consistently as Coleridge and that Thoreau's isolation issues in self-sufficient joy. "Alone, alone, all, all alone, / Alone on a wide, wide sea" seems Coleridge's motto everywhere. The mariner, Christabel, and the personae of such lyrics as "Dejection," "Frost at Midnight," and "This Lime-tree Bower My Prison" victimized by a self-absorption pictured as literal seclusion. Granted, this is only a nadir from which many of Coleridge's speakers rise in such acts of outgoing love as we mentioned in "Dejection." In solitude, that is, they may connect to the "one Life" that affords more of a communal sense than any crowd might. But it is only this affirming paradox that Thoreau adapts in his chapter "Solitude": "I have a great deal of company in my house; especially in the morning, when nobody calls. . . . God is alone,—but the devil, he is far from being alone; he sees a great deal of company; he is legion." In "The Eolian Harp" Coleridge finally denigrates and refuses as unholy his pantheistic vision of the "one Life," that sense of an expanded society among nature, man, and God that Thoreau adopts to people his seclusion. And given Thoreau's version of a

Coleridge reduced to mere dejection by the lyre of another occasion, Thoreau's affirmation of his own company again accuses Coleridge of an unnecessary despair.

Coleridge as the English writer is not only night-sad but over-civilized and every way barred from the spontaneity that is the only good. Thoreau takes the extraordinary measure of repeating his motto in "Where I Lived, and What I Lived For" as if to guarantee our awareness of these implications. He prefaces it by the sentence, "The present was my next experiment of this kind, which I purpose to describe more at length, for convenience, putting the experience of two years into one." "The present" may mean only the present experiment but it also may mean that the experiment of Walden was an attempt to live utterly in the present: as he writes earlier, "to stand on the meeting of two eternities, the past and future, which is precisely the present moment; to toe that line." Given that Coleridge's "Dejection" is named once more in the next sentence, Thoreau's "present" and the packing of two years into one are in vivid distinction to the lassitude of loose moments with which the ode opens and to the general sense of an irrevocable Fall throughout.

Immediate participation is the claim of the motto itself. "I do not propose to write . . . but to brag as lustily as Chanticleer in the morning. . . ." Of course, Thoreau *is* writing, but, as we have noted, *Walden* is arranged so as to avoid anything like the tight structure of an ode, with a simulated and-that-brings-to-mind spontaneity rather than the scene, meditation, initial-scene-transformed movement of Coleridge's poem, much less the rigorous ordering of Coleridge's philosophical writings. Bragging is vocal, part of an earlier, oral mode of transmission, and it is early too in refusing the sublimating restraints upon the ego of a Christian-civilized humility. By such means is Coleridge made all too much a poet. (Thoreau mentions "Ode to Dejection" on one other occasion. In his journal, he describes how a tree may be made more beautiful by a diseased swelling of its tissue. "Beautiful scarlet sins they may be. . . . This gall is the tree's 'Ode to Dejection.'" This is to give compliment to Coleridge's poem as creating beauty out of personal malaise, but the trope implicitly defines Coleridge's mood as an abnormal, insect-infested disease. He elsewhere calls "Art itself a gall." More generally, then, Coleridge's ode simply signifies high art, an injury to inexpressive nature but an injury that is also a benefit. In the context of *Walden*, however, where sublimated acts, including high art, are called into most skeptical question, the paradox of beauty through disruption is removed, and the ode as the incursion of a diseased art into nature is a gall pure and simple. This is so especially in regard to the motto.) And in his motto Thoreau is libidinally potent, as he brags "lustily," a word that might mean simply "with exuberance" were it not connected to Chaucer's rooster. In "Dejection," contrarily, Coleridge accuses himself of general impotence and is apparently barred (as we know he was factually) from the "Dear Lady" he blesses at ode's end just as he is barred from the source of inner joy he celebrates in absentia. This, Thoreau implies, is where the sublimations of civilized life get you, as he leagues in preference with a barnyard animal.

This is the ultimate difference to which Thoreau's allusion points. The poet of lateness recalls a vision that he no longer can experience internally, much less enact to transform the world. Thoreau, as the bard of the early hour when all is possible, wishes to literalize vision as it has never been made literal before. "When one man has reduced a fact of the imagination to be a fact to his understanding, I foresee that all men will at length establish their lives on that basis." From beans will derive a global village of vision, as Thoreau accepts Coleridge's differentiated terms (the imagination is allied to Reason as a self-referential totality transcending the secondary imagination's Understanding in *Aids to Reflection,* a book Thoreau owned) but demands an actualization of the divine I AM on the most common and available grounds imaginable, democratic American earth. The poet of lateness can barely imagine his imagination; he can recall it only. The bard of dawn lives out his now-forming imagination from July 4, 1845, forward "about a mile and half south of the village of Concord" by Walden Pond.

And yet Thoreau does not dismiss Coleridge; he includes the English poet as an item within his emotional range. Coleridge is the poet of night waking owls. "Tu-whit! Tu-whoo!" they cry at the beginning of "Christabel" and ". . . The owlet's cry / Came loud—and hark, again! loud as before" at the beginning of "Frost at Midnight." Thoreau hears in the owls' cries at Walden the words "*Oh-o-o-o-o that I had never been bor-r-r-r-n!*" Thoreau grudgingly acknowledges that they speak to one of nature's many truths, "the stark twilight and unsatisfied thoughts which all have" and thus have their place at a Walden that can afford even despair by placing it within an encyclopedia of other sounds. As McIntosh notes, Thoreau "generally prefers not to exhibit his acquaintance with Wordsworth and Coleridge, Carlyle and Goethe" and so he attributes literary owls to Ben Jonson, while reproducing nearly Coleridge's (admittedly Shakespeare's as well, in the song from *Love's Labour's Lost*) "Tu-whit Tu-whoo" in his next sentence. But when he speaks of the owls' meaning, it is the poet of lateness he attacks. They are "expressive of a mind which has reached the

gelatinous mildewy stage of all healthy and courageous thought. It reminded me of ghouls and idiots and insane howlings." Yet the owl has
its place at Walden and Thoreau can employ Coleridge for incentive. In
"Christabel," recall, "the owls have awakened the crowing cock," though
Coleridge's rooster crows "drowsily," ackowledging English night, while
Thoreau's owl makes Coleridge's night of despair itself "a more dismal
and fitting day."

III

And now another dawn springs of midnoon, as I wish to unsay, or at
least complicate my claim. Coleridge is not the leading figure for England
in *Walden,* but only the most overt. Coleridge stands in for the more
powerful influence of Wordsworth, as Thoreau makes Wordsworth's claim
for the "abundant recompense" of mature age tantamount to Coleridge's
dejection.

Thoreau clearly pairs the two, and both together represent what he
sees as the going idea of literature itself. "This is my lake country," he says
of the ponds surrounding Walden. And later, in an 1859 journal entry,
"There are poets of all kinds and degrees, little known to each other. The
Lake School is not the only or the principal one." Granted, Coleridge is
nominating a sleazy muskrat hunter as yet another poet of sorts, but the
entry assumes an agreement that the Lake School is generally thought to
define poetry, or at least poetry of natural enthusiasm.

But Wordsworth is not merely an afterthought to be included with
Coleridge; it is Wordsworth more. McIntosh quotes an early poem by
Thoreau to "surmise that Thoreau professed so vocally his intention not
to write an Ode to Dejection in *Walden* because he was personally familiar
with the feelings evoked and the questions raised in Coleridge's poem."

The Poet's Delay

In vain I see the morning rise,
In vain observe the western blaze,
Who idly look to other skies,
Expecting life by other ways.

Amidst such boundless wealth without,
I only still am poor within,
The birds have sung their summer out,
But still my spring does not begin.

But the poem bears a much closer resemblance to the second stanza of a different ode, Wordsworth's "Intimations of Immortality."

> The Rainbow comes and goes,
> And lovely is the Rose,
> The moon doth with delight
> Look round her when the heavens are bare;
> Waters on a starry night
> Are beautiful and fair;
> The sunshine is a glorious birth.
> But yet I know, where'er I go,
> That there hath past away a glory from the earth.

The spiritless praising of an animated nature and a guilty sense that the self's preoccupations, in Wordsworth's phrase, "the season wrong" is imitated closely in Thoreau's poem; and McIntosh himself affirms that "For nineteenth-century New Englanders, Wordsworth was *the* poet of nature" and that Wordsworth's ode was the single poem "that seems to have affected Thoreau most strongly." It is the figure of Wordsworth, I believe, beyond any single poem, that engages Thoreau, for Americans tend to think in terms of human representatives rather than texts, in confronting what is English.

Wordsworth appears throughout *Walden,* though always incognito. Like Wordsworth, Thoreau worries that the world is too much with us, and he too recommends not augmentations but a purificatory shedding as the means of hope. Like Wordsworth, who saves his awe for the simple individual who is part of a landscape and who hates the crowdings of cities, Thoreau writes, "we live thick and are in each other's way, and stumble over one another, and I think that we thus lose some respect for one another." Like Wordsworth with his leech gatherer, Thoreau personifies the grandeur of simplicity in a deliberately unheroic-seeming man, the Canadian woodchopper. Thoreau affords his ideal man a more detailed and convincing facticity and allows himself to wonder whether "to suspect him of a fine poetic consciousness or of stupidity." But the woodchopper, like Wordsworth's old man and his other vagabonds, exemplifies that absence of self-consciousness and the concomitant providential assurance that Thoreau directly advises when he writes, "I think that we may safely trust a good deal more than we do. We may waive just so much care of ourselves as we honestly bestow elsewhere." Like Wordsworth too, Thoreau locates a more supernaturally tinged kind of simplicity in the child. Of such as Wordsworth's "best Philosopher," "Filling from time to time his 'humorous stage,' " Thoreau writes, "Children, who play life, discern its true laws and relations more clearly than men."

These are not piecemeal similarities. For both writers, they contribute to a program for earliness. More significantly, both writers travel through a spectrum of descriptions of earliness. This spectrum ranges in each between a love of earliness-as-nature so intense that the self is always seen as too late in relation to it and a love of earliness-as-preexistential vision in which earliest nature itself is too late to fulfill the demands of the imagination. There is a Wordsworth who frolics in a simple natural ecstasy and a more mystic Wordsworth who wishes to look upon natural objects with an eye so intense that object and eye surpass their material condition and we "become a living soul" that can "see into the life of things" ("Tintern Abbey") and reads in a landscape "Characters of the great Apocalypse" (*The Prelude*). Just so, in Fussell's felicitous phrase, "To the end, Thoreau seems undetermined whether he means to be on the frontier or beyond," with his final goal simple, essential living or the employment of that kind of living to achieve an inexplicable bliss of unity with the spirit-source.

As much as Wordsworth, Thoreau praises childhood from a position of privation, the vantage point of adult loss. "I have always been regretting that I was not as wise as the day I was born," Thoreau writes in *Walden*. And his later journal entries that mourn a loss of power could as well quote directly from Wordsworth's crisis poems, as when he writes "Once I was part and parcel of Nature; now I am observant of her." The famous sentence from *Walden*, "I long ago lost a hound, a bay horse, and a turtledove, and am still on their trail," employs images that tease us to identify them while they clearly serve as emblems of a general loss. Just so, Wordsworth in the Intimations Ode confesses to "a Tree, of many, one, / A single field which I have looked upon," both of which speak "of something that is gone," the glory and the dream. And in these instances, natural images are employed to dramatize a loss of something not only natural but preternatural. There is a Thoreau who wishes "to walk even with the Builder of the universe," who "sometimes expected the Visitor who never comes," who speaks Plato-like of "the dark unfathomed mammoth cave of this world," who proclaims that "we are not wholly involved in Nature," and for whom "Time is but the stream I go a-fishing in." Such statements lead to that antinatural extreme epitomized in a journal entry from the period when *Walden* is being written.

> We soon get through with Nature. She excites an expectation
> when she cannot satisfy. The merest child which has rambled

into a copsewood dreams of a wilderness so wild and strange
and inexhaustible as Nature can never show him.

That same Thoreau directly quotes Wordsworth in an earlier journal:
"Methinks my present experience is nothing; my past experience is all in
all. . . . As far back as I can remember I have unconsciously referred to the
experiences of a previous state of being. 'For life is a forgetting'; etc." He
corresponds to the Wordsworth who finally finds not even the Alps sufficient to the human imagination, which is "A thousand times more beautiful than the earth / On which he dwells."

Like Wordsworth, Thoreau represents himself as a walker. His "favorite form," Buell argues, "is the romantic excursion." This natural dynamism is accompanied in both writers by a constant mental travelling between the poles of natural earliness and an earliness that is the ground of
nature but is itself incorporeal, as any thing must be defined by what it is
not. The characteristic tension in both writers is between idealist and naturalist urgings.

We could enlarge our list of similarities that, in part, bespeak Thoreau's acceptance of Wordsworth's teaching. We could discuss in each the
mocking translation of economic terms into considerations of spiritual
cash. We could emphasize in each the dramatizations of a childhood wildness which violates nature for a purpose. Or we could cite the recommen-
dation of relaxed reception, Wordsworth's "wise passivity," throughout
Walden. But it is more to our purpose, as it was to Thoreau's, to discover
crucial differences.

First and simply, Thoreau most echoes Wordsworth or Coleridge
when he speaks of his own insufficiencies and of Nature's, and *Walden* is
predominantly an account of success, the self's ability to find significant
life in the earliness of a capacious Nature. "Both place and time were
changed, and I dwelt nearer to those parts of the universe and to those eras
in history which had most attracted me." Second, although *Walden* is written in the past tense and McIntosh is technically right to attribute to it "a
sense of remembered place," that is not the book's dominant effect. In
such of Wordsworth's lyrics as "I Wandered Lonely as a Cloud," the imaginative memory does not merely recollect earlier experience but augments,
completes, perfects it. That is not true of *Walden*, which carries us quasi-
chronologically through a series of percepts that immediately become concepts. That Walden to which Thoreau attributes a prelapsarian existence
is the Walden that he "in the First person" directly experiences.

The verb "experiences" leads to a third and underlying difference that
Thoreau marks between himself and Wordsworth. In the "Tintern Abbey"

lyric, Wordsworth is surprised to see "pastoral farms, / Green to the very door; and wreaths of smoke / Sent up, in silence, from among the trees!" He imaginatively infers "vagrant dwellers in the houseless woods" whom he implicitly praises for a harmony achieved with nature. But Wordsworth himself is not one of them, just as, seated reflectively beneath a "dark syca-more," he is not immediately part of ever dynamic nature, "of sportive wood run wild": against that contrast, the rest of the poem must struggle toward an affirmation of age. Thoreau is himself one of those "vagrant dwellers." Just as Wordsworth's pastoral farms are "Green to the very door," Thoreau proclaims of his house, "No Yard! but unfenced Nature reaching up to your very sills." Whereas a civilized Wordsworth looks into nature and a remembered natural self, Thoreau locates himself there: "no gate—no front-yard,—and no path to the civilized world."

Thoreau enacts what Wordsworth contemplates. Again: both Thoreau and Wordsworth horizontalize the universe, find high meaning in low ob-jects; but Wordsworth only in contemplation finds at the conclusion of the Intimations Ode that "the meanest flower that blows can give / Thoughts that do often lie too deep for tears" while Thoreau, wishing to know beans, actively cultivates them. Thoreau may allow for characters more primitive than himself, closer to "life near the bone where it is sweetest," such as the woodchopper, but primarily he is himself that Solitary Reaper whose song can inspirit a Wordsworth who is himself too late in time to sing it.

It is not simply that Thoreau describes nature far more particularly than Wordsworth. The claim is that he can be intimately, body-and-soul, amidst nature as the mature Wordsworth spiritually cannot be. When Wordsworth wishes in the Intimations Ode for a simple regression, when he attempts to return to the shores of the ocean of life and leap with the children in festival, the thought of that "Tree" intervenes and reveals the falseness of an adult Wordsworth galumphing about. Yet for the loss of that connection to nature occurs "abundant recompense." Even as a natu-ral child, Wordsworth had felt the loss of an earlier All, and that sense of loss which led to spiritual realization educates him to the good of the pres-ent one. Distance from nature affords imaginative space for Faith, for the "philosophic mind" which best appreciates both nature and specifically human courage. Dawn is done but sunset promises a greater return to the state before and beyond time early or late.

For Thoreau, any loss of connection to nature is absolute loss. Men think they are wiser than children, "wiser by experience, that is, failure" and "with years I have grown more coarse and indifferent." Earliness is all, and the return which Wordsworth finally counts folly is exactly what Thoreau desires. "That man who does not believe that each day contains an earlier, more sacred, and auroral hour than he has yet profaned, has despaired of life, and is pursuing a descending and darkening way." As Charles Anderson succinctly puts it, "Thoreau's search to discover his ideal self becomes a quest to recover his lost youth in a second spring." But at his most optimistic, Thoreau contemplates no loss. It is getting earlier all the time.

From this perspective, Wordsworth's "abundant recompense" is hollow rationalization, and he, as much as Benjamin Franklin, is the target of ridicule when Thoreau continues his rhetoric of dawn by asking, "Who would not be early to rise, and rise earlier and earlier each successive day of his life, till he became unspeakably healthy, wealthy, and wise?" In all, Thoreau accounts himself the worshipper of Hebe, "who had the power of restoring gods and men to the vigor of youth."

Of Hebe, Thoreau continues, "wherever she came it was spring." His confessions of decay are confined to a thoroughly personal voice much subordinate in *Walden* to a self who microcosmically speaks for American possibility. Earliness is made all-portable, all-persistent. "Morning brings back the heroic ages." "Morning is when I am awake and there is dawn in me." The "Bhagvat Geeta" expresses a wisdom that should "be referred to a previous state of existence" and "The pure Walden water is mingled with the sacred water of the Ganges." A return to the early is no more difficult than the return of spring. If dawn is not immediately present, that is not because it is irrecoverably lost in an English past—Wordsworth's cultural implication, if we read his personal mythology as partly a social and historical one as well—but because it is yet to come in an American future. "I have never yet met a man who was quite awake." "We loiter in winter while it is already spring." "Only that day dawns to which we are awake. There is more day to dawn. The sun is but a morning star."

Thoreau vacillates cannily between envisioning Walden as the ultimate earliness, the final good in itself, and envisioning Walden as one of any number of paths to an atemporal good. The latter is his escape clause from too literal and didactic a claim. But he need not decide between the alternatives, for earliness is scope and scope makes everything possible. Walden may or may not be it, but Thoreau is after an attainable ultimacy available to the time of our earth. Such a belief makes of Wordsworth's beyond-sunset faith nothing more than fancy work upon Coleridge's plain dejection. Wordsworth tends to assign his natural intensity to childhood, his mysticism to mature thought (though, we need to add, that mature

thought is informed by the earlier love of plain nature). Thoreau's paradox
of the frontier, whereby he moves forward not to sunset but to sunrise and
makes West East, refuses all ordinary temporality, including historical and
personal aging. His prize term, "The Wild," brilliantly contains his nature-
loving and his spirit-longing aspects, for it means not only *savage, primitive* but also *unconditioned*.

Thus, in *Walden*, as Thoreau "rambles into higher and higher grass,"
the book's seasonal cycle becomes an increasing parabola spinning forward by running backward into the untamed. Thoreau's earliness is not in
a place or at a time. "Any prospect of awakening or coming to life to a
dead man makes indifferent all times and places." Material fact and spiritual law get transformed instantly, as by instinct, into each other so that
earliness becomes less a condition or state than an activity. By its reverse
dynamism, we spin ever more rapidly backward until we pass through a
vortex of the beginning and through an earlier vortex before that and then
an earlier. We must "rise earlier and earlier each successive day" for "each
day contains an earlier, more sacred, and auroral hour" and Thoreau's last
sentence anticipates yet earlier beginnings as "The sun is but a morning
star."

From Beaumont's picture of Peele Castle in a storm, Wordsworth
learns that his early view of the castle as exampling "lasting ease, / Elysian
quiet, without toil or strife" and, most, "silent Nature's breathing life" was
pathetically blind. "But welcome fortitude, and patient cheer, / And frequent sights of what is to be borne!" Thoreau eschews Wordsworth's "hu-
manised Soul," sees it as the spirit of defeat, and in his actualist American
faith teaches of castles a different lesson: "If you have built castles in the
air, your work need not be lost; that is where they should be. Now put the
foundations under them." And that is why, for Thoreau, "Wordsworth is
too tame for the Chippeway."

IV

[Elsewhere] . . . I summarized Sacvan Bercovitch's persuasive theory
of a major difference between Protestant theologies in Old and New England. Calvinism in Britain, however radical, always maintains a distinction between the City of God and the cities of man, a gap that New England was founded expressly to close. New England expects an attainable
earthly paradise, an ending transformation of historical time into a life of
spirit. Especially upon the failure of Cromwell's Commonwealth, Britain
would treat with scepticism any such literalisms.

Once we add to this the far more recent and significant failure of human hope in the French revolution, we are a ways to explaining the differences between the Lake poets and Thoreau. The French disaster would teach a stern lesson on the consequences of confusing internal and individual redemption with political rebellion. For Coleridge and Wordsworth, the lesson only would reinforce a privatism, a scepticism toward the utopian, inherited from their culture. Contrarily, the success of the American revolution, though it might seem all too exclusively political to a mind like Thoreau's, could not but rekindle hope for an absolute merge of personal and national salvation. Wordsworth replaces his political dogmatism with personal recovery. Thoreau secedes from the America of fact to found no private domain, whatever Walden at first may seem, but to revive and live out what he calls "the only true America."

By that, we can account too for a final difference. It concerns the structuring of an audience. Coleridge and Wordsworth typically address a like-minded friend, often each other. The intimate tone creates a society of two in quiet defiance of the loveless crowd, which is the world at large. Thoreau takes a far more public stance, that of a Jeremiah haranguing his neighbors, all of them, the nation. It is conversation on one side of the Atlantic, conversion sermons on the other.

You don't live by what you say and what you say does not say far enough: what I described as the typical American critique of English romanticism suits this case. So too does that habit whereby the American, speaking as a national representative, makes the British writer whom he confronts representative as well. To Thoreau, Wordsworth and Coleridge are England, however much these writers themselves insisted on their separate, private country.

It is not surprising, then, that Thoreau's explicit commentaries on England chime with his implicit criticisms of Coleridge and Wordsworth. "The crop of *English* hay" (Thoreau's italic) "is carefully weighed, the moisture calculated" while the wilds produce "a rich and various crop unreaped by man." When he calls his field, and so *Walden*, "the connecting link between wild and cultivated fields" and "half-cultivated," he seems to compromise. But then "They were beans cheerfully returning to their wild and primitive state that I cultivated," and so earliness is retained, even furthered, and cultivation receives a backward definition.

Linear and historical time, English property, are undone in *Walden*. Thoreau's emphasis on dawn and earliness give special meaning to a jibe like "The government of the world I live in was not framed, like that of Britain, in after-dinner conversations over the wine." And in his role as the

Salem merchant, peddling a "Celestial Empire" that refuses history's claims and reverses time's decay, Thoreau sells "purely native products . . . always in native bottoms."

Given that England is consistently equated with a public world decaying in its accumulations, with a materialism devoid of spirit and, even in its most visionary aspect, with the open despair of Coleridge and the desperate rationalizings of Wordsworth, and given that Walden is an explicitly American experiment, we are at first surprised to hear Thoreau halloo " 'Welcome, Englishmen! welcome, Englishmen!' for I had had communication with that race." And we are as surprised when he links the two nations in despite in his final pages—"It is said that the British Empire is very large and respectable, and that the United States are a first-rate power"—and lectures John and Jonathan alike. But again we are in the midst of a deceptive compromise. We noted that Thoreau sees the public America as having gone English. Indeed, when he welcomes Englishmen, Thoreau may as well mean village visitors, for he has relived the emigration from England in leaving citied New England for the wild. Despite independence, official America has been annexed to the British again.

But the English visit him, not he them. And as Salem merchant, Thoreau does not merely sell his goods, he "will export such goods as the country affords." If John and Jonathan are to save themselves, they will have to awake to a dawn, a sun, a morning that belongs to the wild, the west, American earliness. *Walden* is a counterannexation.

Chronology

1817   David Henry Thoreau born on July 12 at Concord, Massachusetts (he later changed his name to Henry David).

1828   Enters Concord Academy.

1833   Enters Harvard College.

1837   Graduates from Harvard. Begins teaching in the Concord School, but resigns when required to administer corporal punishment. Meets Emerson, and begins writing his *Journal*.

1838   Starts a private school with his brother John. Gives his first public lecture at the Concord Lyceum.

1839   Canoe trip on the Concord and Merrimack rivers with John, described in *A Week on the Concord and Merrimack Rivers*.

1840   Publishes in *The Dial*, the newly started magazine of the Transcendentalists.

1841   Takes up residence at Emerson's home, as tutor and handyman.

1842   Thoreau's brother John dies of lockjaw after cutting his finger.

1843   Tutors in the family of Emerson's brother William, on Staten Island.

1844   Returns home, works at family's pencil-making business.

1845   Begins building a house on the banks of Walden Pond.

1846   First camping trip to the Maine woods. Arrested in Concord and jailed overnight for refusing to pay the poll tax to a government that supported slavery and waged an imperialist war against Mexico.

1847   Leaves Walden Pond and again moves in with the Emersons.

1849   Moves back to his father's house. *A Week on the Concord and Merrimack Rivers* and "Civil Disobedience" published. First visit to Cape Cod.

1850   Travels again to Cape Cod and then to Canada.

1853   Second trip to Maine.

1854   Publishes *Walden; or, Life in the Woods*. Delivers "Slavery in Massachusetts" lecture.

1855   Third journey to Cape Cod.

1856   Meets Walt Whitman in New York.

1857   Fourth visit to Cape Cod. Third trip to the Maine woods. Meets the abolitionist John Brown, who was hanged after a raid on Harpers Ferry.

1859   Delivers "A Plea for Captain John Brown."

1860   Last camping excursion to Monadnock.

1861   Goes to Minnesota because of failing health.

1862   Thoreau dies of tuberculosis on May 6.

1874   Thoreau's body moved from Concord to Author's Ridge at Sleepy Hollow.

Contributors

HAROLD BLOOM, Sterling Professor of the Humanities at Yale University, is the author of *The Anxiety of Influence, Poetry and Repression,* and many other volumes of literary criticism. His forthcoming study, *Freud: Transference and Authority,* attempts a full-scale reading of all of Freud's major writings. A MacArthur Prize Fellow, he is general editor of five series of literary criticism published by Chelsea House.

STANLEY CAVELL is Walter M. Cabot Professor of Aesthetics and the General Theory of Value at Harvard University. His books include *The Senses of Walden, Must We Mean What We Say?,* and *The Claim of Reason.*

JAMES McINTOSH is Associate Professor of English at the University of Michigan. He is the author of *Thoreau as Romantic Naturalist.*

LOREN EISELEY has written books on evolution and anthropology, a biography of Francis Bacon, and several volumes of poetry. He was Benjamin Franklin Professor of Anthropology and the History of Science at the University of Pennsylvania.

PHILIP F. GURA is Associate Professor of English at the University of Colorado. He is the author of *A Glimpse of Sion's Glory: Puritan Radicalism in New England,* and *The Wisdom of Words: Language, Theology and Literature in the New England Renaissance.*

WALTER BENN MICHAELS teaches English at the University of California at Berkeley. He has published many essays on American literature and on contemporary literary theory.

ERIC J. SUNDQUIST is Professor of English at the University of California at Berkeley. He is the author of *American Realism: New Essays* and *Faulkner: A House Divided.*

JOHN CARLOS ROWE is Chairman of the Department of English and Comparative Literature at the University of California at Irvine. He is the author of *Henry Adams and Henry James: The Emergence of a Modern Consciousness*.

BARRY WOOD teaches English at the University of Houston.

RICHARD BRIDGMAN is Professor of English at the University of California at Berkeley. He is the author of *Dark Thoreau* and *Gertrude Stein in Pieces*.

JOHN HILDEBIDLE is Assistant Professor of Literature at MIT. He is the author of *The Old Chore* and *Thoreau: A Naturalist's Liberty*.

MICHAEL T. GILMORE teaches at Brandeis University. He has edited several books on colonial and nineteenth-century literature and is the author of *The Middle Way: Puritanism and Ideology in American Romantic Fiction* and *American Romanticism in the Marketplace*.

ROBERT WEISBUCH is Associate Professor of English at the University of Michigan. He is the author of *Atlantic Double-Cross* and *Emily Dickinson's Poetry*.

Bibliography

Anderson, Charles R. *The Magic Circle of* Walden. New York: Holt, Rinehart & Winston, 1968.

Bishop, Jonathan. "The Experience of the Sacred in Thoreau's *Week*." *ELH* 33 (1966): 66–91.

Bowling, Lawrence. "Thoreau's Social Criticism as Poetry." *The Yale Review* 55 (1966): 255–64.

Buell, Lawrence. *Literary Transcendentalism*. Ithaca: Cornell University Press, 1975.

Cameron, Sharon. *Writing Nature: Henry Thoreau's Journal*. New York: Oxford University Press, 1985.

Canby, H. S. *Thoreau*. Boston: Houghton Mifflin, 1939.

Cavell, Stanley. *The Senses of* Walden. New York: Viking, 1972.

Christie, John Aldrich. *Thoreau as World Traveller*. New York: Columbia University Press, 1965.

Cook, Reginald. *Passage to* Walden. Boston: Houghton Mifflin, 1949.

Dillman, Richard H. "The Psychological Rhetoric of *Walden*." *ESQ: A Journal of the American Renaissance* 25 (1979): 79–91.

Eiseley, Loren. "*Walden:* Thoreau's Unfinished Business." In *The Star Thrower*, 235–51. New York: Harcourt Brace Jovanovich, 1978.

Evans, Robert. "Thoreau's Poetry and Prose Works." *Emerson Society Quarterly* 56 (1969): 43.

Garber, Frederick. *Thoreau's Redemptive Imagination*. New York: New York University Press, 1977.

Glick, Wendell. *The Recognition of Henry David Thoreau*. Ann Arbor: University of Michigan Press, 1970.

Gozzi, Raymond, ed. *Thoreau's Psychology: Eight Essays*. Lanham, Md.: University Press of America, 1983.

Gura, Philip F. "Henry Thoreau and the Wisdom of Words." *New England Quarterly* 52 (1979): 38–54.

———. "Language and Meaning: An American Tradition." *American Literature* 53 (1981): 1–21.

Harding, Walter. *Thoreau: A Century of Criticism*. Dallas: Southern Methodist University Press, 1954.

———. *The Days of Henry Thoreau*. New York: Knopf, 1966.

Hellenbrand, Harold. " 'A True Integrity Day by Day': Thoreau's Organic Economy in *Walden*." *ESQ: A Journal of the American Renaissance* 25 (1979): 71–78.

Hicks, John H. *Thoreau in Our Season*. Amherst: University of Massachusetts Press, 1966.

Hildebidle, John. *Thoreau: A Naturalist's Liberty*. Cambridge: Harvard University Press, 1983.

Holland, Joyce. "Pattern and Meaning in Thoreau's *A Week*." *Emerson Society Quarterly* 50 (1968): 50.

Houde, Carl. "Nature into Art: Thoreau's Use of His Journals in *A Week*." *American Literature* 30 (1958): 165–84.

Howarth, William. *Thoreau's Life as a Writer*. New York: Viking, 1982.

Howarth, William, and Robert Stavell, eds. *A Thoreau Gazetteer*. Princeton, N.J.: Princeton University Press, 1970.

Johnson, Paul David. "Thoreau's Redemptive Week." *American Literature* 49 (1977): 22–34.

Kellman, Steven G. "A Conspiracy Theory of Literature: Thoreau and You." *The Georgia Review* 32 (1978): 808–19.

Kronick, Joseph G. *American Poetics of History: From Emerson to the Moderns*. Baton Rouge: Louisiana State University Press, 1984.

Kumin, Maxine. "With Thoreau in Darkest Maine." *Harper's*, July 1986, 63–66.

Lebeaux, Richard. *Young Man Thoreau*. Amherst: University of Massachusetts Press, 1977.

Lewis, R. W. B. *The American Adam*. Chicago: University of Chicago Press, 1955.

Lyon, Melvin E. "Walden Pond as Symbol." *PMLA* 82 (1967): 289.

McIntosh, James. *Thoreau as Romantic Naturalist*. Ithaca: Cornell University Press, 1974.

Matthiessen, F. O. *American Renaissance: Art and Expression in the Age of Emerson and Whitman*. New York: Oxford University Press, 1941.

Meyer, Michael. *Several More Lives to Live: Thoreau's Political Reputation in America*. Westport, Conn.: Greenwood, 1977.

Miller, Perry. Commentary on the *Lost Journal*. In *Consciousness in Concord: The Text of Thoreau's Hitherto* Lost Journal. Boston: Houghton Mifflin, 1958.

Moller, Mary Elkins. *Thoreau in the Human Community*. Amherst: University of Massachusetts Press, 1980.

Nash, Roderick. "Henry David Thoreau: Philosopher." In *Wilderness and the American Mind*, 84–95. New Haven: Yale University Press, 1982.

Neufeldt, Leonard N. "Henry David Thoreau's Political Economy." *New England Quarterly* 57 (1984): 359–82.

Paul, Sherman. *The Shores of America: Thoreau's Inward Exploration*. Urbana: University of Illinois Press, 1958.

———, ed. *Thoreau: A Collection of Critical Essays*. Englewood Cliffs, N.J.: Prentice-Hall, 1962.

Porte, Joel. *Emerson and Thoreau: Transcendentalists in Conflict*. Middletown, Conn.: Wesleyan University Press, 1966.

Ruland, Richard, ed. *Twentieth Century Interpretations of* Walden. Englewood Cliffs, N.J.: Prentice-Hall, 1968.

Sayre, Robert. *Thoreau and the American Indians.* Princeton, N.J.: Princeton University Press, 1977.

Seybold, Ethel. *Thoreau: The Quest and the Classics.* New Haven: Yale University Press, 1951.

Shanley, J. Lyndon. *The Making of* Walden. Chicago: University of Chicago Press, 1957.

Simon, Myron. "Thoreau and Anarchism." *Michigan Quarterly Review* 23 (1984): 360–84.

Smith, Herbert. "Thoreau Among the Classical Economists." *ESQ: A Journal of the American Renaissance* 23 (1977): 114–22.

Stein, William Bysshe. "Thoreau's *A Week* and OM Cosmography." *The American Transcendental Quarterly,* no. 11 (1971): 24.

Stoller, Leo. *After* Walden: *Thoreau's Changing Views on Economic Man.* Stanford: Stanford University Press, 1957.

Sundquist, Eric. *Home as Found: Authority & Genealogy in Nineteenth Century American Literature.* Baltimore: Johns Hopkins University Press, 1979.

Taylor, Carole Anne. "Authorship without Authority: *Walden,* Kierkegaard, and the Experiment in Points of View." In *Kierkegaard and Literature: Irony, Repetition, and Criticism,* edited by Ronald Schliefer, et. al. Norman: University of Oklahoma Press, 1984.

Thoreau Quarterly (formerly the *Thoreau Journal Quarterly*), 1968–.

Van Doren, Mark. *Henry David Thoreau: A Critical Study.* New York: Russell & Russell, 1961.

Wagenknecht, Edward. *Henry David Thoreau: What Manner of Man?* Amherst: University of Massachusetts Press, 1981.

West, Michael. "Thoreau and the Language Theories of the French Enlightenment." *ELH* 51 (1984): 747–70.

———. "Scatology and Escatology: The Heroic Dimensions of Thoreau's Wordplay." *PMLA* 89 (1974): 1043–64.

Whitaker, Rosemary. "*A Week* and *Walden.*" *The American Transcendental Quarterly,* no. 17 (1973): 12.

Acknowledgments

"Words" by Stanley Cavell from *The Senses of Walden* by Stanley Cavell, © 1972 by Stanley Cavell. Reprinted by permission of the author and Viking Penguin, Inc.

" 'The Shipwreck': A Shaped Happening" by James McIntosh from *Thoreau as Romantic Naturalist* by James McIntosh, © 1974 by Cornell University. Reprinted by permission of Cornell University Press. Quotations of Thoreau are from *The Writings of Henry David Thoreau* (Walden Edition, 20 volumes; Boston: Houghton Mifflin, 1906).

"Thoreau's Vision of the Natural World" by Loren Eiseley from *The Star Thrower,* edited by Howard Chapnick, © 1974 by Howard Chapnick. Reprinted by permission of Grosset & Dunlop.

"Thoreau's Maine Woods Indians: More Representative Men" by Philip F. Gura from *American Literature* 49, no. 3 (November 1977), © 1977 by Duke University Press. Reprinted by permission.

"*Walden*'s False Bottoms" by Walter Benn Michaels from *Glyph* 4 (1977), edited by Samuel Weber and Henry Sussman, © 1977 by the Johns Hopkins University Press, Baltimore/London. Reprinted by permission.

" 'Plowing Homeward': Cultivation and Grafting in Thoreau and the *Week*" by Eric J. Sundquist from *Home as Found: Authority and Genealogy in Nineteenth-Century American Literature* by Eric J. Sundquist, © 1979 by the Johns Hopkins University Press, Baltimore/London. Reprinted by permission.

" 'The Being of Language: The Language of Being' " (originally entitled " 'The Being of Language: The Language of Being' in Thoreau's *A Week on the Concord and Merrimack Rivers*") by John Carlos Rowe from *Through the Custom House: Nineteenth-Century American Fiction and Modern Theory* by John Carlos Rowe, © 1982 by the Johns Hopkins University Press, Baltimore/ London. Reprinted by permission.

"Thoreau's Narrative Art in 'Civil Disobedience' " by Barry Wood from *Philological Quarterly* 60, no. 1 (Winter 1981), © 1982 by the University of Iowa. Reprinted by permission.

"Rags and Meanness: Journals, Early Essays, Translations, and Poems" by Richard Bridgman from *Dark Thoreau* by Richard Bridgman, © 1982 by the University of Nebraska Press. Reprinted by permission of the University of Nebraska Press.

"Suspectable Repetitions: *Cape Cod*" by John Hildebidle from *Thoreau: A Naturalist's Liberty* by John Hildebidle, © 1983 by the President and Fellows of Harvard College. Reprinted by permission of Harvard University Press.

"*Walden* and the 'Curse of Trade'" by Michael T. Gilmore from *American Romanticism and the Marketplace* by Michael T. Gilmore, © 1985 by the University of Chicago. Reprinted by permission of the University of Chicago Press.

"Thoreau's Dawn and the Lake School's Night" by Robert Weisbuch from *Atlantic Double-Cross: American Literature and British Influence in the Age of Emerson* by Robert Weisbuch, © 1986 by the University of Chicago. Reprinted by permission of the University of Chicago Press.

INDEX

Modern Critical Views